GROWING AMERICAN ROOTS

GROWING
AMERICAN
ROOTS

WHY OUR NATION WILL THRIVE
AS OUR LARGEST MINORITY
FLOURISHES

SENATOR
BOB MENENDEZ

A CELEBRA BOOK

CELEBRA
Published by New American Library, a division of
Penguin Group (USA) Inc., 375 Hudson Street,
New York, New York 10014, USA
Penguin Group (Canada), 90 Eglinton Avenue East, Suite 700, Toronto,
Ontario M4P 2Y3, Canada (a division of Pearson Penguin Canada Inc.)
Penguin Books Ltd., 80 Strand, London WC2R 0RL, England
Penguin Ireland, 25 St. Stephen's Green, Dublin 2,
Ireland (a division of Penguin Books Ltd.)
Penguin Group (Australia), 250 Camberwell Road, Camberwell, Victoria 3124,
Australia (a division of Pearson Australia Group Pty. Ltd.)
Penguin Books India Pvt. Ltd., 11 Community Centre, Panchsheel Park,
New Delhi - 110 017, India
Penguin Group (NZ), 67 Apollo Drive, Rosedale, North Shore 0632,
New Zealand (a division of Pearson New Zealand Ltd.)
Penguin Books (South Africa) (Pty.) Ltd., 24 Sturdee Avenue,
Rosebank, Johannesburg 2196, South Africa

Penguin Books Ltd., Registered Offices:
80 Strand, London WC2R 0RL, England

First published by Celebra,
a division of Penguin Group (USA) Inc.

First Printing, October 2009
10 9 8 7 6 5 4 3 2 1

CELEBRA and logo are trademarks of Penguin Group (USA) Inc.

Library of Congress Cataloging-in-Publication Data:

Menendez, Robert, 1954–
    Growing American roots: why our nation will thrive as our largest minority flourishes/Senator Bob Menendez.
        p. cm.
    ISBN 978-0-451-22805-5
    1. Hispanic Americans—Social conditions. 2. Hispanic Americans—Government policy.
3. Hispanic Americans—Education. I. Title.
    E184.S75M455 2009
    973'.0468—dc22   2009018001

Set in Adobe Garamond
Designed by Ginger Legato

Printed in the United States of America

Publisher's Note
While the author has made every effort to provide accurate telephone numbers and Internet addresses at the time of publication, neither the publisher nor the author assumes any responsibility for errors, or for changes that occur after publication. Further, publisher does not have any control over and does not assume any responsibility for author or third-party Web sites or their content.

To the joys of my life, my daughter, Alicia, and my son, Rob, who are both deepening their American roots and already proudly contributing to our country; to my mother, Evangelina, whose courage started our journey here in America; and to my sister, Caridad, who is an angel here on earth.

CONTENTS

GROWING AMERICAN ROOTS

What's past is prologue.

—WILLIAM SHAKESPEARE, *The Tempest*[1]

---

1 Note that the statue says "What *is* past is prologue." No contraction, as it reads in the Shakespeare itself. I'll leave that to my editor.

INTRODUCTION—
THE LESSONS OF HISTORY

Every so often, I set off down Pennsylvania Avenue from my U.S. Senate office in Washington to visit the National Archives, where the founding documents of our nation are on display—the Declaration of Independence, the Constitution, and the Bill of Rights—which enshrine forever the spirit in which we pursue a more perfect union, and which declare those freedoms we all cherish.

Preparing to write this book, I made another visit to that imposing classical structure and paused before one of four massive statues commissioned by the building's great architect, John Russell Pope. The statue is named *The Future*, designed in 1933 by Robert I. Aitken. It is the image of a young woman, carved from a block of limestone and weighing 125 tons. She is clad in Roman garb, her right hand holding a book open in place on her lap. She seems to have paused to consider what she had been reading, gazing into the beyond. Larger than life, she is seated on a pedestal inscribed with a line from Shakespeare's *Tempest*: "What is past is prologue."

The heroic statue and its simple message are a powerful reminder that our country is still changing. We are the product of our history, our efforts set out to reflect the highest values of our heritage; we are always renewing ourselves, seeking to live up to the promise of the Founding Fathers. Our past, our history, is the story of people who heard the call and came in search of that more perfect union. Let us consider the wonder and never forget the accomplishments of our country since the Constitution was enacted in 1787. Such is the glory of the United States, born of a desire by people eager to build a new life and a world-changing system of democracy.

I stood in the nation's capital in the presence of that document, a child of proud but poor immigrants who had only a grade school education and came here half a century ago. Now their son, the first member of the family to ever graduate from college, is a member of the United States Senate. I am proud of my accomplishment, but I am equally proud and moved by the fact that this country could allow something so remarkable to take place.

That visit to the National Archives helped me focus on what had been a vague notion that I had something to say about Latinos and my role in this society. I knew what I did not want to do: write a memoir of my life. I'll tell you in passing about myself by way of introduction, but it is a bit early in my life and career to be writing a memoir. No, I had something else to say. I recognized that the statue named *Future* sums it up: I could not think of a better image to help refocus and redefine the promise of our country.

America's future is built on the history of its people—the greatest part of the equation is that we have united, have grown together, and continue to change. As I consider my public service, the one contribution I can make toward creating a more perfect nation is to speak close to the heart—the issue of who we are as a people. Quickly I turn to my own background, to the story of the immigrants who have come here. Let this serve as a reintroduction to the history, role, contribution, and future of Latinos of the United States. In part, this is a process of breaking down barriers at a key moment of our history. Who are the Latinos of this country? Let us recognize their collective contribution, their long-lasting involvement in the creation of this country. Let us also look at their changing role in years to come.

There at the National Archives, as I reflected on our history, a corollary was obvious—as much as the past is prologue, the future is our promise. When I say that, we need to pay close attention to the pronouns. I'm talking about all of us—we cannot afford to make artificial separations among the human beings struggling to make the best of life in this country, or anywhere in the world, for that matter.

And so, this book is a portrait of Latinos in America and our integration into the larger American family. I'll talk about three steps along the way, past, present, and future. First, we need to remind ourselves and the rest of America about our long presence here. Too often, with characteristic humility, we have not boasted enough about our accomplishments. From the earliest days of our republic—indeed well before the Revolution—Latinos have been part of the establishment of this country; it would do well for all Americans to have access to that history. We need to enhance the teaching of the story of Hispanic life in America; we need to encourage changes in schools around the country so that they include in their curricula Latino contributions to the building of America. All Americans should have access to and understand the building blocks of our history in all its detail and glory. The stories of our Hispanic ancestors, meanwhile, offer a sense of pride to a new generation, Latino children who are making it, and the disadvantaged, who can be inspired by our place in the story. Latino patriots have fought in every American war; we are artists and dancers and singers who have added spice and beauty to the cultural life of this country; we are scientists, and teachers, more frequently than ever businessmen and entrepreneurs essential to the nation's economy.

Second, we need to understand accomplishments and where we fall short; Latinos constitute a thriving community, mostly born in the United States, who have contributed mightily and continue to do so. Without wanting to drown in statistics, I'll describe a bright present and prospects for an even brighter future. Millions of Latinos are graduating into the middle class; more Latino children are going to colleges and universities than ever before; Latinos are serving increasingly in public office and in key areas of the economy. But at the same time, despite progress in education, too many Latino children drop out of school, too many families are struggling to make ends meet, and too many of our families suffer from a lack of adequate health care.

Turning to one overriding, controversial issue in this country, we need to set the record straight on immigration. Americans, out of their sense of common justice, must put an end to discrimination against and mistreatment of immigrants. Latinos have been under attack unfairly, as if they were somehow different from any other immigrant group that came before them. Every reliable piece of analysis shows that Latinos enter the American experience in the same ways and on the same trajectories as other generations of immigrants who came to these shores. My goal is to shed light on the positive and the negative; prejudices and outrages and plain injustice have no place in America.

We are too far down the road to build up false ideas—that some Americans somehow drag back the rest of us, or that one group suffers as a result of another. We are living already in the world of the American rainbow, all of us of every gender, preference, and ethnic background—together.

Third and most important, this is a book about planning for that future. "Growing American Roots" means recognizing our past, acting now, and preparing the road for those new generations. We need sweeping efforts to improve education for Latinos and all American children, specific programs to bring along children who have fallen behind in school. Their families need comprehensive health care, and elder care, and economic opportunity, and on—the same rights that all Americans deserve. And we must have broad immigration reform, legislation that will guarantee equitable and humane means of dealing with Latinos and all immigrants. We must recognize that Latinos not only deserve such treatment but also must be protected: They will play a key role in our economic future.

This then is our Latino manifesto. We are here, and we are not some isolated segment of the population. Most of us are native-born Americans, and we are part of the fabric that makes this country great. We share the aspirations, goals, and patriotism of all Americans. I am a member of the group, one of forty-five million Americans known as Latinos or

Hispanics,[1] people whose ancestors migrated here from Spain and from the south, territories below the Rio Grande, across the Caribbean, from throughout Central and South America. A few of our families have been here since before the creation of the United States; others of us are arriving here every day, seeking success and liberty that they have never known. Just like our forebears, we are here to build a new future: the past is prologue.

As much as we all are Americans, we are a nation of immigrants. Except for those of us who descend from the peoples who lived in America centuries before Europeans arrived, we are the children of immigrants. Some of our ancestors made the voyage on the *Mayflower* four hundred years ago; others stepped off a ship at Ellis Island in the late nineteenth or early twentieth century; millions of us are the descendants of people who arrived forcibly as slaves; millions more, like me, are the children of Hispanic parents who came to this country fleeing tyranny and searching for freedom. Despite our varied histories we have come here with the same goals—a dream, the opportunity to prosper, security for our families, an environment to fulfill our God-given potential, or, as Thomas Jefferson said it most powerfully, life, liberty, and the pursuit of happiness.

Over the 233 years since Jefferson penned the Declaration of Independence, immigrants joined in a common purpose and a common language and became Americans. We look forward, confident that generations of new Americans will continue to bring new vitality. Together, we are always building the new America.

I often quote a famous line by the governor of California who, ad-

---

1 I've decided to use the words Latino and Hispanic interchangeably, even though there is sometimes controversy about the use of these and other terms. I'm using both terms because the U.S. Census and other branches of the government use them both. The federal government determined in 1997 that it would use both terms; the Office of Management and Budget at that time decided to use the terminology "Hispanic or Latino," for statistical purposes, and said that it considered the word "Hispanic" as more dominantly used in the Eastern United States, while "Latino" was more prevalent in the West. So when I mention either of the terms, I am referring to people in the United States whose origin is either Spanish, or those from Mexico, the Caribbean or Spanish-speaking countries of Central and South America.

dressing an event for Latino leaders, said: "It's your time to stand in the sun, and I want to be a part of it." He was right. We are, in fact, already here, some of us for generations, just one component of the tapestry of America. We should make this a declaration of interdependence: It is our time in the sun; Latinos have arrived. We are people of all creeds, colors, and nations, working together to lead this nation and the world to new heights of health, security, and equality.

The governor's simple statement is somewhat complicated when you examine the details. It was addressed to all Hispanics in the United States, and ultimately to all Americans. The hitch is that it was spoken not by Arnold Schwarzenegger in 2009 but by Jerry Brown in 1978. Brown acknowledged the role of Latinos in American life when there were only about twelve million Hispanics in the United States. With almost four times that amount in 2009 Latinos were living and working and thriving in every state of the Union, participating at all levels of American life.

A SNAPSHOT OF OUR COUNTRY reveals a stunning view—there are more Latinos in the United States than there are people in Canada. In fact, there are more Latinos here than there are people in Canada, Croatia, and Costa Rica combined. Most Latinos in this country are U.S. citizens, representing dozens of countries and ethnic groups. Many live hard lives barely at the poverty line, a growing number have reached the ranks of the middle class, and a significant number have become prominent, well-to-do beneficiaries of the American dream.

We have a huge stake in the marketplace, turning the corner in 2009 on one trillion dollars of purchasing power. That represents a lot more than tortillas, rice, and beans. We are out there buying computers, tractors, refrigerators, Priuses, and Mercedes-Benzes—have a look at an average hour of prime time on Spanish-language television. But don't be fooled to think that most of us speak only Spanish; a younger generation of Latino children all speak English as their first language.

We work in the factories and companies and stores that produce some of those products and increasingly we own them—in 2009 five of the top hundred Latino-owned businesses in this country had revenues over one billion dollars. Our lives are tied to the economic well-being of our country. When we buy things, we feed the economy of the United States, and when we make things, we keep the engine turning.

We are the youngest and fastest-growing ethnic group in this country. We make up seventeen percent of high school students in this country. Two Latino last names, Garcia and Rodriguez, are among the ten most common names in the United States.

Already, our celebrities have made history: Christina Aguilera, Eva Longoria, Jennifer Lopez, Carlos Santana, and other Latin personalities are at the top of the charts; Plácido Domingo leads the Washington Opera. I am one of twenty-eight senators and members of Congress of Latino heritage now serving; there are more than five thousand federal, state, and local elected Latino officials in the United States. A generation from now, perhaps a Latino will be president of the United States. After the elections of 2008, we know that can happen.

Our stories of immigration and the saga of our parents and grandparents blend into the American story. We arrived here, we worked hard, and we have helped create a new world. Hispanics and those we refer to as minorities are already a powerful force and represent the largest component in population growth in this country.

So it is fair to say *hemos llegado*—we have arrived. However, we have been contributing to and have been part of the American tapestry for hundreds of years. We fought for the United States in the American Revolution. Latinos fought and died on both sides of the American Civil War and have participated in every war since then. A majority of Latinos were born in this country as American citizens, and many of their families have been here for generations.

Demagogues would divide Americans from one another, claiming that Latinos are somehow a threat to the American way of life. This is dangerous nonsense.

"It was once said that immigration is taking jobs away from America," said Jeffrey Passel, the chief statistician and an authoritative source at the

Pew Hispanic Center, a Washington-based organization. "This has disappeared from discussion, because it is clearly not true."

Divisive people pervert and distort the record, especially on the airwaves; would-be populists promote their ideas about immigration with a fearful public. When economic times are good, the din is quieter, but in 2009 in the midst of a frightening economic collapse, the misconceived rabble-rousing has grown. Moving forward, reforming the economic system, we will move on to a new generation, acting and reacting with some common sense.

I am pained by the injustice against Latinos in this country—distortions by pseudoscientific treatises that defend our country as a white Protestant state, as if immigration were something new. We face abuse based on ignorance and racism, and outrageous indifference to suffering, to lack of equal opportunity, to the basic rights of our nation.

This land now has a chance to restore itself—to reestablish itself as the center of world respect for its individual freedoms, the force of its example, not the example of its force. My aim is to fill in the divide between Hispanic advancement and public understanding. While there has been progress since the governor of California's pronouncement, Latinos in the United States have been a mystery to the broader populace of this country. We have just begun to break into the American consciousness. The coming generation will bring even greater prominence to Latinos in this country.

My entry into politics was born of my need to redress injustice. Injustice directed at one group is not just a matter of prejudice—it is wrong. This nation, where the only natural-born Americans were tribes of Native Americans, has a blemished history in dealing with immigrants to this land of opportunity. Americans have been forced to fight off oppression and injustice all the way along the road. It has been our challenge since the first settlers fought and displaced indigenous Americans, since the slave traders brought millions of Africans to these shores under barbaric conditions, since waves of immigrants came here, seeking justice, inspired by those words "of the people, by the people, for the people."

Latinos, like all Americans, want to succeed and share the wealth of progress. Talk about family values—Latinos in the United States emphasize strong ties of marriage, taking care of their children, tending to the aged and infirm. This is a group that doesn't cause problems; it provides power to the economy, and stability to our communities. Despite the misconceptions, prejudice, and ignorance, the truth is, Latinos are Americans in search of the same dream of progress, education, safety, and health for their families. Latinos represent more than fifteen percent of the U.S. population, people whose diverse origins are in Mexico, the Caribbean, or Central or South America, all working toward the same dream.

Americans have every reason in the world to tune in and learn more about Hispanics in this country. As with Europeans of another age who brought their languages, their religions, and their customs, and African-Americans, who gave us art and music and a sense of justice, we Latinos are leaving our mark. We are working toward integrating America's Latino population, guaranteeing parity in health care and employment, empowerment, and full participation in the political system. Somehow, despite the injustices suffered by some, we labor together, Hispanics, African-Americans, Native Americans, all of us, a nation of immigrants, to reach that unattainable perfection.

In fact, the Latino minority in this country will change dramatically one generation from now, and by 2042, the minorities—Hispanic- and African-Americans, Native Americans, Pacific Islanders, and Asians—will become the majority.

By 2050, there will be 130 million Latinos in the United States, a majority under thirty years old. We will be one-third of the U.S. population; our hard work and our influence will blend into the American experience. We will speak English, we will honor our shared heritage; we will recall our heroes—George Washington and Simón Bolívar; Abraham Lincoln and José Martí. Our parents will look at us with pride; they have worked hard to give us a solid foundation. And all the while, we were growing American roots. There is no turning back.

Once we set the record straight, all Americans will move on together to solve the common issues of equality, the right to health care, decent housing, education, and protection for the old and infirm. These are issues for all of us. As much as the past is prologue, the future gives us the chance to make things right.

It has never been more obvious that the needs of one minority are the needs of all. If all of us work hard enough, most Hispanic-Americans, like Italian-Americans, Polish-Americans, and Scandinavian-Americans, will be speaking English as their first language, while still valuing our cultures and our second languages from the old country. The dynamic mix will add to the richness of American society.

THE CHALLENGE IN 2009 AND beyond is the one we have had throughout our history. When an immigrant is mistreated, or the member of a minority group receives less than his due, we must work harder, fight and vote for change. When high school football players in Pennsylvania beat and kill a young Latino, or when a Chinese immigrant dies in a U.S. detention facility, his pleas for medical help amid screaming pain unanswered, something is wrong.

While reasonable minds can differ on some aspects of the immigration debate, Americans must not employ ignorance and lies in the media and spread hatred. Hatred breeds intolerance, violence, and death. Allowing sick people to suffer and die in our prisons and detention centers without treatment or humane care is unacceptable and violates the most fundamental standards of American justice. Looking back, a generation from now, we will be able to say we repaired the system and answered the call of history.

These are the Hispanics of America, people who long ago began setting their roots in this society; others now join them, adding their labor and their ingenuity to the equation that is America. A generation from now, our debate will have overcome demagoguery and fearmongering, in favor of understanding and working for equality among all Americans. Always changing, we will welcome the orderly arrival of yet a new generation of immigrants; like those before them, they will be bringing unique abilities, and will serve as catalysts for change and progress and success.

Immigrants have been and will continue to be a resource for American progress. We can all work together toward these goals. This is a call to reaffirm our values, to provide for opportunity for all, demand responsibility from all, and create a sense of community for all.

CHAPTER I

A NEW AGE IN POLITICS

One of these days, the younger generation will come knocking at my door.

HENRIK IBSEN,
QUOTED BY FORMER VICE PRESIDENT AL GORE

After the great transitional election of 2008, we can now say that all possibilities are open to us. Barack Obama, the forty-fourth president of the United States, has crafted a new body politic in this country. Just as with the image of the Muse of History at the National Archives, you consider the past, create a foundation, and then dream of what might be.

When I was campaigning in the fall of 2008 for then-candidate Obama in Florida and around the country, I spoke frequently on his behalf on Spanish-language television and radio. My argument was this: In addition to all the merits of his campaign and the value of his positions on the critical issues of the day, I would say that for us as a community, to paraphrase the president's own words, if a tall skinny guy with a funny name who happens to be an African-American can rise to the greatest position of the land, then every barrier is broken for the rest of us. The names Sanchez, Gonzalez, and Menendez won't seem anywhere as unfamiliar as did the name Obama; neither will consideration of heritage nor the skin hues of the people campaigning for our attention seem to matter anymore. It would then be easy to think that a Latino might be president by the year 2030, maybe even earlier.

BEYOND ANY PREDICTION OF THE ethnic background of some future leader, we now know that the merits and the power of the ideas of an individual are the qualities that are going to propel him or her into office. I told my listeners to understand the importance of the moment: When Barack Obama becomes president of the United States, the message toward the future goes far beyond his personal history, even beyond the great, legitimate pride and emotion of African-Americans in this country. His arrival at the presidency really means that the door of opportunity has been flung wide open and now everything is possible. Think about what it means to live in an America in which maybe the glass ceiling of limitation has been broken. That is what Barack Obama's election means to the United States.

We now know from experience that a person of color can strive for anything in this country. There is no limit to our imaginations and our ability to move toward a more perfect union.

TIME AND AGAIN, THE PRESIDENT has tuned in clearly to the moment. Before a vast throng in Chicago on the historic night of his election, he said:

> If there is anyone out there who still doubts that America is a place where all things are possible, who still wonders if the dream of our founders is alive in our time, who still questions the power of our democracy, tonight is your answer.
>
> It's the answer told by lines that stretched around schools and churches in numbers this nation has never seen, by people who waited three hours and four hours, many for the very first time in their lives, because they believed that this time must be different, that their voice could be that difference.
>
> It's the answer spoken by young and old, rich and poor, Democrat and Republican, black, white, Latino, Asian, Native American, gay, straight, disabled, and not disabled—Americans who sent a message to the world that we have never been a collection of red states and blue states; we are, and always will be, the United States of America.
>
> It's the answer that led those who have been told for so long

by so many to be cynical, and fearful, and doubtful of what we can achieve, to put their hands on the arc of history and bend it once more toward the hope of a better day.

It's been a long time coming, but tonight, because of what we did on this day, in this election, at this defining moment, change has come to America.

By the middle of the twenty-first century, maybe even sooner, a person of Hispanic origin may be next. And we know we've even broken the gender gap, so why not predict that a woman of Hispanic origin will also be president of the United States? Somewhere, this very moment, a young person in this country is coming of age; give him or her an economic foundation, a secure environment, and educational opportunity, and he or she will already be dreaming. Our young people need role models; we must encourage them to harness the strength of their dreams, help them strive toward a goal.

HERE'S THE KEY: WE HAVE to go beyond the declaration of change—we need to promote and inspire the enthusiasm that will produce the changes we seek; Americans need to help lift up those members of our society who are struggling to succeed, because they work with us and among us, supporting American life every day—and their children are the seeds of the future. Meanwhile, members of this generation must reach back and help their brothers and sisters catch up. Government has a responsibility and so does each of us individually.

There are many ways to serve. Some of us serve in government or in business to propel the American economic machine. Some are teachers or doctors, citizens all, contributing to society to the best of their abilities. And one special group serves courageously in our armed forces; we honor the proud veterans who have fought and sacrificed to preserve our liberties.

We seek, in turn, the good judgment of leaders who will respect the sacrifices of our military. They do that by focusing on the basic principles of our democracy, on the need for consultation, diplomacy, and good sense, with a goal that future wars are always a last resort rather than a preemptive choice.

Our schools are crying out for the service of dedicated teachers. The safety of our streets depends on brave policemen and firemen. Our hospitals need doctors, nurses, and technicians to restore our health. Our places of worship need clergy to lift our spirits and give us hope in our darkest hours. And more than that, our own homes ask us for service, as devoted big brothers, fathers, and sons.

We have to be teaching about ideals, and living them. This is a country in which men and women should have the means to get ahead through the power of their intellect and the strength of their own hands. They may not start out wearing the best clothes, or able to afford an iPod or a fancy car; if they have a goal, if we create the opportunity, they should be able to succeed. If you have a goal, and the willingness to put in some sweat equity, your achievement should be unlimited.

Politics alone won't discover a new source of energy, or design a fuel-efficient car, or develop a cure for Alzheimer's. Those breakthroughs will come through service in other fields. But politics can play a part. It's about setting the right priorities to allow those breakthroughs to happen.

We don't just get the government we deserve. We get the government we work for. Our participation makes all the difference in the world. And with this new generation of leadership, we have a chance to move toward the future, serving our communities, combining our talents, insights, and dreams for causes greater than ourselves.

IN THE 2008 PRESIDENTIAL ELECTIONS, we faced a new reality in American political history. Once again, we have to take a reality check. New voters, young voters, registered; there was a groundswell of support for Barack Obama. And once again, Latinos and people of color brought home the victory.

Almost 10 million Latinos voted on Election Day, representing about eight percent of the American electorate, according to the National Association of Latino Elected and Appointed Officials (NALEO). In 2004,

7.6 million Hispanic citizens reported voting in the presidential election.[1] One thing is clear, however. Latino voters played a crucial role in contributing toward Barack Obama's victory. "The record turnout among Latinos solidifies this emerging electorate as an important voting bloc among U.S. voters," reported the NALEO Educational Fund. "Latino voters also helped to reshape the political map by helping President-elect Barack Obama and Democrats win key states in the Southwest, Florida, Indiana, and Virginia."[2] Statistics show that applications for citizenship increased significantly in 2008 over 2007 and the indication is that a majority of Latinos registered as Democrats. A coalition of organizing groups, the Mi Familia Vota Educational Fund, the NALEO Educational Fund, the National Council of La Raza, and Spanish-language media companies, including Univision, Entravision, and ImpreMedia, were committed to Latino voter registration, under the banner *Ya Es Hora* (It's Time). There are no secrets here. Early in the Democratic primary campaign, Hillary Clinton had strong support from the Hispanic community, a product of long relations with the Clinton administration. Much of that support transferred over to the candidacy of Barack Obama. It wasn't easy of course. He was unknown to Latinos, and as they say, a presidential primary race is a good way for a candidate to shake out his or her weaknesses.

IN THE 2008 DEMOCRATIC PRIMARY, things looked different—Governor Bill Richardson of New Mexico, a Mexican-American, was in the presidential race. He and Senator Chris Dodd of Connecticut, a fluent Spanish speaker from his days in the Peace Corps, were favorites among Latino voters, as was Hillary. Latino voters remembered the warm relationship between President Bill Clinton and their community in the 1990s. The problem facing Senator Obama was that he was little known in the community.

---

1 "Latino Voters in the 2008 Presidential Election: Post-Election Survey of Latino Voters," www.naleo.org/downloads/Post-Election%20Survey.pdf
2 NALEO Educational Fund, "New Post-Election Survey Provides In-Depth Analysis of Latino Vote," November 21, 2008, http://www.naleo.org/pr11-21-08.html

Perhaps later than he should have, but successfully nevertheless, Obama paid attention to Latinos. Hispanics for Obama organizations emerged throughout the United States. After Obama consolidated his victory in the primaries, he dedicated a twenty-million-dollar program aimed at attracting Hispanic voters in every state[3] in what was described as a landmark advertising campaign in Spanish-language media, and brought in members of Congress and others to spread the word. The hope was that the enthusiasm among Latino voters for Hillary during the primaries would translate to the Democratic standard-bearer. "That love that the Latino community had for Hillary and has for Hillary is also a love for true change in America," said my Democratic colleague in the House José Serrano, of the Bronx.[4]

Obama began reaching out to Latinos across the board, speaking in television ads during the primaries in Puerto Rico, and dealing with issues among Mexican-American voters in California. He was endorsed by *La Opinión* in Los Angeles and a host of other Latino media outlets, and ran far ahead of John McCain. Surveys have said that seventy-two percent of Latino voters chose Obama. Interestingly enough, the youngest Latinos—second-generation children and Spanish speakers—gave even more support to the new president, eighty percent choosing him over McCain.

As a result of the elections, we added a new member of the House of Representatives. Ben R. Luján, the former New Mexico public regulation commissioner, became the first Latino from that state in Congress since Governor Bill Richardson was in the House from 1982 to 1996. Until 2009, we had a high-water mark of three Latino senators—Ken Salazar of Colorado, my Republican colleague Mel Martinez of Florida, and me. Ken Salazar left the Senate when President Obama chose him as secretary of the interior. It is not only a great honor; it is also a great step for all Americans. Weeks after his appointment, Ken and I paid homage to

---

3 Jared Allen, The Hill (thehill.com), http://thehill.com/campaign-2008/hispanics-embrace-obamas-20-million-outreach-2008-07-29.html, "Hispanics Embrace Obama's $20 Million Outreach," July 29, 2008.
4 Ibid.

the immigrants of America on a visit to the Statue of Liberty. Ken's job is central to the future of this country. The Interior Department includes the Bureau of Land Management, the U.S. Fish and Wildlife Service, among others, and he has regulations to repair and work on after years of neglect.

Also overseeing the National Park Service, he also is involved in promoting and focusing on our history and the nation's heritage. Ken told me he is studying the future establishment of a museum in the nation's capital that will commemorate the Hispanic experience in this country. It is a long time coming.

History was made on May 26, 2009 when President Obama nominated Sonia Sotomayor to the U.S. Supreme Court. What could more poignantly symbolize the growing presence, influence, and participation of Hispanics in this country? What a proud moment, that the nation's first African-American president could stand before the nation and nominate an eminently qualified federal judge who happens to be of Hispanic heritage.

It filled me with pride to have the opportunity to cast a vote to confirm this groundbreaking nominee. Born to a Puerto Rican family, Judge Sotomayor grew up in public housing in the South Bronx. Inspired and spurred on by her mother, she excelled, graduating as high school valedictorian, then summa cum laude from Princeton University and serving as editor of the Law Journal at Yale Law School. In short, her ethnic background was not the justification for her nomination. Judge Sotomayor brings more federal judicial experience to the Supreme Court than any justice in one hundred years, and more overall judicial experience than anyone confirmed for the Court in the past seventy years.

BEYOND THOSE SERVING IN WASHINGTON, more than 240 Latinos serve in state legislatures. The numbers are certain to increase. Thousands of others serve as mayors and council members, and on local school boards everywhere. Those are numbers, but within the statistics we see the reality; Hispanics are making an impact on society every day. They vote on increased budgets for local schools, on measures to offer preschool education, on transportation for the elderly, on expanding libraries, on housing and commercial projects throughout the land. What greater testament can there be toward creating deep roots for our shared American future? With unprecedented population growth, Hispanics are projected to be almost one-third of the U.S. population by 2050. There are about thirty million Hispanic adults in this country, divided about half-and-half between foreign- and U.S.-born. About fourteen million of these people were registered to vote in 2008, approaching ten percent of the U.S. electorate.

And when you bore down into the numbers, the role of Latinos becomes even more evident. Not only Florida, with its twenty-seven electoral votes, but four other swing states with significant Latino populations were in play—Arizona, Colorado, New Mexico, and Nevada, with a total of twenty-nine electoral votes. President Obama won all but Arizona, and one could envision future victories for the Democrats there as well, when a Republican favorite son is not vying for the presidency.

IN SHORT, WE CAN SAY that the road to the White House came through our community—Hispanic voters were pivotal in the outcome of the 2008 presidential election. The Obama victory was a result of this overwhelming support, joined in a coalition with African-American voters, and an overwhelming youth vote across the board. One thing is clear: Without that coalition, the Democrats could have been defeated in enough states to produce an Electoral College victory for John McCain and Sarah Palin.

IT WOULD BE FOLLY FOR any party to avoid the chance to court Hispanic voters, and President George W. Bush had some success in doing so by playing up traditional social values in his 2000 and 2004 political campaigns. He seemed to be recognizing this in an interview with Fox News in the waning days of his presidency in January 2009. He said the Republican Party "should be open-minded about big issues like immigration reform, because if we're viewed as anti-somebody—in other words, if the party is viewed as anti-immigrant—then another fellow may say, well, if they're against the immigrant, they may be against me."[5]

The warning by the outgoing president was neither a surprise nor anything new. Republicans refused to join Bush and most Democrats in promoting comprehensive, rational immigration reform. Latino leaders, meanwhile, decried an alternate immigration bill offered by Wisconsin Republican Rep. Jim Sensenbrenner, which passed the House in December 2005. The bill, supported by the Republican majority, appeared to force mass deportations of undocumented immigrants, among other draconian measures. Latinos and their supporters, alienated by the Republican stance, demonstrated against the bill in Washington and around the country. The bill did not pass the Senate.

REPUBLICANS APPEARED TO BE MAKING a generation-changing mistake. Matthew Dowd, the Bush campaign's strategist and pollster in 2004, understood the urgent need to recognize and accommodate Latino political power.

"The Latino vote in this country is the fastest-growing demographic of the electorate—it's grown 400 percent in the last 20 years," he told the *Wall Street Journal*'s *The Journal Editorial Report*. "And I think both political parties understand that it's a demographic that is probably one of the most important—you know, who's going to have majority status in this country."[6]

As the Republicans reorganize for the future, one would think they'd be keeping the issue in mind—among other things, there is at least one other Bush waiting in the wings. Although the former president's brother Jeb decided in late 2008 not to run for Senate from the state of Florida, he is perennially considered as a future presidential candidate. Jeb, the former governor of Florida, has strong credentials in the Latino community. His wife, Columba Garnica Gallo, is of Mexican heritage, and one

---

5 *Fox News Sunday*, interview by Brit Hume, Fox, January 11, 2009.
6 Immigration Reform and the GOP, *The Journal Editorial Report*, quoted at http://origin.foxnews.com/story/0,2933,190286,00.html, April 3, 2006.

of their sons, George P. Bush, is a young lawyer who carries an impressive name, along with Latino roots.

Nevertheless, I have seen astonishing signs that Republicans still don't get it. At a time when it seems evident that politicians need to focus on dealing equitably with Latinos, they are staying close to the old formula—pandering to their anti-immigration allies. We need look no further than the Republican obstructionist response to the Democratic measure to restore health benefits to legal immigrants under twenty-one years old. President George W. Bush had twice vetoed our efforts to redress this inequity for children of legal immigrants, who were being forced since 1996 to observe a five-year waiting period for Medicaid and state health insurance. Republicans voted almost in lockstep against this provision, part of their effort to demand onerous verification procedures for immigrants—mostly Latinos. The Republicans in Congress seem to be oblivious to reality—their party was roundly whupped in 2008 and they are willing to cast aside a major part of the populace—and the electorate.

I want to stress repeatedly with emphasis that in talking about the future of Latinos in this country, you cannot segment off one group from the interests of all. We are the same people and have the same needs. According to opinion polls, two-thirds of Latino voters in 2008 saw the economy as the most imposing, immediate need facing the nation. They are no different from the larger population.

Despite that overwhelming concern shared by all Americans, Latino voters are expecting a sweeping change on immigration policy. More than two-thirds classify reform as an important issue for the immediate attention of the Obama administration, according to a survey released by NALEO. For us, this is our central civil rights issue. This concern is pivotal for all of us, our generation, our children, and their descendants. Certainly, equitable immigration reform cuts across all segments of our community, from Mexico through the Caribbean and Central and South America. But the larger issue involves the role of Latinos as full participants in American society, and demands a rejection of treating them as second-class citizens.

Clearly, Latinos are not giving their support to the Democratic Party by default. They expect President Obama and the 111th Congress to come to the rescue. The NALEO report said, "Strong support for the President-elect and the new Democratic-majority in Congress comes with high expectations from Latinos. Nearly 70% of Latino voters expect the Latino community to see improvements under the new Obama Administration. These hopes are even higher among immigrant voters with 3 out of every 4 expecting something better."[7]

THE RECENT HISTORY OF IMMIGRATION reform has shown at least some bipartisan interest. John McCain, one of the times that he equaled his maverick reputation, teamed up with Teddy Kennedy on an attempt to promote rational immigration reform. After bipartisan agreement on such issues as tightening border controls and enforcement measures against employment of undocumented workers in the Republican-controlled Senate in 2006, House Republican leaders pushed for hardline enforcement and rejected compromise proposals. As immigration reform collapsed for that session,[8] Republican-inspired ads around the country compared Mexican immigrants to Islamic terrorists.

McCain at the time said this in favor of the bill that bore his name: "Without enactment of comprehensive immigration reform as provided for under this bill, our nation's security will remain vulnerable. That is why we must pass this bill, and reach a meaningful final product through conference deliberations. He [Senator Kennedy] and I spent many months working to develop a comprehensive, reasonable, workable legislative proposal, much of which is contained in the bill before us."[9]

The Republican Party platform of 2008 said something quite different, and did not use the key phrase "comprehensive immigration reform." It focused instead on national security and existing laws. "Our determi-

---

7 New Post-Election Survey Provides In-Depth Analysis Of Latino Vote, NALEO Educational Fund, November 21, 2008, http://www.naleo.org/pr11-21-08.html
8 Council on Foreign Relations, "The 110th Congress and Immigration Reform," February 13, 2007, http://www.cfr.org/publication/12628/#2.
9 John McCain, statement, *Congressional Record*, May 25, 2006, http://www.c-spanarchives.org/congress/?q=node/77531&id=7461086

nation to uphold the rule of law begins with more effective enforcement, giving our agents the tools and resources they need to protect our sovereignty, completing the border fence quickly and securing the borders. . . . Experience shows that enforcement of existing laws is effective in reducing and reversing illegal immigration."[10]

WHILE RUNNING FOR PRESIDENT, McCAIN also backed away from his initial support for comprehensive reform (and the bill he cosponsored) and stressed enforcement only. At the time, he was titular leader of a party whose platform opposed a pathway to legalization for undocumented workers.[11] McCain's position, which looked like a tactical decision to cozy up to the Republican right, was hardly expected to gather support among immigration advocates. Some of McCain's aides said privately that he still supported comprehensive reform, but the confusion and waffling did nothing to help his standing among Latino voters.

As I said at the time, citing the Spanish saying "Del *dicho* al *hecho hay un gran estrecho*," there's a big difference between what people say and what they do.

The Democratic position does not condone illegality, but it seeks a rational, safe, legal, and orderly way to deal with a broken system that hurts the American economy, and does little to deal with the substance of national security.

NALEO's post-election analysis[12], by the way, shows that forty-six percent of Latino voters in 2008 were born outside the United States. And fifteen percent of the nearly ten million Latino voters were casting their ballots for the first time. Latinos come in many flavors, but overwhelmingly they share in Democratic social values—health care, Social Security, the right to work, and a fair playing field for all Americans. Latinos turned out in record numbers during the primaries, and seventy-eight percent of those voting were Democrats. It is clear that Hispanics

---

10 2008 Republican Party Platform. platform.gop.com/2008Platform.pdf, page 3
11 2008 Republican Platform, http://www.gop.com/2008Platform/NationalSecurity. htm#Def5, page 3
12 NALEO, Op. Cit. http://www.naleo.org/pr11-21-08.html

will be taking an increasing, often decisive role in electoral politics in this country.

One thing has been abundantly clear—when political parties invest time and energy in listening to Latino voters and talking to them, they do better.

There has been some very interesting analysis about voting trends by the Hispanic Project of the New Democrat Network. The project talks about diversity, and says that there cannot be a single strategy in attracting Latino voters. In the 2004 elections, according to a project report, President Bush made inroads with Hispanic voters, but "Democrats did much better in the states with aggressive Hispanic campaigns, and actually picked up ground in Colorado and Florida."[13]

I agree with the conclusions of the project, that Democrats must communicate more with Latino voters, recognizing that there is no national consensus or single voting bloc. Democratic officeholders should pay attention to Latin American affairs and issues close to Hispanics in the United States, and build long-term relationships among various parts of the community—political organizations, community-based organizations, businesses and chambers of commerce, and the most grassroots level.

It was always assumed that Latinos in this country would be reliably and overwhelmingly Democratic. But this has been changing so far in the twenty-first century, and the Democratic Party was slow to realize and react. Hispanic voters in many parts of the country amounted to a significant swing-voting bloc. Early on, the Bush administration took a series of steps that were attractive to Hispanic voters. The result was that the Republican share of the Hispanic vote increased from twenty-one percent in 1996 to forty percent in 2004. Among the key parts of the Republican drive for the Latino vote was an effort to promote the victorious senatorial campaign of Mel Martinez in Florida. Martinez preceded me by two years in 2004 as the first Cuban-American senator in U.S. history.

---

13 "Learning from the 2004 Campaign in the Hispanic Community," Hispanic Project, New Democrat Network, December 13, 2004.

*　　*　　*

MUCH FOCUS WAS GIVEN TO George W. Bush's appointment of Alberto Gonzales—his longtime general counsel and secretary of state when Bush was Texas governor—as attorney general. Gonzales was appointed to the Texas Supreme Court before being named White House counsel in 2001. He served about two and a half years as attorney general in Bush's second term, but resigned amid serious allegations of perjury and misuse of his office. Among the charges: that he used appointments of U.S. attorneys and other Justice Department posts for partisan politics and lied about it before Congress. There were other serious charges about malfeasance and misuse of his office in the pursuit of the war on terrorism.

Nevertheless, the fact that the Bush administration was choosing Latinos for high positions not traditionally accorded them resonated among some. Bush also traveled to Latin America in his second term, and appointed Carlos M. Gutierrez, a Cuban-American, and the former chairman of the Kellogg Company, as secretary of commerce.

INTERESTINGLY ENOUGH, DEMOCRATS SAW LOSSES in areas where they'd had strong supporters such as New Mexico and Nevada. And interestingly, with changing demographics in Florida, an influx of non-Cuban Latinos brought significant new Latino support for the Democratic presidential ticket. Analysis by the New Democrat Network noted that support for President Bush among Hispanics decreased from the 2000 election to the 2004 election, even among Cuban-American voters. But much of the gain for Democrats came from non-Cuban Latinos, whose numbers increased to fifty percent of the total Latino vote.

MY FRIENDS SIMON ROSENBERG AND Sergio Bendixen have done excellent work on voter trends. Simon is the head of the New Democrat Network and Sergio is one of the preeminent analysts of Hispanic polling trends.

Polling figures from 2006 show that an influx of immigrants to Florida from Puerto Rico, Central America, Argentina, Colombia, Brazil, and other Latin American countries has changed the dynamic. Non-Cuban Hispanics actually have a higher percentage of the statewide Latino vote than do Cuban-Americans. NDN reported that in the 2006 governor's race, the non-Cuban Latino vote went two to one in favor of Democrats. In summary, the Florida secretary of state reported in 2008 that Hispanic voters are now majority Democratic, an important shift where both presidents Bush won the state's electoral votes four times.

BEYOND REGIONAL POLITICS, HISPANICS ARE taking an increasingly significant role. Bill Richardson, now the governor of New Mexico, was appointed the chief deputy whip of the House, a top leadership position, and I succeeded him when President Clinton named him U.S. ambassador to the United Nations. It was actually the highest position a Latino has ever achieved, but it was still an appointment. Then I ran for and won the post of vice chairman of the Democratic Caucus, the first time a Latino won an elected Congressional position in either party in the history of the United States. I then went on to become the chairman of the Democratic Caucus in 2002, making me the third-ranking Democrat in the House. And now I've taken on the additional task of heading the Democratic Senatorial Campaign Committee, hardly a nonpartisan job.

But the point is that with the maturing of the political environment for the Hispanic community nationwide, we had the clout to come to the leadership table and say we deserved representation, as members of the broader system. As prominent Latinos and Latino organizations spoke out on the major issues of the day, they were also demonstrating that people like me were just plain qualified for the job. All this went beyond my being one congressional member from one district from New Jersey. It gave me a national leadership role on what issues were going to be highlighted. And it gave me an opportunity to talk about some of these issues not only from a New Jersey perspective but also in terms of a national Hispanic perspective. As a result I started traveling around the country, seeking to bring more Latinos to Congress, at the same time helping other members who had growing Latino populations in their districts, identifying what the issues were, how to campaign and engage. I get a wider picture in this way, not purely from a Mexican-American, Cuban-American, or Puerto Rican–American standpoint. We're dealing at the same time with issues particularly linked to Central and South Americans coming to the country in increasing numbers. Latino issues have their nuances in the West versus the East, South versus the North. In the case of Mexican-Americans, more than most, we find a multigenerational history, as with Interior Secretary Ken Salazar, of Colorado, whose family first settled in the vicinity of Santa Fe, New Mexico in the late sixteenth century. Ken's roots in Colorado alone go back to four generations of farming the same land, El Rancho Salazar. Talk about growing American Roots—Ken's family could not be more part of the fabric of our country and is not an exception. During our time together in the Senate, Ken and I often discussed how Hispanic heritage has often been omitted from the American saga. He recalls that in elementary school, he never heard about the real story of Hispanics in this country. "When I went to school," he told me, "I was taught that my parents came across on the *Mayflower* to Plymouth Rock and somehow they moved westward and through Manifest Destiny had ended up 'from sea to shining sea.'

"It was only when I went to college I began to study the real history of America and I discovered there was another history, that Mexican Americans in the southwest had come into California, Texas, Arizona, New Mexico and Colorado, long before Jamestown was settled. Part of my family helped settle Santa Fe in 1598. Part of my family had a major land grant from Spain, that included the territory from San Antonio, Texas all the way to Nuevo León in Mexico. We had many oral stories in our tradition and our history, yet it was never taught in the schools."

IT IS WORTH STOPPING TO discuss Ken's role at the Interior Department, placing him, along with Hilda Solis, the new secretary of labor, among the highest-ranking Hispanic members of the executive branch in U.S. history. A Latino legislator does not govern on behalf of his or her community, but serves as a representative of the group for the greater service to America. It is wrong to limit or assume parochial perspectives among the thousands of Latinos serving in government across the United States. In my case, when I'm asked what I'm doing for Latinos in my role as an elected official, or when news media have tagged me as a senator who focuses on Hispanic affairs, my answer is simple and succinct and my record is ample proof. I serve all the people.

The same is to be said for Ken Salazar, who served with me in the Senate representing Colorado until President Obama summoned him to the cabinet. Ken's responsibilities range from national parks to the Fish and Wildlife Service to the Bureau of Indian Affairs. What we expect of our leaders and what we will receive from Ken is the highest level of concern and service based on his experience as a legislator and as a state attorney general and an attorney specializing in water and environmental issues. Our role as government officials of Latino descent is basically this: We hear and we understand the sensitivities of our communities, born of heritage and environment. So as we go about our days, we apply our lessons and our unique perspectives in ways that others might not. In the end this is nothing less than the glory of our multicultural, multiethnic society.

He says that the Department of Interior "has a major role with respect to covering and displaying the history of all Americans." He aims to make sure especially that young people will have access to information and opportunities offered by the department, recreation, history, environmental studies. "We're creating opportunities for young people of all backgrounds, including underrepresented groups, including Hispanics."

I hear in his words much the same responsibility I first felt as a local elected official in New Jersey. We are not only expected to represent all Americans, we also do so with a great sense of pride and patriotism.

Much the same can be said about Hilda Solis, the twenty-fifth U.S. secretary of labor and the first Hispanic to serve in that role. She is a former California state legislator—the first Latina to serve in the California state senate—and was a member of Congress from 2001 until her designation by the president. She has dedicated herself to providing affordable health care for all Americans and to establishing programs to help working families. I feel a certain bond with the new labor secretary; like me, she is a first-generation Hispanic-American, the child of Nicaraguan and

Mexican immigrants. She has worked on behalf of labor unions and the poor and has described her support for "affirmative action in educational settings." She has said: "Encouraging more women and minorities to enter into a wide variety of fields will produce the qualified candidates needed in the public and private sectors. With the growing diversity of our country, our workforce and government will need to reflect and understand our population. I continue to encourage women and minorities to run for office."[14] Her perspective on human rights, unions, and the need for a sustainable living wage will inherently help build an equitable future for Latinos in this country.

In a historical perspective, recent immigrants arrive in different circumstances and even as they obtain citizenship have a new way of looking at things, compared with Latinos whose families arrived generations back. A prior generation of Latinos was striving for equal opportunity in the mid-twentieth century under the flag of equal opportunity and civil rights. That was the era of César Chávez of the United Farm Workers, rallying for equal rights, seeking power to transform the role of government in people's lives. Now the new immigrants also seek economic parity and opportunity, but arrive from places where they were deeply suspicious of the role of government.

This new group could be more susceptible to Republican ideas on social values, abortion, and gay rights, appealing to their conservatism in religious views, customs, and culture. Also, as people who have come to this country with a strong work ethic, they tend to be responsive to another portion of the Republican agenda: The government is there to offer an opportunity, but you get nothing unless you work hard for it on your own. An immigrant from a country with a history of official corruption, or with political strife or inefficiency, is used to making it on his or her own. "Do it on your own—you'll make it" are the bywords, and these communities are incredibly hardworking.

As I travel and listen to these different groups, I sense another type of

14 "Congressional Conversations," interview with Deva Kyle, Young Women's Task Force, September 2006, http://www.ywtf.org/YWTF/Programs/CongressionalConversations.aspx.

diversity, not just among those who come from Mexico or Colombia or El Salvador, but also in terms of how long their families have been here, versus those who are newly arrived. Sergio Bendixen recognized the dichotomy during polling he conducted during the Bush-Kerry presidential campaign. Multigenerational Hispanic-Americans have a different view of government and their relationship to government versus new citizens who come from countries where there is a distrust of government. One of the key factors is clearly the proficiency of use of the English language.

It's not that new immigrants don't want to master English, just that they haven't been able to do so yet, and sadly there hasn't been adequate classroom space to meet the demand. There's a significant need for extending English-language training and literacy courses for immigrants, an investment that will pay off mightily over time.

Literacy programs, cultural training, and transitional support for newly arrived immigrants are part of the story. We promote citizenship training, we educate our children to participate in the political process, we stage voter-education drives, and we encourage and train many people to become the leaders of the future. In the process we add to the numbers of Latinos who are graduating toward full participation in our democracy. The Latino community deserves the understanding of all Americans— Latinos strive only to take their rightful place in society. As more of us vote, enter the workforce, become teachers and professionals, the American union is not at risk; on the contrary, our society is enhanced. Many Latinos have come to the United States from countries where their rights were limited and curtailed; their safety and livelihoods were in danger. They are here to realize the dreams of freedom and popular democracy. As Latinos become more of a political and social force, they pitch in and enhance the values that all Americans aspire to; their experience of discrimination and injustice or their thirst for opportunity brought them here and they are already seeking a firm base in expanding and promoting our democracy.

CHAPTER 2

GOOD TEACHERS
AND GOOD FORTUNE

That's the point. It goes like this: Teaching is touching life.

JAIME ESCALANTE

We build the future one person at a time. In my case, a strong family set my life course—parents who wanted me to succeed in the new homeland they had chosen—and the good fortune of being nurtured by mentors at a young age. I submit to you the idea that we need to replicate the positive aspects of life in our immigrant communities— sacrifice by one generation dreaming of new opportunities for their children and descendants, school systems that attract and inspire and encourage those children—and we need to ensure the stability of an economic and social system that allows such things to happen. On that basis, I write about myself, reflecting on how to best inspire the success stories that must come from the Hispanic community, and from throughout the immigrant populations across our country.

I grew up poor in a tenement in Union City, the first in my family to go to college. I was not in a likely trajectory that would lead to my being one of only a hundred United States senators in a country of three hundred million people. But I was fortunate enough to get a big push toward a life of service early on, surrounded by family, by nurturing teachers and mentors. I was lucky enough to see America's promise fulfilled for me, and now I'm working as hard as I can every day to make sure that promise exists for future generations of Americans.

Back in elementary school a teacher told me the story of a man who was walking along a beach, and the beach was filled with starfish that had been swept ashore. The man saw another man picking up the starfish and saving their lives by throwing them back into the sea. The first man said, "Why are you even bothering to do that? There must be thousands of starfish. You can't possibly save all of them—you can't possibly make a difference." The second man picked up another starfish, tossed it back into the water, and said, "Well, it just made a difference for that one."

I'VE COME A LONG WAY from being that chubby latchkey kid doing his homework and waiting for his parents to come home to a tenement apartment in Union City. They were the rock of stability that gave me a chance to dream. The future is in the hands of solid hardworking people in this country, immigrants among them.

My parents, Mario and Evangelina, moved to the United States from Cuba in 1953. My mother was the driving force behind the decision. She didn't like living under the right-wing dictator General Fulgencio Batista, who had been in power on and off for twenty years, and she wisely sensed danger and instability in the air. Fidel Alejandro Castro Ruz, a twenty-seven-year-old law school graduate, had led a rebel attack on the Cuban army base at Moncada that year, killing a number of soldiers.

My mother dreamed of stability and safety for her children. She made a momentous decision—she wanted to create a future for her family in the United States.

It took some convincing with my father. He was working in a tie company and didn't want to leave, or to lose the little money and few possessions they had. But my mother was adamant. Life was tough, but she sensed worse times were coming. She told him, "I don't want my children growing up here in this set of circumstances." There were two kids already—my brother, Reinaldo, who was born in 1945, and my sister, Caridad, born in 1943. My parents were hard workers; you could place them in the lower middle class. Life was hard, and work wasn't always available.

With my mother's insistent argument about the uncertain future, he finally agreed. They packed up and set off for Puerto Rico. My mother wasn't happy there, though. Luckily, a few months later, the tie company my father worked at offered him a chance to work in the United States. By the fall of 1953, my father, mother, brother, and sister arrived in New York, my mother already pregnant with their third child—me. When they got to New York, they had close friends waiting for them—soon to become my godparents. It is so often that way with immigrants. They welcomed our family and helped them get established.

I WAS BORN ON NEW Year's Day 1954. I was too young to remember anything when we moved out of New York City a few years later. We crossed the Hudson River, first to Hoboken, and then to Union City, which became my hometown. Union City had been a city of immigrants since the late eighteen hundreds, a base for a succession of nationalities— Austrian, Swiss, German, Irish, and Italian. A small number of Cuban immigrants were in the latest wave, attracted by manufacturing jobs. Union City was known for the manufacture of Schiffli lace, a fine machine-made embroidery. My mother started working as a seamstress and my father took on itinerant carpentry work.

Unfortunately, by the time I was entering public school, downtown Union City had become a ghost town, symptomatic of the postwar urban flight to the suburbs. I didn't realize it, but the city was on the decline; shops along Bergenline Avenue, the main drag, were boarded up and closed. People were working hard and long hours, but few of our neighbors were well-off.

Our family had been in the vanguard of Cuban migration to the United States. This was beyond the vision of an elementary-school child, but I could see that there weren't a lot of kids around like me—Cuban, with a family that spoke Spanish at home. That was already starting to change, though. Waves of Cubans started coming to the United States, following Castro's overthrow of Batista in 1959. Many of those arriving in Union City in this new round of Cuban immigrants came from Fomento in central Cuba, whereas we were from Havana; frequently with immigrants, new arrivals tend to reach out to friends and families and create mini communities of people who lived close together back home.

The embroidery industry attracted the new arrivals, ready to work long hours with as much overtime as they could get, pushing themselves to make it. Their children descended on the local schools, and the structure of the schools began to change. Whereas I was one of the few Latinos in the early years, by the time I got to second and third and fourth grades, there were many more children like me. Some were arriving in the so-called freedom flights, others through Operation Peter Pan, sponsored by the United States and the Catholic Church. About fourteen thousand children came to the United States under Operation Peter Pan between 1960 and 1962. One of the most prominent beneficiaries of the flights, by the way, was my Republican colleague in the Senate, Mel Martinez of Florida.

With the long hours, my parents got up early and were home late, and my brother and sister, much older than me, were also out of the house during the day. So when classes were over, I was on my own. The order of the day was to go home, lock myself in, and do my homework until my parents arrived. I was a classic latchkey child.

We lived at 4607 Hudson Avenue, a few blocks from Bergenline Avenue, and just down the street from Roosevelt Elementary School. We were on a block of two rows of tenements. But across the street was a row of narrow two-family houses with garages. To my young eyes, it looked like those rich people were living in Shangri-la. That block—a couple of streets from the Hudson River and just north of the Lincoln Tunnel— was my tiny world. I didn't have a bike, but if I wanted to go exploring, I was sometimes allowed to borrow a bike from one of my friends and ride up and down the street.

But my permitted range stopped at the next corner, and I could go that far only when my mother got home. My mom and dad were very protective parents, and that was not unusual in the society we were part of. The whole Cuban-culture lifestyle was quite restricted. First things first: You had to do well in school. That meant there was no time to play until homework was done—stay in and study. Even when I was allowed to go out to play, I was being watched and the rule was fixed: I was not to go past the end of the block. Life, according to my parents, was dangerous. I can still see the image of my mother, and, if not her, the mothers of my friends, leaning over the windowsills, gazing to the street below and monitoring us all the time.

Our parents didn't have a lot of money. We ate well and I never experienced hunger or the fear of poverty. Our apartment was small, but our family was tightly knit. There was a lot of love. The biggest extravagance I can remember is having the chance once in a while to walk down to the bodega on the corner and buy five cents' worth of candy. My impression is that I got special treatment because I was the youngest of the three children; my parents did as much as they could and struggled, as I remember, to make sure I had Christmas presents every year. That's not to say that we were spending lots of money on extravagances, but I was never wanting.

DURING THE SCHOOL YEAR, MY mother came home in the late afternoon, cleaned, cooked, and did the laundry. Busy as she was, she would always take the time to find out about my homework. She didn't speak English or read it very well, but she questioned me about my assignments and whether I had finished absolutely everything. "What were you supposed to do?" she asked in a nightly routine. "And what did you really do?" After the interrogation, she turned the job over to my sister, Caridad, telling her, "This is what he told me he did. Make sure it's done."

Failure was not an option in my home and bad grades in particular were a major issue that would not be tolerated. This was my mother's attitude: He was born here, he has the best chance, he's got the best shot among all the children, and that's what he has to do. I think that my mother regretted that Caridad and Reinaldo didn't have the same opportunities I did. My brother started college, but didn't finish. He needed to make money, and went to work with my father in his carpentry.

My mother's message came through loud and clear. "You have one job and one job only. You are the one who has the unique opportunity for an education." Even at the earliest age I recognized that I had been given a big responsibility, and I took it seriously. I wanted to do what I was told, and it will be no surprise that, as a result, I brought home good grades.

So every day when school let out, I walked down Hudson Avenue and locked myself in the apartment. I would eat my *merienda*—a little afternoon snack—and then start my homework, methodically doing all my reading and assignments with the understanding that my mother was going to grill me about homework. This is what I remember—the importance of school, homework, building responsibility by something so basic as taking out the garbage. After that, I could think about managing a quick bike ride before nightfall, then starting over again the next morning.

It was a fundamental set of values, enforced by mother and father with their vision of how to build a future for their youngest child. If only we could bottle that formula and sell it to every parent in every immigrant community in this country.

One of my earliest clear memories about the outside world was the assassination of President Kennedy in 1963. I wasn't even ten years old, but I remember sitting with my family riveted to the television set. There was absolute silence, except when my mother said, "I can't believe that this could happen in the United States." I was really not aware enough about current events at that tender age. All I can summon up about the Cuban missile crisis the year before was that we had strange air-raid drills in school. Every so often the teachers would order us to duck our heads under the desk or crouch over.

By the time I reached eighth grade, I had a vague sense that I wanted to accomplish something in the world, not knowing exactly what that meant, or how to summon the wherewithal to make it happen. I did get somewhere that year—my teachers chose me as the head of the junior police crossing guards. I was very proud.

I was a shy kid when I got to Union Hill High School in 1969, and wasn't much into socializing or sports. I was a studying machine, but by then current events had invaded my world. I was deeply affected by the deaths of Martin Luther King and Robert Kennedy a year earlier. I sensed that things in the country were not going well and that America needed to look for change.

By junior year, things had changed. I had new mentors, especially my history teacher, Tom Highton, who had strong opinions and was especially vocal about the right to vote. Voters' rights for young people that year, 1970, had become a major issue. We were in the middle of the Vietnam War, but most soldiers were under twenty-one and too young to vote. Tom Highton encouraged debate and discussion among his classes, asking a simple question: "How can an eighteen-year-old be old enough to die for his or her country," he asked, "but not old enough to vote?"

His argument was pure and simple, and I was impressed. Tom's brother-in-law, John Mielo, was also a teacher and encouraged students to think about politics. They both nurtured me, and said I had the capacity to be a leader. In short order, I'd gone from being a wallflower to being brave enough—once they planted the idea—to run to be president of the student council. I won and started looking for causes I could support.

Meanwhile, my academic advisers had notified me that because of my ability and grades I had qualified for the high school senior honors program. The only hitch was I was told I'd have to purchase the books for the assignments—which cost two hundred dollars. Quite an honor, but the only problem was that my parents didn't have anywhere near two hundred dollars to spare. The answer from the school was, no money, no honors program. For the life of me, I couldn't understand how, if I had the ability and the grades, I could actually be barred from the honors program because I couldn't afford it. I created such a ruckus that the school administration got sick of arguing, told me to shut up, gave me the books, and put me in the honors program.

That wasn't good enough, because I felt guilty. The school was still being unfair to other students, many of them my friends, who also had the ability and the grades, but also didn't have the money. They didn't get into the honors program—the only difference was that they hadn't spoken up and made a nuisance of themselves like I had. The case was clear—the system was unjust and skewed, in this case against my friends because they hadn't spoken up.

One of my first political acts, and one of my first trips to Washington, was accepting an invitation from our local congressman, Dominick V.

Daniels, to testify before a House education committee in the late 1960s on the perspective of a student about the validity of so-called "impact aid." As a result of U.S. policy toward Cuba, especially after the failed Bay of Pigs invasion under President Kennedy, tens of thousands of refugees and thousands of children were entering the country. The sudden influx of children in places like Union City, elsewhere in New Jersey and New York, and throughout South Florida was overwhelming the school systems, and people argued there was a basis for obtaining federal funding to alleviate the crowded conditions.

Speaking in public was a nightmare. I was a good student, but a total introvert. I was horrified to find out from my guidance counselor that one of my last graduation requirements was to take a public-speech course, focusing on extemporaneous speaking. I refused.

"What's your problem?" the counselor asked.

I didn't tell him that I was afraid. My answer was succinct. "I don't want to do that."

I ended up taking the class and did all the assignments, but still refused to stand in front of the class. I lived in a little world by myself with my mother and father and brother and sister. When the neighborhood kids went outside to play after school or socialize, I was locked in the house studying. We had a routine, isolated and comfortable. I would have been content to remain in the background, but my public-speaking teacher kept forcing the issue.

"You have no choice," she said. "It just won't work to do the assignments and not get up in front of the class."

I still refused. And then she lowered the boom.

"You're either going to do this or fail."

She said the word "fail"; it was like hearing someone in the movie *Back to the Future* call Marty "stupid." She'd hit upon my mother's mantra: "Failure is not an option." So I went along. My teacher started working with me after school, giving me coaching and encouragement. Slowly, she coaxed me toward the goal. First, she said, "Write a short story and read it to me." Nobody was in the room. Then she said, "Write a poem, read it again. There's nobody here."

After all the coaching, she was managing to loosen me up. But then came the ultimate test.

"You're going to be the narrator in the school Christmas program," she announced one day. I almost fainted. At our school that meant that everyone from the ninth to the twelfth grade would attend—eight hundred people watching the Union Hill Chorus.

The bottom line is that I swallowed hard, marched onto the stage, and managed to stand in front of all those people. After the first chorus, I looked around and said to myself, "Oh my God, I can do it." I was a success and suddenly was hooked by the idea that I could stand up and speak in public.

Years later, I had the chance to talk to this unsung hero, Gail Harper, my public-speaking teacher, who was not unsung for me. She told me that everything she'd done for me had been planned out and on purpose, that she'd looked at my writings and seen promise. Challenging me with failure made the difference.

So when I talk about role models and encouraging students to go beyond themselves, I think of personal experience. We need to encourage such mentors, with higher pay for teachers, and the kind of training that reproduces millions of times over the process I experienced.

I GRADUATED FROM UNION HILL in 1972 and was accepted to Saint Peter's College in Jersey City. All the while, I had been mulling over the broken politics of the school board, and when I got to Saint Peter's, I decided to do something about it. I was now eighteen, a new voter. So I started a petition drive for a referendum to change the composition of the Union City School Board; it had always been a closed set of political appointees chosen by the mayor. My proposal was to allow Union City voters to elect the school board. With the help of like-minded friends, we put together thousands of signatures, placed the referendum on the city ballot, and succeeded in passing it.

And when election time came around a year later, I was on the ballot for a seat on Union City's first elected school board. I figured that I would be a solid candidate, since I had helped sponsor the referendum that forced the new voting system. Not so fast, Menendez. I was concerned when I found out that the minister of a local church was running for the same slot. How do you beat a man of the cloth with a built-in base and— one could only assume—God on his side?

Well, I venture to say that neither of us used negative advertising; it wouldn't have been prudent, as George H. W. Bush might have said. I ran on merits and somehow managed to win. I was twenty years old. The local daily newspaper, the *Hudson Dispatch*, sent over a reporter to write a profile when they determined that I was the youngest school board member ever elected in the state of New Jersey. Their question was, "Kid, what do you want to do when you grow up?"

I didn't hesitate, telling the reporter, "I want to be a United States senator."

We took our job seriously on the new elected school board and brought significant changes. One of the first orders of business for me was a great success: no more charging students for things they deserved but couldn't pay for. We went much further: We also set out to change the teaching approach and diversify the teaching staff, choosing applicants from a broad spectrum of colleges. Previously, most teachers came from one or two New Jersey state schools. We reached out to other schools in the state, and beyond. We also initiated changes in district business practices. It was a period in which the school budget was getting more complicated; the district had grown rapidly and considerably with the influx of Latino students.

In a larger view, the school board changes were an example of American democracy at its best. At the same time, the decision to adopt an elected school board had wide repercussions in the city. The school board's power was still limited; the Union City Commission had veto power over the district's budget. We often heard complaints about cronyism coming down from the mayor's office. Those complaints grew to the establishment of a new organization, Project 70, which defeated Mayor William Musto's bid for reelection in 1970 on a pledge of civic reform.

From my point of view, the new crowd ended up being worse than the administration they had replaced. My two mentors from high school,

Tom Highton and John Mielo, agreed with me and put together a movement to reform the reformers. They teamed with Musto, who served at the same time as New Jersey state senator, and helped him return to office in 1974. I ended up working for Mayor Musto as an aide.

Meanwhile, I had been elected to a second term on the school board. I had graduated from Saint Peter's and was on my way to Rutgers Law School in Newark. My colleagues on the school board asked me to assume the role of board secretary, a paid job, unlike my elected position. I accepted the post, which basically made me the chief financial officer of the school district.

The restored city government under Mayor Musto did well in its first term, from 1974 to 1978. It stabilized the city finances, made the streets a lot safer, and approved the school board's request for a much-needed school-construction program. I continued to serve as school board secretary, with the assignment of performing much of the school board's business.

Musto and the Commission were reelected in 1978, and I started to see serious trouble. Coming back from a vacation trip, I found that a series of checks had been issued for a particular contract without my approval. I protested, asking how checks could be issued without my authorization, and without confirmation from the architect involved that the work had been completed. There was no satisfactory answer. The more I dug into it, the more concerned I became. The construction projects were ringing up questionable cost overruns, but the school board didn't listen to my complaints. I was their employee with no independent authority; the school board kept passing the resolutions. It became evident that the president of the school board was working on shady projects with the mayor; the mayor, in turn, had other construction plans, such as trying to sell the city's most popular park, two square blocks across from St. Michael's Monastery, to build a department store. I protested even more, arguing that the park was important to the lives of residents of Union City, the most densely populated city in the United States.

I refused to look the other way, and began to complain in public about illegal financial dealings. The issue developed as a major local news story. The FBI began investigating, and the U.S. attorney filed federal corruption charges against the mayor and others involved with him. I was called to testify for the prosecution, received death threats, and wore a bulletproof vest for a month. Musto was convicted of racketeering.

In the process, I was working with friends on a housecleaning campaign to wipe out corruption on the City Commission and the school board. Despite the corruption conviction, the mayor and his allies were up for reelection to a third term in 1982. I ran against the mayor's Commission ticket and lost by several hundred votes, the only election I have ever lost. The crowning irony was that the mayor won reelection two days after he was sentenced to seven years in federal prison. What better evidence of the difficulty of breaking a powerful political machine. They were convicted on racketeering charges, sentenced, and reelected. It was a well-oiled machine—we lost by very little, but we lost.

I was frustrated and disillusioned by losing under such circumstances. If the public thought more of an incumbent mayor who had been sentenced to seven years in federal prison on the eve of the election, I resigned myself to the idea that my role in life would be to promote social reform and equality through the law. Up to that time, a lot of my legal practice had been pro bono. Now I went back to it, ready to challenge injustice and corruption where I found it.

But some people in Union City were lobbying for yet another reform movement, angered as I was by the corruption. They included schoolteachers, firefighters, police, and other public employees, many of whom had supported me and were fired wrongfully by the city, even though they should have been protected as civil servants.

They came literally knocking at the door of my law office, saying, in effect, "We believed in you, we followed you. What are you going to do about it?" We assembled wrongful-dismissal cases in court, charging that the city had violated the rights of the fired civil servants, and those cases started to be won.

Mayor Musto, meanwhile, was serving jail time, but maneuvered to have his wife take over his seat on the Commission. I had sworn off politics, but was persuaded by my friends and colleagues to run again for the

Commission. I was elected in 1986, and we threw out the remains of the machine. The five-member Commission chose me as mayor.

We inherited a city on the verge of bankruptcy and the first day of office I had to lay off dozens of civil servants; when we discovered the magnitude of the financial problems, we laid off a third of the workforce. It was especially painful. Union City was by now a majority-Latino city; these people, who never had many opportunities in public life, now had an advocate, and the advocate, under civil service rules, had to let them go, since most of the recent hires were Hispanic. It was a bitter moment, but we saved the city from bankruptcy; in the medium term, we turned the city around and brought many people back to work.

One of my proudest achievements as mayor was the establishment of our nationally acclaimed day-care program. Working with Dana Berry, long at the forefront of day-care issues, we put together a versatile program that included early-childhood-education job training for day-care workers. Most of the children were Hispanic, and many of their mothers were either working or on welfare. By taking in their children and working with the mothers, we helped them break out of the welfare cycle. We also reached out to grandmothers in the community, retired senior citizens, and trained them to work at the day-care centers. Our reasoning was that grandmothers use a lifetime of experience and love, while we gave them part-time employment. This intergenerational concept fought poverty, helped children and their families, and produced a new cadre of day-care professionals. What I liked about it was that it mirrored the way a Latino family functions: one generation helping another, even living together, with Grandma nurturing her children and grandchildren, all in the same system.

We put together an impressive team of teachers to train our new day-care workers, creating a formal course of study and a graduation program. I was always moved when I attended graduation, especially seeing these seniors having a new sense of purpose in their lives. We went one step further, establishing a home day-care component, with an additional training course for the seniors.

The program won national awards, and was recognized for its joint goals of breaking the welfare cycle, offering work to a new class of trained people, and providing options for parents who work.

We brought back Little League baseball to Union City, which had been abandoned for years. We rebuilt a county park and convinced the county to lease it to us. Baseball, of course, is huge in many sectors of Latin culture, and the program was a tremendous success.

We started observing José Martí Day in Union City, and it has developed into a big celebration. That actually caused me one of the occasional problems I encountered as the city's first Latino mayor. At some point, a news photographer took a picture of me in my office near a portrait of José Martí. Sometime after that, a woman approached me while I was out campaigning on the street.

"You know, there are a lot of American heroes. You don't need José Martí in your office; you should have some great Americans."

"Well, if you come to my office," I answered, "you'll see there is a portrait of George Washington on one wall, and a picture of Abraham Lincoln on the other. But José Martí fits in the category—he was a great man of the Americas, one who believed in the same principles of democracy and freedom that we share, and everything he did was inspired by the United States."

My goal in such cases was to disabuse people of the idea that Hispanics were somehow less worthy, less American, or less patriotic. My point has always been this—Latinos are among the latest wave of immigrants who have come to these shores because they cherish and want to share these same ideals.

My view of such things was based on experience. I knew I was Cuban, and I was very proud of that. My family was Cuban, our neighbors in our apartment building were Latinos, and we were poor. Most of the families across the street in what I saw as palatial two-family homes were not Latinos. I knew something about being needy before I could describe it. Yet I didn't particularly consider that I was living the life of a Cuban-American. My knowledge of Spanish wasn't all that good; certainly I didn't speak it as well as I do now. I spoke some form of Spanglish when I spoke it at all, because my parents insisted on English, English, English;

my father spoke English pretty well, but my mom never did, although she understood when spoken to.

As a Hispanic growing up in the United States, I knew that prejudice and misunderstanding were always close to the surface. Even though I always spoke English perfectly well, it was clear that bias would come close to me in my personal and professional lives. I'm grateful that my heritage has allowed me to recognize and bridge cultural misunderstandings. I always recall my time as the young mayor of Union City, New Jersey, the first Latino to hold the job at a moment when an increasing number of Puerto Ricans, Cubans, and other Latin Americans were moving to the city. The cultural differences were evident. We had, for example, a police chief right out of central casting, a law-and-order man of European background. At one point, he wanted to conduct a sweep of the streets, to put an end to what he considered to be loitering. He saw poor Latinos hanging around outside, talking in groups, playing games, sitting on park benches, and he concluded such street activity was a menace. We clashed heavily on the issue and I shut him down for all the right reasons. When I observed the same scene, I recognized the vibrant sights and sounds of the kind of central plaza found in every village, town, and city in Latin America. Miraculously, the same energy had been transferred to the streets of Union City. Hispanic life is highly social; the plaza is the center of Latino life, full of political debate, recreation, gossip, and courting, even business deals. Take that away and the *sabor* and vitality of the community is lost. I'd like to take readers to the typical Latino plaza in America so they can sense the dynamic, loving sights and sounds.

Another defining moment came during a hearing at city hall. A woman in the audience was struggling to make a comment in broken English, and from the dais, I switched to Spanish, asking the woman to tell me her problem. My gut reaction was to help someone with a problem, but my choice brought controversy. People objected to the idea that their mayor should ever speak Spanish, complaining that the city's business should be conducted exclusively in English. At that point I called a recess. After the break, I invited those present down to the Union City official archives and showed them some dusty minutes from the late eighteen hundreds. The transcripts were sometimes unreadable—the proceedings of city meetings were often conducted in German.

My sympathy for the lady at the council meeting came from deep knowledge of the problem. And the broader Latino view could not be separated from a basic sense of fairness. As soon as I was elected to the school board and throughout my career, I had Spanish-speaking constituents asking for help. I was driven to want to speak to them, and I improved my Spanish skills. My understanding came as a result of civic engagement. Hispanic constituents came to me as their only resource, and they taught me in return. In their view, they sought someone to speak to as a friendly face with similar roots, because I was Latino as they were. And since I was the only Latino serving as an elected official at the time in local government, people came to see me as a natural outlet to try to resolve their own challenges.

We forget too often our early lessons and sometimes need to be reminded that this is a nation of immigrants. Today's immigrants—as with Europeans of another age, and African-Americans, although their arrival has a divergent history—share the same goals. All want to succeed, to create and share the wealth of progress.

After winning the 1986 election and becoming mayor, I spent a lot of my time at the capital in Trenton, lobbying to avoid Union City's falling into bankruptcy. It was evident that many people didn't understand the challenges and pressures of cities like mine. We needed to provide well-paying jobs, adequate housing and education, money for public safety. I decided to run for the state legislature in 1987, concurrently as mayor, which was then a common practice in the state. I won, and for once it was not a first for Latinos—there had been a Republican Latino in the assembly once before for a single two-year term. Three years later, in 1990, I won a state senate seat and became the first Hispanic and for a long time the only one to serve. Finally, in 2007, Maria Teresa Ruiz, a first-generation Puerto Rican–American, became the first Latina to serve in the state senate.

I have of course always been proud to serve as an elected official of Hispanic descent in the United States. In my career, many people have taken me as a symbol, and as their own representative even far beyond the borders of my constituency. People have tended to see me as a vehicle for their aspirations and as playing a role in helping them meet their challenges. But it is essential and basic for me to say that I have always represented all my constituents. Throughout my career, it's interesting to note, I've never been elected in a constituency that was majority Hispanic in voter registration. At the same time, I have a great feeling of pride: Just as we have been represented by non-Hispanics, I am privileged to represent all the people. And it is also a sign of the times that I can do so.

I HAVE SERVED IN THE context of an agenda for all people from my city, and state, and all of America. Educational opportunity was a real challenge for everyone, but disproportionate numbers of Hispanics were dropping out of school. Crime was a big issue and it wasn't unique to one community—all people in New Jersey were concerned.

I had this internal dialogue while I was in the state legislature: I knew where I came from, but I now had a unique opportunity for the Thirty-third Legislative District of New Jersey; I didn't get here for ethnic reasons, nor did I intend to represent just the Latino point of view. On the one hand, I didn't want to be defined as a one-issue politician. But I also knew that I had an obligation to the community as a spokesperson.

I was sometimes chagrined when reporters came to talk to me. They wanted to talk to me as the Latino legislator about welfare or dropout rates, because in their minds, these were the issues I was supposed to be dealing with. They had this narrow-minded focus about what Menendez was up to. I wanted to go beyond issues of class; I wanted to talk about the overall state economy, broader issues of education and health care. So I broke free. I recognized that Latino officials are not elected to deal with parochial matters; they are elected because they are participants in the system and deserve a significant voice, and should emphasize their greater role in all aspects of local and national affairs. In this case, I sponsored, for example, the state's telecommunications act, which came to be known as the "fiber optics bill." The goal was to make New Jersey the best-wired state in the nation, and to link the high-speed communications to educational opportunities. Thus, I could serve both facets of my job at the same time. Within this overarching bill, a landmark piece of legislation, I found a way to make sure that disadvantaged schools were not overlooked. We set up a pilot program at the Christopher Columbus Middle School in Union City, among the first to be wired with fiber optics. The school system assembled a broad spectrum of students, many disadvantaged and bound to fail or underperform—poor, Anglo, Hispanic, and African-American. They created a multimedia learning system that included a home-teaching component, integrating technology with teaching. The students in that pilot program outperformed their peers in statewide tests, and their attendance and graduation rates soared to ninety percent. President Clinton and Vice President Gore came to visit, and Bill Gates wrote about the program in his book *The Road Ahead.*

"It's no surprise that the program has been expanded from the seventh grade now to include the entire middle school," Gates wrote. He noted that the system was installed with help from Bell Atlantic, whose CEO said the result was "a true learning community in which the home and school reinforce and support each other."[1] Even Newt Gingrich wrote about it.

The U.S. Census in 1990 resulted in redistricting of congressional districts in New Jersey and around the United States. Frank Guarini, whose seat in Congress included Union City, decided to resign rather than campaign in a newly drawn district that included portions of four New Jersey counties and sixteen cities, adding in portions of Newark and Elizabeth.

I decided to run and soon found myself in a bizarre Democratic primary race. Winning the Democratic primary in a predominantly Democratic district was tantamount to victory in the general elections. I had the support of state and Democratic leaders, but my opponent played the ethnic card. He put out word on the street, especially in parts of Bayonne and Jersey City, where the Irish-American population was significant, that I didn't speak English, and wore a sombrero and a serape.

---

1 Bill Gates, *The Road Ahead* (2006), 232–33.

It sounds funny, but at the time, it was potentially effective negative campaigning. I wouldn't stand for it, nor would I accept the implication that a Hispanic wasn't going to pay attention to Bayonne or the rest of New Jersey. First he put out a campaign flyer with a burning cigar on the cover, connecting me to Cuba, and saying "we need to stop this!"—in essence we need to stop a Hispanic from winning. So I decided to deal with the problem head on. I went straight to Bayonne and gave a speech; I pledged that, if elected, I would keep open the satellite congressional office there. After making that promise, I went on to talk about the issues I thought were important. When I finished, a woman approached me and, speaking with an Irish brogue, said she was very glad that she came to hear me speak.

I thanked her, and asked what had most impressed her. I've never forgotten the answer. "It's not so much what you said, but the fact that you can speak English. I'm going to vote for you." I didn't know how to respond, but smiled and thanked her again. Take the votes any way you can.

I won the primary and was elected in November. Dennis Collins, the former mayor of Bayonne, helped me follow through on my campaign pledge and became a key aide. "Bob," he said, "the more they know you, the more they love you."

My arrival in Washington in January 1993 coincided with the start of the Clinton administration. It signaled several changes and new firsts. I was the first Hispanic member of the House from New Jersey, and the first Cuban-American Congressman from any state who was a Democrat. Also in the new freshman class for the 103rd Congress was Nydia M. Velázquez from Brooklyn, the first Puerto Rican woman to enter the House. In 2006, she was named chairwoman of the House Small Business Committee, making her the first Latina to chair a full congressional committee. Also coming to Congress was Luis V. Gutierrez of Chicago, also of Puerto Rican descent, and who now plays a key role in dealing with immigrants' rights in the United States.

We all joined the Congressional Hispanic Caucus, which at the time was overwhelmingly Mexican-American. The arrival of three Democrats with roots tracing back to the Caribbean changed the dynamics. This, in turn, attracted José Serrano of the Bronx, a Puerto Rican who had arrived in 1990 to replace retiring congressman Bobby Garcia, but had not been fully engaged in the caucus.

The resulting change was interesting. Some of the Mexican-Americans from the South had a conservative slant and did not always agree with liberals from California and the East Coast. Yet there were few differences of opinion about core concerns facing Latinos—and many other minorities—whether it was high school dropout rates health care for seniors or discrimination based on who people were, or what they looked like. It was shocking to all of us, for example, that for a long time in the United States Mexican-Americans who served in the armed forces of this country were barred from being buried in military cemeteries. They had gone through a long, humiliating period of discrimination, something that attacked the very notion of service, despite the fact that they were clearly loyal to the concept of military service.

I was clearly the member of another subset among the Hispanics in Congress. I was from the Caribbean, but I was a Cuban-American, and the only Democratic Cuban-American for that matter. This brought interesting differences in nuance. The Republican Cuban-Americans and I shared one core point of agreement: We opposed the Castro regime equally and totally. But after that, we had divergent views of the national agenda.

I have always faced opposition from Cuban Republicans in New Jersey, who have continually looked for ways to challenge me. Their main method of attack—using themes they figured would work on Democrats—has been policy on Cuba. But since my view on U.S. policy toward the Castro regime is largely the same as theirs, they've always hit a brick wall on that one. The next effort has been to criticize me, as a result, for being a Democrat at all—"You should really be a Republican"—which is ridiculous because my broader position on social issues is firmly Democratic. By the time I got to Congress, the serious sniping was a nonstarter. You can't get beyond being mayor of Union City, New Jersey, or running from my district for the legislature or anywhere else, without cutting your teeth on the Cuba issue. By the time I got to the House of Representatives, it was abundantly clear that there wasn't an iota of separation between Republicans and me on Cuba policy. It was equally clear that I differed openly with significant members of my own party, and that was that. My position gave me an opening, not only to develop personal support among voters, but also to help raise support for other candidates.

South Florida Cuban Republicans, if they're honest, will tell you they don't enjoy my visits down there. I'm probably the only national Democrat who can get on local Spanish-language radio and TV stations, because my credentials are impeccable. And as a result, I am trusted as a friend in the community to campaign on behalf of Democrats, who, in turn, pay more attention to Cuban-American concerns.

There has been a natural affinity for Democratic Party principles among Cuban-American and other Latino immigrants to the northeastern United States. The profile of those immigrants tended to be working-class and they were looking for progressive, pro-union, pro-worker agendas. Cuban-Americans in the North held and still hold the same view as their brethren in Miami regarding the Castro regime and policy back in Cuba, but they've tended not to look at their lives solely through that prism. People like me came to office in terms of the broader view of serving public life, and it was natural for me not only to be a Democrat but also to serve a constituency that was interested in Democratic programs.

Cuban and other Latino voters have always reacted a bit differently up North, in part because of the Democratic Party's attitude there. Democrats in the decades of Latino migration were committed to engaging the community directly and created a strong bond on the social and economic issues that most concerned them. They worked closely on helping immigration and resettlement into the community. Democrat-led school systems were accommodating to the newly arrived immigrants; business and local politicians championed economic opportunities for them; immigrants had easy access to the manufacturing sector, slowly expanding the mercantile class. In other words, Democratic officials dominated in a majority of Northern areas that hosted immigrants, and officials worked hard to make immigrants welcome.

I have been successful in my local and statewide campaign in New Jersey, not only for my advocacy for Latino issues, but also for my advocacy as a Democrat. In fact, each of my campaigns was conducted in areas where the Latino population was not large enough to give me a majority of the votes. My successors in each position—mayor, state legislator, and member of the House—have also been Democrats.

My experience gave me insight into voting patterns helpful to recent Democratic presidential campaigns. It was clear to me that if you set the Cuba issue aside—or if you make it clear that you stand solidly with Cuban-Americans on the issues of freedom, democracy, and human rights in Cuba, there is a meeting of interests. The Cuban community in most ways is a very progressive community.

The political evolution of the Cuban-American community is not unlike that of other ethnic groups, for example, Jewish Americans who are concerned about fair U.S. policies toward Israel. These groups are generally socially progressive and they care about a whole host of other issues, including issues of separation of church and state. But especially the older generations, who are perhaps more tied to the history they and their parents experienced, can get caught up on single-issue voting. If they view a politician as being wrong on that basic issue, he or she can't get past the rest of it. So the Cuban-American story is not unique in that sense.

In any case, I have never thought it was right to separate the Latino agenda from the larger American agenda. I have always been proud of my heritage, but I knew that the U.S. system must solve Latino issues as part of the larger picture. From my first awareness of politics and public service, I had a moral and fundamental view of what was right and wrong. So when something didn't pass the test, the judgment was not based on my role as a Latino—it was just plain wrong.

I found that Latinos needed and still need the same things that all Americans want: a safe neighborhood, educational opportunities for their children, health care. In 2009, there are forty-seven million Americans who have no health-care coverage, and the biggest single group is Latinos.

From my earliest days in Union City, I was convinced that the role of a legislator or politician of Hispanic descent is to serve all the people and the greater good. That certainly is my mantra in my role as U.S. senator; I have never wanted to be pigeonholed with the moniker "Latino legislator" in the Senate, as if I had limited, tunnel vision. Rather, as I serve all my constituents, I will implicitly provide the sensitivity of one who rose up in the ranks, who knows the issues of my community and serves as a proud member of that minority.

Today, we are entering a new era in which we can ensure that Latinos have a greater seat at the table of national discourse, commensurate with our numbers and our growing significance. Representation and recognition of Latinos will amount to a change in the course of our nation for the better. If we do it the right way, we can seize the moment, build a strategy that will enhance the lives of Latinos, and in turn help make America a more secure, thriving, and hopeful society. The timing and the approach are logical. Latinos are the largest minority group in a country in which, one day soon, the minorities will make up the majority. How so? How do Latinos help mold the future of this country? How do you convert the rallying cry to action?

CHAPTER 3

THE TAPESTRY OF AMERICAN LIFE

A private sin is not so prejudicial in this world, as a public indecency.

MIGUEL DE CERVANTES

One of my goals is to guide all Americans toward a new understanding of Latinos in this country, to assert once and for all that we are full participants in the dream, not some recently arrived crowd imposing a foreign culture on this land. Hispanics in America predate the Revolution, and our contributions in sweat and blood have helped make the country great and will continue to do so. To push away from the excesses and the injustices that distort reality, we need to accentuate the real story as it is. We must strike down the idea that Hispanic culture in America is overtaking the United States—Latinos are a natural blend within American culture. Only in this way can we cast away misguided anger and realize that these American roots are conjoined and shared by all.

Too often, Latinos haven't done the work of promoting themselves, and I want to change that. There are at least two things we can accomplish by doing a better job. First, each and every American should know the history of Latinos in the United States, to understand the contribution we have made ever since the American Revolution. Second, we Latinos have a special need to know our own story and draw pride from that long narrative. It is especially so for young Latinos and all youth; we should introduce them to the stories of people who may inspire them, the prominent members of our community who have made history; our heroes set the example for new generations. Let us then cut through the idea, once and for all, that the Hispanic component in our culture is new or invasive, and from there, with education, Latinos can be motivated to act. It is a process of identifying examples, recognizing, honoring, and following the examples of history.

It should go without saying that you can't generalize about Latinos any more than you can generalize about anyone in this world. We are doctors, lawyers, farmers, and politicians. Some of us are teachers; some are philanthropists; some fall short; a few without doubt are thieves. But there are astrophysicists, and union leaders, and nurses and office workers and field laborers. And there are recent arrivals whose children will soar as high as the dreams of their parents. One may be a president or a Supreme Court justice. All things are within grasp in this country. So let us put the issue of immigration in perspective. We are welcoming in a new generation of hardworking, freedom-seeking people, who, just as in the past, will include major players in the future of our country. In other words, Latinos are incorporated in the fabric of the American experience every day. We are America.

Today, Latinos are at the forefront, though not alone, in the wave of immigration. But the current generation of Latino immigrants joins a group of Hispanics in this country who were here before the start of the republic. Before we can talk about where they are going, and how we can enhance the story, we need to know who these people are—we need to understand one another to break down barriers.

Latinos are a blend of cultures and ethnic backgrounds, religious and political persuasions, and are among the earliest inhabitants of North America, and some lived in this country before it was the United States. In a very real sense a great number of Mexican-Americans are neither immigrants nor the descendants of immigrants. Spanish-speaking explorers came to North America in the sixteenth century. Some settled in Florida; others settled in Mexico. I hesitate to say this, but an explorer[1] who is a namesake of mine, Pedro Menéndez de Avilés, settled in what we now

---

1 Craig Wilson, "Florida Teacher Chips Away at Plymouth Rock Thanksgiving Myth," *USA Today*, November 21, 2007, http://www.usatoday.com/life/lifestyle/2007-11-20-first-thanksgiving_N.htm.

call St. Augustine, Florida, and on September 8, 1565, celebrated a Thanksgiving with the local Indians.

Not wanting to usurp legends, I would also point out that some scholars say that another explorer, Don Juan de Oñate, also convoked a Thanksgiving feast near El Paso in West Texas or eastern New Mexico in 1598, years before the Pilgrims broke turkey with Indians at Plymouth, Massachusetts, in 1621. In any case, let us all agree that settlers from Europe, whenever or wherever they landed, had reason to celebrate their safe arrival in a land of such expanse and promise.

Mexicans settled in what is now known as New Mexico in the early sixteen hundreds. Spanish rule and Mexican settlements advanced north and east for two hundred years after that, throughout Texas, up to Arizona and California. Wherever the settlers went, missionaries were there too, establishing a series of missions that stretched from San Antonio to San Juan Capistrano. Mexico won its independence from Spain in 1821, and lived relatively peacefully alongside the United States until the countries went to war over the Texas territory. Ironically, the war was waged in part because the Mexican government was concerned that too many Americans were crossing the border to work the land and live in Mexico. After the U.S. victory in 1848, Texas, California, and parts of Arizona, Colorado, New Mexico, Nevada, and Utah became parts of the United States. Six years later, the United States and Mexico agreed to the Gadsden Purchase, with the United States paying ten million dollars for part of Arizona and New Mexico. The president during the treaty was Franklin Pierce, who had been a brigade commander in the battle of Mexico City during the war with Mexico. In less than ten years, the United States grew in size, and the people who had been living in Mexican territory were suddenly American residents, and they were never immigrants at all. Their descendants are as homegrown in this country as anyone can be.

Mexicans were always part of this country, though later generations have also fled north for economic reasons, or to escape danger and instability. In one way or another, that is the story of most immigrants to the United States.

Puerto Ricans, the second-most numerous individual group of Hispanics in the United States, were declared U.S. citizens under the Jones-Shafroth Act in 1917. They have participated in all aspects of American life. Puerto Ricans still living on the archipelago participate in the presidential primary system—in fact, with the close race between Barack Obama and Hillary Clinton during the 2008 primaries, both Barack and Hillary visited the archipelago. Large numbers of Puerto Ricans came to the United States, many to New York, in the twentieth century, especially in the 1950s, seeking a better standard of living.

Some Latinos in this country are political exiles, making the best life they can when they are wrenched from their homes and their lives. Such is the case with people who came here from Central America and from Cuba. Cuban-Americans in this country have thrived, with an impressive list of accomplishments. More than half the Cuban-Americans in this country live in South Florida, exiles who have fled the Castro regime on the Caribbean island over the last fifty years. They have built a vibrant presence in this country, participating in politics and the economy beyond Florida and enclaves such as my hometown of Union City. In fact, our history in the United States goes back much further. Seventy-five years before hundreds of thousands of Cubans fled Communism, there was another exodus. By the nineteenth century, Cuba had been a Spanish colony for hundreds of years. Cuban aspirations for independence grew progressively in the mid-nineteenth century and exploded in a call for revolution. The ten-year-war from 1868 to 1878 killed an estimated fifty thousand Spanish soldiers and Cuban rebels. Some Cubans fled the island, seeking freedom first in Key West, later in Tampa, which became a significant center for Cuban immigrants. Cuban cigar makers and their families moved to Ybor City, which became part of Tampa. Ybor City still retains the colorful heritage of those early Cuban settlers.

Few people realize how many American icons actually have Latino roots. I contend that declaring those roots and embracing our joint American heritage is a crucial point of departure on the road to change—we are Americans among the broader American family. Most people realize that someone with the family name "Menendez" would have a Hispanic connection. But last names don't tell the whole story: Anthony Quinn was born Antonio Rudolfo Oaxaca Quinn in Chihuahua, Mexico; Sammy Davis Jr.'s mother was Puerto Rican; Raquel Welch was born Jo Raquel Tejada, and has Bolivian heritage.

One story close to my political life is the case of Bill Richardson, the governor of New Mexico and former U.S. ambassador to the United Nations, secretary of energy, and candidate in the Democratic presidential primaries. Step by step, barrier by barrier, we are breaking down the unspoken rules that have limited full participation in our system. In Bill's case, there was a humorous, more immediate goal. He had a basic problem as the first Latino candidate for president from a major political party—with the last name Richardson, few people realized that he was a Latino. He told reporters in 2007, speaking in Spanish at the time, "Because my name is Richardson, many Latinos don't know I'm Latino."[2] Bill's mother, María Luisa López-Collada Márquez, was born in Mexico City, and his father, William Blaine Richardson Jr., was born in Nicaragua. Bill has joked that he should change his name to López, his mother's name, to resolve the confusion among members of the public. When the story is finally told, a future Latino or Latina president of the United States will honor the role of Bill Richardson in being a trailblazer along the way.

That's how it's been for Latinos in this country. This is how we measure progress. I've argued throughout this book that a path toward a successful future is built on a firm foundation, as in that wonderful image of the Muse of History holding the book and imagining what might be.

César Estrada Chávez, a Mexican-American, was one of the great role models of my generation, and his importance transcends any ethnic or cultural line. His life and work on behalf of the poor have been compared to the grassroots campaigns led by Lech Walesa in Poland, Rachel Carson, the American activist who warned about the dangers of pesticides, and Chico Mendes, the Brazilian environmentalist and labor organizer

2 Kathleen Hennessey, "Richardson Targets Hispanic Vote," Associated Press, August 23, 2007.

who was assassinated by landowners as he sought rights for indigent rubber tappers in western Brazil.

Hilda Solis, our new secretary of labor, has recognized Chávez's role in society, saying that, like Mahatma Gandhi, he embodied "the willingness to sacrifice."

The legacy of César Chávez offers us hope and a beacon toward the future. "César Chávez changed the course of history for Latinos and farm workers," said Secretary Solis. "As a result of his actions, many have been empowered to fight for fair wages, health care coverage, pension benefits, housing improvements, pesticide and health regulations, and countless other protections for their health and well-being. These changes have meant considerable improvements to the life of the farm worker, three-fourths of which are Latino."[3]

All Americans can be inspired by his hardscrabble story that ends in triumph. If you focus at length on César's life story, you see a journey shared by the American generation devastated by the Great Depression, but that survived with grit and fortitude.

César was not an immigrant—he was born in Arizona in 1927—but he and his family did suffer anti-Mexican discrimination. His father, Librado, was a second-generation farmer in Arizona along the border with California and Mexico. Librado's father, Cesario, in turn, had fled to Arizona from Mexico in the 1880s, and worked his way up from menial jobs in mining territory to owning his own eighty-acre spread. The family hit hard times in the aftermath of the Depression, fell into debt, and was forced into migrant life, picking vegetables, fruits, and nuts in California farm country. It was César's introduction into the harsh work forced upon tens of thousands of workers, moving from harvest to harvest and hoping there was enough work and fair pay. It was a cruel classroom that became the seed of an idea.

The saga of César Chávez takes place during the cruel period of American history chronicled by John Steinbeck's *Grapes of Wrath*. Poverty and

---

3 Hilda L. Solis, "Honoring the Legacy of César Estrada Chávez," The Huffington Post, April 2, 2008, www.huffingtonpost.com/re-hilda-I-solis/honoring-the-legacy-of-ce_b_94769.html.

suffering are not demarcated by ethnic boundaries, nor is heroism; César exemplified the Greatest Generation. He spent two years in the navy during World War II, but found himself, like so many of his fellow Mexican-Americans, back in the fields after that, a victim of prejudice and the whims of wealthy landowners.

His path in life changed in 1952 when Fred Ross, a community organizer, arrived in the impoverished Santa Clara valley, near San Jose, California, where César had moved with his new wife, Helen, after the war. Ross had set about educating the Chicanos of the region, reaching out to individuals, churches, and community groups, encouraging them to ask questions and finally to seize the greatest power they had as Americans, the right to vote. Ross reached out to Chávez and his neighbors in their poor barrio, with the tragic-ironic name Sal Si Puedes, "Get Out If You Can." He won over the trust of people used to the derision and arrogance of Anglos, and convinced César and his friends. The goal was self-respect, desegregation, and strength in numbers to stand up to power—often wielded unjustly by politicians, banks, business, and the police. Ross convinced Chávez to begin organizing with him, and their friendship endured. After working together throughout the 1950s, challenging farm executives, organizing workers to demand their rights, Chávez rose to be executive director of the Community Service Organization in 1959. Ross then introduced him to Dolores Huerta, a young woman born in Mexico who had grown up in that part of California. Together, Huerta and Chávez set off to found the United Farm Workers.

In 1965, Huerta and Chávez decided that their organization would join a wildcat strike by grape pickers in Delano, California. The five-year strike, including five thousand Filipino and Mexican-American farmworkers, brought groundbreaking changes, and significant rights to laborers on the land. They eventually won the rights to be recognized as union workers, to bargain for their conditions and wages, to be protected from dangerous chemicals, violence, unfair practices, and exploitation.

Chávez demonstrated tirelessly for the rights of farmworkers and staged a series of subsequent strikes, including boycotts, participating in hunger strikes to attract attention to his cause. Significantly, the fourteen-year grape boycott caught national attention, and for a time showed that appeals to consumers by workers could be effective.

Americans of every background and stripe, labor organizers, community workers, and volunteers look to the example of Chávez and Huerta, who fought for the basic rights of all Americans. It is a legacy of standing up for equitable working conditions for all Americans.

Wherever one looks around the country, grassroots community programs portray the diversity that goes beyond stereotypes. Those communities and the dedicated individuals working with them motivate us. That's the message I take from César Chávez; in the Latino community, but also for Native Americans, or for poor Anglos in the Midwest or African-Americans in major cities, we need economic opportunity—a good job; we need equitable health care, to be able to care for the elderly; we need secure lives and a chance to give a better opportunity to our children. It is the history of the United States.

Latinos come from varied backgrounds, united originally by language and heritage, and eventually by the communities in which they live. There are inherent differences among Ecuadorans, Mexicans, Puerto Ricans, and Dominicans, sometimes ethnically, often culturally. They are no less than the differences among Americans of Australian, South African, Kenyan, Jamaican, and other national origins. We speak the same language, but from that point we must look for our common interests.

What unites Latinos from dozens of countries, African-Americans, and immigrants from elsewhere is the treatment they receive in society. I've pointed out, beyond that, that all Americans share in the same core values, and we must get beyond differences toward a unified way of seeking solutions to the economic, political, and social problems we face.

We are linked as Latinos by language, but also by our desire to be united as Americans.

Let us be proud to recognize the success stories in this country—scientists, artists, public figures who contribute to the United States. Sometimes Latinos from one group have left an indelible impact on some parts of the country, such as Mexican-Americans in Texas and California, or Cuban-Americans in South Florida, or Puerto Ricans and Dominicans in New York. But we have moved around all the fifty states, and all of us are contributing to the American story.

My colleague Representative José E. Serrano, a proud member of Congress from the Bronx, says rightly that the Puerto Rican community has left an indelible mark on New York City. His words exude the pride of *boricuas*, as Puerto Ricans are known in Spanish. With joy and humor, Puerto Ricans have given a vibrant beat to New York and the nation.

"Through the middle of the twentieth century, an exodus of victims of difficult economic times looking for new opportunities moved to New York and transformed the city's and nation's culture forever.

"We developed the salsa that pulses from stereos from Los Angeles to Caracas. We created a market for Spanish-language and Latino-themed film, television, radio and publications. We pioneered bodegas. We fought for bilingual education. We fought for the right to play our sports in the public parks while our artists pushed boundaries to showcase their talents in ways no Latinos had done before.

"Today, New York is in no small part a Latino town. Latinos continue to sacrifice for our community's future, but one can only imagine how much more difficult it would be were it not for the foundation laid down by those New Yorkers who came before."[4]

Latinos have played a role in U.S. politics since the beginning of the republic. Technically, José Marion Hernández was the first Latino in Congress, serving briefly from 1822 to 1823 as a delegate from Florida before it became a state in 1845. Romualdo Pacheco of California eked out victory by one vote in 1876 as the first Hispanic member of the U.S. Congress. The first Hispanic senator was Octaviano Larrazolo of New Mexico, who served briefly in 1928 before resigning because of ill health. Another New Mexican, Dennis Chávez, served in the Senate from 1935 to 1962.

Prominent Latinos have served with distinction in the fields of applied science and research. There have been three Latino Nobel Prize

---

4 Rep. José E. Serrano, "Salute Your Roots," *New York Post*, no date given. Cited at http://serrano.house.gov/Newsdetail.aspx?ID=457

winners from the United States: Luis W. Alvarez, of Spanish and Cuban heritage, a physicist who won in 1968; Mario J. Molina, a scientist born in Mexico, cited for his work in studying the dangers of the ozone hole over the Antarctic; and Severo Ochoa de Albornoz, born in Spain, a biochemist who won the award in 1959.

Eleven astronauts have been Hispanic-Americans; the first was Franklin Chang-Díaz, born in Costa Rica, who moved to the United States when he was in high school. After getting his Ph.D. at the Massachusetts Institute of Technology, Chang-Díaz flew on seven space missions. He later became director of NASA's Advanced Space Propulsion Laboratory.

Also prominent at NASA was Dr. Orlando Figueroa, once named by *Hispanic Business* magazine the most influential Hispanic in the United States. Dr. Figueroa, a graduate of the University of Maryland, was director for Mars exploration at NASA. He came to the United States after graduating with an engineering degree from the University of Puerto Rico. He began his career at NASA in the 1980s. He once was chosen Federal Employee of the Year; a colleague described him as someone who knew how to "cut through the tape and get the job done."

Let's think about some of the top achievers in this country, who happen to be Latinos. We can take inspiration from their stories not only because of their successes but also because of the adversity some had to face in the process. These stories are not well-known, but they should be; they are a powerful reminder of the role of Latinos who established roots, flourished and contributed to the lives of all Americans. Few could be more instructive or more stirring than that of Dr. Alfredo Quiñones-Hinojosa, who crossed illegally from Mexico to California when he was a teenager and has been paying this country back ever since. A graduate of Harvard Medical School, Quiñones is director of brain-tumor surgery at Johns Hopkins Hospital in Baltimore, one of the most prominent neurosurgeons in the United States.

He first worked as a farmhand in California's San Joaquin Valley, then learned English, then attended the University of California, Berkeley, and eventually became an American citizen. Not that he advocates the path he chose. Dr. Quiñones told a CBS interviewer in 2007, "All that I had on my mind was just to make a little money, send it back to my parents.

"The last thing that I want is for people to think what I have done is justified," he said. "The only thing I can do is try to pay back with every single thing I do."[5]

All along the way, he harbored the dream of becoming a doctor; it must have seemed a long, impossible task.

"My very first job was with these very same hands—the very same hands that do brain surgery now, back then they pulled weeds."[6]

His goal now: to find a cure for brain cancer. Now, what would have happened if Dr. Quiñones had been deported before he ever became a doctor? Who would have benefited and who would not have been saved on the operating table?

It would be hard not to mention a friend of mine, Dr. Salomon Melgen, a prominent, well-respected, enterprising ophthalmologist based in south Florida.

Dr. Melgen was already a physician when he came to the United States from the Dominican Republic in 1979, determined to make a life in this country. He had a simple reason: "I knew that the best medicine in the world was practice here in the United States, and this is where I wanted to train and live."

The obstacles were many—among other things, he hadn't learned English yet, and he faced prejudice from people who said he would never make the cut. Meanwhile, getting a permanent visa was arduous and frustrating. It took years to establish permanent residency; he is now a proud U.S. citizen.

His initial goal was to complete his education, specializing in ophthalmology. He was a top student in Santo Domingo—summa cum laude at the medical school of the National University Pedro Henríquez Ureña. He wanted to be a world-class physician.

---

5 Christine Lagorio, "The Amazing Doctor Q," *CBS Evening News* Web site, May 18, 2007, http://www.cbsnews.com/stories/2007/05/18/assignment_america/main2827109. shtml.
6 Ibid.

"Everybody was discouraging me, asking why I had come to this country. I was looking for a job, but they were telling me you're not going to get anything. It wasn't very encouraging." Although a doctor already, his first job in the United States was as a medical assistant, while waiting to pass proficiency exams.

Through persistence, he showed doubters that he could master English and pass the required tests. By 1980, he was an intern at Yale University's Danbury Hospital; within five years, he progressed through residency at the University of Missouri and by 1985 was chief fellow at the Massachusetts Eye and Ear Infirmary at Harvard Medical School.

Perseverance and internal fortitude paid off in the face of insults. Especially before he could speak English well, other doctors in training even "laughed at me, treated me like nothing." Dr. Melgen said that the insults somehow didn't distract him from his goal. "I had an inner feeling that I was going to do whatever I had to do to make it. And I was trying hard."

Since 1988, he has been chairman of the organization that he founded, Vitreo-Retinal Consultants in West Palm Beach, and is a specialist in treating macular degeneration. He is also chief of ophthalmology at St. Mary's Hospital in West Palm Beach.

Why should we not be looking at these stories? I think there's a young man or woman in Los Angeles or Tucson or along the Texas border who needs to hear this story, and who can take solace in his or her humdrum life and shoot as high as the sky. They need to get the message, a story, a song, or a movie that touches the spirit and the mind, but reaches far beyond.

MUSIC IS A PERFECT MEDIUM for spreading the cultural word and for synchronizing American roots, as has happened; a perfect blend has been adapted in the United States and transformed the larger culture. Salsa, Cumbia, Tex-Mex, and Latin hip-hop play from Madison Square Garden in New York to the Hollywood Bowl, at music festivals across the country any given evening. You might see Luis Miguel, Los Lobos, Shakira, and Enrique Iglesias on tour. Kat DeLuna, a New Yorker of Dominican heritage, born Kathleen Emperatriz DeLuna, is in her early twenties and making an impact. Christina Aguilera is a trailblazing singer, representing a growing generation of mixed heritage—her father was born in Ecuador; her mother is of Irish descent. Plácido Domingo, the great Spanish tenor, has performed for four decades and is director of the Washington National Opera.

Latin categories for all the charts and awards add dramatic proof of Latin influence on our culture—Celia Cruz, Gloria Estefan, Juanes, Ricky Martin, Rubén Blades, so many other artists who have crossed over beyond Latino audiences.

My friend Moctesuma Esparza is one of the most interesting participants in, and analysts of, Latino pop culture. Moctesuma produced a film in 2006, *Walkout*, with Edward James Olmos as the director. It tells the story of Mexican-American students in East Los Angeles in 1968 who boycotted classes to protest academic conditions for Latinos. The movie is poignant—more so because he was one of those students and so was Antonio Villaraigosa, now the mayor of Los Angeles. In the process, Moctesuma remained active in promoting education rights, encouraging Hispanic students and their families to demand the best possible education. "I feel blessed to be associated with a powerful rebirth of social consciousness in my community. That's how I feel."

Moctesuma's thirty-five-year career includes the films *Selena*, *The Milagro Beanfield War*, and *The Ballad of Gregorio Cortez*. A Positive Image Award presented by the Hispanic Outreach Taskforce rightly honored him in 2007. He has dedicated his work to creating and accurately portraying Latino and minority characters in Hollywood.

FILM OFTEN RIDES ON THE forefront of cultural change and understanding. A remarkable 2008 documentary, *Calavera Highway*, about Armando Peña's road trip in search of his roots, is a classic document of the immigrant experience and American life. The film, by Renée Tajima-Peña, Armando's wife, and Evangeline Griego, presents Armando's journey for answers about his family. He was one of the seven sons of Rosa Peña, a migrant worker and single mother who lived in Texas border towns in Hidalgo County, one of the poorest counties in the United

States. The film follows Armando and one of his brothers, Carlos, on a trip to reunite their siblings years after the death of their mother. Their journey never strays far from the struggles of migrant workers in this country and the pressures of family life in those circumstances. It is also a search for the father they never knew.

Television has been the great cultural influence of the last generations. Many young people might not know the name Desi Arnaz, the first prominent Latino of the TV age, an actor who both introduced and humanized our culture to audiences of the 1950s. Arnaz came from a prominent place in Cuban society—one ancestor was a mayor of Santiago de Cuba, and a grandfather helped found the famed Bacardi Company. His parents fled the regime of Fulgencio Batista, twenty years before my parents did the same. Desi became a musician and played for a time with Xavier Cugat before teaming up with his wife, Lucille Ball, to break barriers. Exaggerating his Cuban accent, but humanizing the Latino experience, he and Lucy took pratfalls and tumbled into the hearts of Americans in the 1950s. With warmth and humor, Desi used early television to herald the arrival of Latinos to Middle America, at a time when it seemed almost a taboo to hear someone on television speaking with a Spanish accent. As time went on, it became increasingly common to see Hispanic actors both on television and in film. Among others, we recall Cesar Romero and Mel Ferrer, and more recently Raul Julia, Cameron Diaz, Eva Longoria and Benicio del Toro.

Literature always has its special role in chronicling our lives—storytelling has been important in describing the Hispanic experience in this country. The list of Latino writers in the United States is long, among them Anaïs Nin, Richard Rodriguez, and Oscar Hijuelos.

Hijuelos, a Cuban-American born in New York, was the first Hispanic to win the Pulitzer Prize for fiction with his book *The Mambo Kings Play Songs of Love*, which tells the story of two Cuban brothers who bring their music to New York in the 1950s.

Junot Díaz, born in the Dominican Republic, won the Pulitzer Prize in 2007 for his novel *The Brief Wondrous Life of Oscar Wao*. Díaz, who teaches creative writing at the Massachusetts Institute of Technology, is from my home state of New Jersey and attended Rutgers University.

Díaz, like Hijuelos, writes about the immigrant experience in the United States. *Oscar Wao* portrays the brutal history that brought many Dominicans to the feeling of unsettled identity, existing on a cultural divide. At the same time Díaz's story is uniquely American, one of a new generation of Latino artists in this country.

There are dozens more—to name a few, Isabel Allende, a Chilean-American, whose books include *The House of the Spirits*; Francisco Goldman, award-winning author of *The Ordinary Seaman*, whose mother was born in Guatemala; and Marie Arana, a Peruvian-born editor and novelist, whose book *American Chica* was a finalist for the National Book Award.

Can you think of a greater image for the future of the new melting pot, this latest influx of immigrants who are changing the face of America and give us new vibrancy?

To GET A READING OF the liveliness of Hispanic culture today, check out the airwaves in this country. Latino television and radio are thriving. The New York–based Spanish-language Univision was the top-rated prime-time network among eighteen- to thirty-four-year-olds thirty-one times in 2007, beating ABC, CBS, Fox, and NBC. Moreover, according to statistics, Univision local newscasts every night were tops in major cities around the country, including Los Angeles, Houston, Miami, and San Francisco. The network news anchors Jorge Ramos and María Elena Salinas are as recognizable to Latinos, if not more so, as Katie Couric or Matt Lauer or Brian Williams on English-language television.

Both have written popular books. Salinas's memoir, *Yo soy la hija de mi padre* (*I Am My Father's Daughter*), published in 2006, refers in the title to the fact that she learned as an adult that her father was a Roman Catholic priest. Ramos has written a number of books in English and Spanish, and has written stories about immigrants to this country like him. He waited tables for a time before getting his first broadcasting job with Univision in Los Angeles in 1984.

Hispanic radio in the United States is at least as energetic as television. Debates on Cuban-American stations in Miami could be more heated or controversial than anything on English-language stations. And in Los Angeles, Mexican-American radio host Eddie Sotelo, better known as El Piolín, is an influential force, syndicated in dozens of cities. In 2006 and 2007, El Piolín rallied listeners to protest unfair immigration policies and to sign petitions in favor of reform.

El Piolín is representative of the kind of media diversity that needs to be encouraged and protected in this country, in terms of programming and ownership. The result is news and information with a vibrant accent that we need. It provides a window into communities, into languages, views, and values that otherwise might be suppressed. Minority-owned media report regularly on health-care issues in their communities, but the implications go beyond local problems. These concerns can be generalized. We might not otherwise hear about hospitals being closed down in inner cities around America, a dangerous situation that harms and limits health-care options for African-Americans—and we might not hear about the Hispanic and African-American medical professionals working long hours to take care of sick patients.

Throughout the nation, we know that schools and colleges face spending cuts and budget crunches, but minority media report on the specific challenges Hispanics face. I have repeated the fact that Latinos face a higher high school dropout rate than any other group; searching for solutions, good local reporting provides positive stories about Hispanics and Asian- and African-Americans who take the lead in organizations such as Teach for America.

While demagogic TV hosts repeatedly try to link crime to minority immigrants, minority news outlets report on the facts; research shows that immigrants are generally less likely to commit crimes. With mean-spirited people spouting lies, minority newspapers, radio, and television look for the facts. In the face of invented and sensationalistic stories about immigrants with leprosy, street gangs, or Mexican plots to reconquer the United States, we need to be able to flip to stations where we can hear about Asian-American CEOs who are revolutionizing their industries,

African-American doctors saving lives, and Hispanic soldiers, many of whom are not yet citizens, bravely fighting overseas under the flag of the country they're proud to call their own.

Increasingly, those stations and other news media are as likely as not to be providing their information in English. The median age of Latinos in the United States is about twenty-seven years old, about ten years younger than that of the overall population. Younger second-generation Latinos, children of the most recent wave of immigration, are attending school, learning English, speaking it along with Spanish at home, but preferring the language of their peers.

A 2007 report[7] by two researchers at the University of Miami, Paola Prado and Walter McDowell, said that "a false impression fostered by Latino media is that these important audiences can be reached only through Spanish-language programming." They reported that "a substantial portion of Latino audiences watch English-language prime-time television programming."

They cited reports that "Latinos increasingly consume both English- and Spanish-language television" and quoted the respondent to one poll: "Most second-generation Hispanics aren't watching *Sábado Gigante*. [For those of you who haven't heard of the long-running variety show, it has been hosted since 1962 by the perennially popular Chilean television host Mario Kreutzberger, better known as Don Francisco.] They're watching *CSI*, *Entourage*, etc., just like regular white folk."

WHEN IT COMES TO PORTRAYALS of minorities in the media, we are often subjected to perceptions that border on hysterical. Nothing has the power to neutralize those hysterics like the actions of our communities' most heroic individuals.

Heroism is displayed not just in the stories told by minority journal-

---

7 Paola Prado and Walter McDowell, "Acculturation and Media Preference: Exploring the Popularity of English-Language Television Programs among Latino Audiences in the U.S." (paper, annual meeting of the Association for Education in Journalism and Mass Communication, Washington, D.C., August 8, 2007), http://www.allacademic.com//meta/p_mla_apa_research_citation/2/0/3/2/0/pages203209/p203209-1.php.

ists but also in the work of the people who own the radio and television stations that employ them. Ernesto Schweikert, for example, is the owner of Radio Tropical Caliente, a small AM station in New Orleans. When Hurricane Katrina devastated the city, even after power had failed, Schweikert and Radio Tropical bravely went on the air with the help of a generator, and he read news by candlelight. Schweikert, a Guatemalan-American, translated all the news he received into Spanish—and became a lifeline for the 180,000 Spanish-speaking people of New Orleans, who otherwise probably would have had no idea what was going on, and where to go for help. For years afterward, people would approach Schweikert on the street and say, "You saved our lives."

In 2006 the National Association of Hispanic Journalists recognized Schweikert and his station for their work. He said that the radio's listenership grew significantly as people began rebuilding after Hurricane Katrina. He likes talking about New Orleans's deep Hispanic roots.

Schweikert said, "If you go look at any roof in any part of the metropolitan area, you are going to see Hispanic people rebuilding the homes and the buildings and cleaning up.

"Why do you think Latinos like New Orleans? Because we feel at home."[8]

Rather than stopping with the success of his radio station, he leveraged the increased role of Latinos in New Orleans to establish the city's first Spanish-language television station, KGLA-TV, which became an affiliate of the Spanish-language Telemundo network. Spanish-speaking viewers are now able to watch a ten p.m. local newscast on weeknights. "It's like a news magazine," said Schweikert. "We're doing local, national and international news, and we're also doing sports."[9]

Schweikert and others in the media business are more than broadcasters—they function as advocates for the communities that de-

8 Greg Flakus, "Spanish-Language Radio Station Profits from Hispanic Influx in New Orleans," VOAnews.com, September 7, 2006, http://www.voanews.com/english/archive/2006-09/2006-09-07-voa23.cfm?CFID=48022789&CFTOKEN=70881851.
9 Dave Walker, "FEMA Refuses to Help Local PBS Affiliate Rebuild," Times-Picayune, August 26, 2008.

pend on them. There is more work to be done in supporting minority media. Minorities comprise about one-third of the U.S. population, but minorities own only about eight percent of radio stations and three percent of television stations.

The National Association of Hispanic Journalists does much to support minority journalists and media business. The organization cited the work of María Hinojosa, television and radio journalist, for her work in giving voice to minorities and the disadvantaged. In accepting her award, she said, "I don't practice advocacy journalism; I simply tell the truth."[10]

Others receiving 2008 awards from NAHJ included Jim Avila of ABC News, who reported about the plight of undocumented farmworkers during wildfires that ravaged Southern California in 2007; Leticia Espinosa of *Hoy Chicago*, for her story about Elvira Arellano, an undocumented immigrant who had sought sanctuary in a church to avoid deportation; and Mario Barraza, who filmed images of children trying to cross the Mexican border alone.

The Hispanic journalists' organization works closely in turn with similar groups—the National Association of Black Journalists, the Asian American Journalists Association, and the Native American Journalists Association. Every four years, the groups hold a Unity Conference, exploring minority issues, and trends in journalism and politics. Thousands of people attended the 2008 convention in Chicago, which included a closing speech by then presidential candidate and senator, Illinois' favorite son, Barack Obama.

Together the organizations describe their mission thus:

> The journalism industry has an obligation to deliver a complete, fair and representative picture of the communities and world in which we live. In order to achieve this, diversity in the newsroom and in coverage is fundamental. We envision a nation in which newsrooms are inclusive and reflect the communities they

---

10 María Hinojosa, 2008 National Association of Hispanic Journalists, http://www.nahj.org/events/2008/noche/2008NochePressRelease.shtml.

cover, and where people of color hold positions of influence. To achieve this we will conduct research, convene people and advocate change by offering attainable solutions to the industry.[11]

We can mention, by the way, one prominent member of the media, Soledad O'Brien of CNN, who is a member of both the National Association of Hispanic Journalists and the National Association of Black Journalists. Soledad's mother is Afro-Cuban, and her father is Australian of Irish descent. Her life is a perfect illustration of the blending of cultures, and more and more what our American roots are about. We honor our European ancestors and our Latino ancestors, and make a combined future.

While we often mention prominent artists and people who have stood on a broader stage, it is sometimes people who take a simple, courageous stance in life that offer the great lessons with profound repercussions. Such is the case of Sylvia Mendez, of Puerto Rican and Mexican heritage, who had a prominent role in American history by winning the right to go to a decent neighborhood school like any other child in this country.

Her parents, Gonzalo and Felicitas Mendez, had settled in the town of Westminster in Orange County, California, in the 1940s. When Sylvia and her brothers, Gonzalo Junior and Jerome, were old enough to go to school, there were two elementary schools in the town. One was Seventeenth Street Elementary, a nice-looking building, landscaped with lovely trees and a well-manicured lawn. The other choice was Hoover School, a dilapidated wooden structure. "Everybody knew" what was unspoken: Latinos went to Hoover School, because the Seventeenth Street School was intended for Anglos.

Segregation was something that Gonzalo and Felicitas could not accept, and something that an eight-year-old couldn't comprehend. "I didn't understand why they wouldn't let my brothers and I in the nice school," Sylvia Mendez recalled in an interview.[12]

---

11 Mission Statement, Unity, Journalists of Color, Inc, http://www.unityjournalists.org/mission/index.php.
12 Fermin Leal, "A Desegregation Landmark," *The Orange County Register*, Wednesday, March 21, 2007. Quoted at http://www.mendezvwestminster.com.

When their parents tried to enroll Sylvia, Gonzalo Junior, and Jerome in the building one fine day in 1944, they were turned away. The parents sued the Westminster School District, charging that it was unconstitutional to force Mexican-Americans to go to schools segregated from other children. A federal appeals court ruled in their favor three years later. The California legislature passed a law as a result, ending the practice of segregating Mexican or Mexican-American children. Governor Earl Warren signed a bill in 1947 ending the practice.

Tellingly, Warren was chief justice of the United States seven years later when the Supreme Court ruled in a sweeping unanimous decision, *Brown v. the Board of Education*, that segregation of any kind was unconstitutional in the United States. The court decision cited the case of Sylvia, Gonzalo Junior, and Jerome in its landmark decision. Simple acts of conscience can resonate for all time. We dedicate ourselves to honor the memory and struggle of such people and exhort our community to reach even higher.

The richness of Hispanic life in our country is now regularly and increasingly commemorated, as it should be. Latino history is showcased every year through Hispanic Heritage Month, September 15 to October 15. The dates are significant in Latin American history, surrounding the key dates of emancipation from Spanish rule. It's refreshing to note the numerous school programs around the United States, and the support from corporate and media sponsors.

To gauge and distinguish our progress in the fight for equality, we must recall episodes of official intolerance and discrimination against Latinos. The National Register of Historical Places, for example, lists an impressive neoclassical building in Miami, Arizona, the Bullion Plaza School. Built in the 1920s, it was designated for Mexican-American children, who, if they did not "appear" to be Anglos, were allowed to enroll only in certain schools. According to National Register files, "Mexican-American students could attend the white Inspiration Addition School if they (or their parents) 'looked white,' spoke English exceptionally well, or were persistent in asserting their rights to attend the same schools as their Anglo neighbors. Exactly how and when desegregation was accomplished in Miami remains a mystery, not only because of missing school records, but also because the local newspaper, the *Arizona Silver Belt*, did not acknowledge the segregation of Mexican-American students or report challenges to the practice." In the early 1950s, the concept of separate Mexican schools was abandoned, as a broader consensus was developing that would strike down "separate but equal" principles and demand school desegregation across the land.

Such stories speak to courage, and to the enterprise of those among us. By writing about our heritage, the heritage of all Americans, we preserve the roots of our lives. But for a long time, the contributions of Latinos were little known; our triumphs deserve to be celebrated. In some ways the most dramatic and heroic part of the story of the Latinos in this country spotlights the sacrifices of the few. While focusing on the personalities who move us by their unique accomplishments, we also must stop and pay special tribute to those who have contributed to our armed forces. Throughout American history, Latinos have fought in every war; among them were people born in the United States, immigrants, and children of immigrants, and those who fought even before they were legally admitted into the country.

There was a time when Latino history was sliced out of our history books, and children never learned about anything more than Davy Crockett and the Alamo. The story of those Latinos who fought and died for our freedom has now won a place in history.

We have every reason, like the Muse of History, to consider our past as we march on toward a promising future. Let us reflect on our heritage, honor our history, and find inspiration in those who lead the way and who have come before us.

CHAPTER 4

THE HONOR ROLL

I have but one lamp by which my feet are guided, and that is the lamp of experience. I know of no way of judging the future but by the past. . . .

Patrick Henry

One winter morning less than a week after President Obama's inauguration in January 2009, I attended a departure ceremony for three hundred members of the New Jersey National Guard who were being deployed to Iraq. Many of the soldiers, members of the 1-150th Assault Helicopter Battalion, were going off on their second deployment in three years. The next day, I saw a touching photograph in a local newspaper showing one of the members of the Guard, Sergeant Zelene Díaz, in her camouflage uniform, hand in hand with her four-year-old son, David.

Governor Jon Corzine and my New Jersey colleague in the Senate, Frank Lautenberg, accompanied me at the event. I said a few words that I thought summed up the moment.

"These are historic times for our nation, historic for the challenges we face at home and abroad, but also historic for the sense of optimism that millions of Americans have even in the midst of these great challenges. . . .You are the men and women who will help us rise to the occasion in the face of our international challenges."

We shook hands with many of them and I couldn't help glancing at the nameplates over their pockets. Many of these young men and women were Hispanic, with names such as Sergeant Díaz, Martinez, Rodriguez, and on. And so in this respect, here we are: Our collective security depends on a very small group of people; many of them happen to be Latinos. Some of our soldiers, in fact, are not even U.S. citizens.

They are permanent residents, and can't vote for the commander in chief who sent them to serve, and do so willingly, proud to represent our country. All the more dismay for me when I hear uninformed, malicious words repeated about immigrants broadcast incessantly on the airwaves. One would hope that those words would be tempered by the sense of gratitude that we feel. We should understand: This is a community of our proxies guarding sentry posts somewhere halfway around the world, on our behalf. Let the concept sink in and let us hope that reason and good sense will prevail. Latinos do their part in the protection of this country.

However, let us also understand the context in which our soldiers serve in the U.S. military in 2009. We owe it to Sergeant Díaz and her family and our entire active military to understand our priorities and to judiciously measure the risks and dangers we place before them.

Six years after George W. Bush ordered the invasion of Iraq on the false premises that Saddam Hussein was in the process of preparing weapons of mass destruction, we've lost more than four thousand soldiers; tens of thousands have been wounded and otherwise scarred; Iraqi casualties are estimated in the hundreds of thousands.

Our soldiers do not question their service to their country, but on their behalf we need to ask the ultimate cost. Let us imagine how much more Americans would have gained if they had pursued and cornered Osama bin Laden and Al-Qaeda instead of pursuing this ideological, mistaken war. Imagine how many lives would have been spared.

We must also consider costs beyond the immediate human dimension. For the hundreds of billons of dollars spent, Americans could have had universal health coverage—every single American. We could have been spending money on vaccination programs, medical research, the improvement of our crumbling infrastructure, education, jobs, green energy, helping the middle class make ends meet, supporting the lives of poor and working families; with the hundreds of billions spent on President Bush's war, we could have helped spark and enhance opportunity for all Americans.

We know the extent of the failures of President Bush's invasion of Iraq, and what could have been done judiciously, not recklessly; we have learned from those mistakes. With the new Obama administration, we are working in a measured way toward important changes that will protect our future. Of course we need strong measures to defend our nation at home and abroad; our aspirations, our dreams, depend on a solid base of safety and security. It is undoubtedly clear that when twenty-first-century dangers threaten us, Latino citizens will play an increasingly important role. Our ranks in the armed forces, in police forces, in fire and first aid corps, are steadfast. We stand united with them.

One need go no further than the honor roll of those who died and the rescuers who came to the aid of the wounded in the terrorist attacks of September 11, 2001. They were from all walks of life. We lost mothers, fathers, and children; brothers lost their sisters; neighbors lost their friends. So many communities were affected in so many different ways— not the least of which was the American community. It felt like a day when there were no borders between us. Terrorists tried to engulf us in the smoke of fear and hatred, and for a moment, we felt like the whole world went dark. But the light of heroism burst through. Individuals rushed into burning buildings, risking their lives to save others; strangers opened their homes to help people they didn't even know; men and women all over the country rushed to give whatever they could to help those in need. We honor them deeply. Our heroes triumph every day. Their supply of courage has never run out.

The Latino contribution to our military has been considerable, and citing the details is more than just listing accomplishments. Latinos have been driven over time by a sense of patriotism and service to their country, particularly those for whom this became their adopted country. Often, they've seen their parents serve before them, and that has made them even more likely to serve.

As a group, Latinos have faced adversity and don't shrink from a fight; this instinct carries onto the battlefield, where they often perform with great heroism. Throughout history Latinos have received more Purple

Hearts than any other ethnic group.[1] At the start of 2008, there were 20,328 soldiers in the U.S. Army who had permanent residence status but were not American citizens, according to Pentagon records.[2] Of those, about twenty percent were serving in Afghanistan and Iraq. Immigration law allows all immigrants who serve honorably during wartime to apply for immediate citizenship. According to PolitiFact, a Web service of the *St. Petersburg Times*, about one-quarter of those 20,328 soldiers holding green cards have Hispanic backgrounds. The Web service also reported in 2008 that 10,533 naturalized citizens serving in the military were born in Spanish-speaking countries. According to the National Immigration Forum, more than six hundred thousand immigrants of all backgrounds served as of 2004 on active duty in the U.S. Armed Forces.

FOLLOWING IN THE LONG HISTORY of their participation in all aspects of American life, more than two hundred thousand Latinos were members of the U.S. Armed Forces and reserves as of 2008, and about eighteen thousand were officers.[3]

More than 440 Latinos were killed in Iraq as of the fall of 2008. One poignant fact: One of the first U.S. combat casualties in Iraq in 2003 was an immigrant, José Gutierrez, twenty-two, a Marine lance corporal. A Guatemalan-born permanent resident, he died hours after the invasion in a firefight on March 21, 2003. Gutierrez, whose parents died in Guatemala, entered the United States in 1999 as a teenager, hopping freight trains through Mexico and crossing the border into California. Detained by immigration authorities, he became a ward of the state, eventually learned English, and finished high school. Jackie Baker, a member of one foster family that sheltered him, said Gutierrez joined the Marines because he "wanted to give the United States what

1 Col. Gilberto Villahermosa, "America's Hispanics in America's Wars," *Army Magazine*, September 2002, http://www.valerosos.com/HispanicsMilitary.html.
2 PolitiFact.com, http://www.politifact.com/truth-o-meter/statements/509/.
3 DRS #21421, prepared by the Defense Manpower Data Center, August 20, 2008.

the United States gave to him. He came with nothing. This country gave him everything."[4]

At one time, American textbooks did not include stories about Mexicans, or Cuban highlights in U.S. history, or the contributions of other Hispanic-Americans over the last 250 years. The fact is that even before the Revolution, Hispanic leaders played a role in colonial America.

Increasingly, we now find references to Bernardo de Gálvez, a Spanish army officer and the governor of Louisiana from 1777 to 1785, who played a role in blocking British advances against George Washington in the American Revolution. His contribution was among many acts of courage and sacrifice by Latinos during the War of Independence. Soldiers from Spain, Cuba, Mexico, Puerto Rico, and the Dominican Republic helped colonists in the battle for independence. Galveston, Texas, is named for Gálvez.[5]

Jorge Farragut, the father of the Civil War hero Admiral David Farragut, was a Spanish ship captain who came to America and fought for the colonies against the British. Admiral Farragut is known as the first admiral of the navy, and for his famous rallying cry, "Damn the torpedoes, full speed ahead!" I would imagine that as they drive by and walk past the majestic statue of the admiral in Farragut Square in downtown Washington, D.C., every day, few people know this history and that Admiral Farragut was Hispanic.

HISPANICS FOUGHT ON BOTH SIDES of the American Civil War, and in all subsequent wars. There are forty-three Hispanic-Americans on the rolls of military Medal of Honor winners, which testifies to the Latino participation in American defense, a role that continues in the Iraq War. The Medal of Honor was created by Congress in 1862 during the

---

4 Marin Kasindorf, *USA Today*. "One of the first U.S. servicemen killed in combat in Iraq was not a citizen of the country for which he sacrificed his life," quoted at MilitaryCity.com http://www.militarycity.com/valor/256506.html, *USA Today*.

5 My preferred source on the subject is *Hispanic Military Heroes*, Virgil Fernandez (Austin: VFJ Publishing, 2006). Fernandez has assembled a colorful look at Hispanic military contributions to the creation of the United States and profiles of the forty-three Hispanic Medal of Honor winners.

Civil War and was to be given to a soldier who "distinguished himself conspicuously by gallantry and intrepidity at the risk of his life above and beyond the call of duty while engaged in an action against an enemy of the United States. The deed performed must have been one of personal bravery or self-sacrifice so conspicuous as to clearly distinguish the individual above his comrades and must have involved risk of life."[6]

Three Hispanics received the medal during the Civil War. John Ortega was the first Hispanic to be awarded the honor. Ortega had migrated from Spain to the United States, settling in Pennsylvania. He was a sailor for the Union forces, and signed aboard the USS *Saratoga*; in 1864, the warship was part of the effort to interdict goods and war matériel to the Confederacy. Ortega participated in landing parties that staged raids into South Carolina, taking prisoners and destroying Confederate infrastructure.

Another Hispanic sailor, Philip Bazaar, was born in Chile; he joined the Union navy in Massachusetts as an ordinary seaman on the USS *Santiago de Cuba*. He received the medal in 1865, with this citation: "As one of a boat crew detailed to one of the generals on shore, O.S. Bazaar bravely entered the fort in the assault and accompanied his party in carrying dispatches at the height of the battle. He was one of six men who entered the fort in the assault from the fleet."[7] A Union army corporal, Joseph H. De Castro, received the honor for his actions fighting the Confederate Pickett's charge at Gettysburg on July 3, 1863. As a volunteer flag bearer in the Nineteenth Massachusetts Infantry, De Castro seized a Confederate flag during battle and gave it to General Alexander S. Webb, himself an eventual Medal of Honor winner for defending against Pickett's charge. General Webb wrote about De Castro: "At the instant a man broke through my lines and thrust a rebel battle flag into my hands. He never said a word and darted back. It was Corporal Joseph H. De Castro, one of my color bearers. He had knocked down a color bearer in the enemy's

6 Code of Federal Regulations, Title 32, Volume 2, Section 578.4. U.S. Government Printing Office. Revised as of July 1, 2002. Pages 395–396.

7 http://www.history.army.mil/html/moh/civwaral.html

line with the staff of the Massachusetts State colors, seized the falling flag and dashed it to me."[8]

There were at least ten thousand Mexican-Americans fighting for the Union during the Civil War, and a number of others fighting for the Confederacy. One of the more folkloric characters emerging in the Civil War was Loreta J. Velazquez, who was born in Cuba, and who claimed that she disguised herself as a male lieutenant and fought against Union forces at several battles, including the first battle of Bull Run. She later claimed to have worked as a spy for the Confederacy.

Even in the Spanish-American War, a dozen Latinos were among Theodore Roosevelt's Rough Riders,[9] despite divided loyalties in the conflict among Spain, Cuba, and the United States. One of the best-known Hispanic Rough Riders was Maximiliano Luna, a member of a prominent Republican family in New Mexico.[10]

In World War I, an army private, David Cantu Barkley, of Laredo, Texas, of Mexican descent, volunteered to penetrate German lines in France and, with a comrade, drew maps of German troop locations and supplies. Barkley drowned on the return trip, but his partner carried back the logistical information. Praised by General John J. Pershing, he won the Medal of Honor.

More than nine thousand Latinos gave their lives during World War II. There were thirteen Medal of Honor winners[11] among the half a million Hispanics who served in the armed forces between 1941 and 1945, from the Aleutian Islands to the South Pacific and the war in Europe in every branch

---

8 John Austin Stevens, Benjamin Franklin DeCosta, Henry Phelps Johnston, Martha Joanna Lamb, Nathan Gillett Pond, William Abbatt, *The Magazine of American History*, with notes and queries, compiled by William Abbatt, Volume 23, July–December 1887, page 18.
9 Charles H. Montgomery, *The Spanish Redemption: Heritage, Power, and Loss on New Mexico's Upper Rio Grande* (Berkeley: University of California Press, 2002).
10 Ibid, 77.
11 Wikipedia, the Free Encyclopedia, s.v. "list of Hispanic Medal of Honor recipients," http://en.wikipedia.org/wiki/List_of_Hispanic_Medal_of_Honor_recipients. The Hispanic World War II medal winners: Joseph P. Martinez, Rudolph Davila, Lucian Adams, Macario Garcia, Jose Mendoza Lopez, Jose F. Valdez, Cleto Rodriguez, Manuel Perez Jr., Silvestre Herrera, Ysmael R. Villegas, Harold Gonsalves, David H. Gonzales, and Alejandro Renteria Ruiz.

of the service and every campaign.[12] Among the heroes of World War II was marine PFC Guy "Gabby" Gabaldon, who won the Navy Cross Medal for capturing more than a thousand enemy soldiers in the South Pacific during the summer of 1944. The honor and patriotism of each of these soldiers cannot be overstated; the story of Alejandro R. Ruiz, an army private who fought at Okinawa, epitomizes their commitment to our country and the tragedy some of them endured. His Medal of Honor citation noted his "conspicuous gallantry and intrepidity above and beyond the call of duty. . . . When an enemy soldier charged him, his rifle jammed. Undaunted, Pfc. Ruiz whirled on his assailant and clubbed him down. . . . Leaping from one opening to another, he sent burst after burst into the pillbox, killing 12 of the enemy and completely destroying the position. Pfc. Ruiz's heroic conduct, in the face of overwhelming odds, saved the lives of many comrades and eliminated an obstacle that long would have checked his unit's advance."[13]

He wrote this letter:

> I never questioned my duty since I believe that as Americans we have a responsibility to serve our country and preserve our way of life and freedoms. Too many people take our freedom for granted and expect the benefits without giving back in service. But no community or country can survive or become great if our citizens take that attitude.
>
> All I can say is that I did what I had to do. Someone had to take this action or the lives of my men and my own would have been sacrificed. When you are in battle, you have to rely on your men. You have to count on one another. So my only thought was to save my men.
>
> During the White House ceremony, President Truman awarded me the medal and as Commander in Chief saluted me and told me that he would rather have the medal than be president.

---

12 Robert Menendez, Latino Leadership Link, "Commemorating Memorial Day: Honoring the Military Service of America's Latinos," http://menendez.senate.gov/latinoleadershiplink/.
13 http://www.history.army.mil/html/moh/wwII-m-s.html

But upon my return to El Paso, Texas, where I was stationed at Fort Bliss, I was not allowed to eat in the restaurant when I took my wife out to eat to celebrate. They had segregation at the time and there was a sign that said, "No Mexicans or Dogs Allowed."[14]

Latinos were represented in every branch of the U.S. Armed Forces in Europe and in the Pacific. There were renowned units, such as El Escuadrón 201, a Mexican World War II fight squadron known as the Aztec Eagles. Attached to the Fifty-eighth Fighter Group of the United States Army Air Forces, the squadron participated in the liberation of Luzon in the Philippines in 1945.

The Puerto Rican Sixty-fifth Infantry Regiment, the Borinqueneers, also saw significant action. The mostly Hispanic unit began as a volunteer regiment in 1899 and participated in World War I, World War II, and the Korean War.

More than three hundred Hispanics died in the Korean War, and eight Latinos received the Medal of Honor.[15] The Borinqueneers fought in nine major campaigns during the Korean War, and its members received four Distinguished Service Crosses.

THE STARK NUMBER OF DEATHS in the Vietnam War always gives us pause, astonishment, and a sense of humility; of the 58,195 names on the Vietnam War Memorial, there are more than 15,600 names of Hispanic soldiers. An estimated eighty thousand Latinos fought in the Vietnam War. Seventeen Latinos received the Medal of Honor.[16] Navy Com-

---

14 Virgil Fernandez, *Hispanic Military Heroes* (Austin: VFJ Publishing, 2006), page 41.
15 The Latino Medal of Honor winners from the Korean War: Baldomero Lopez, Eugene Arnold Obregon, Joseph C. Rodriguez, Rodolfo P. Hernandez, Edward Gomez, Fernando Luis Garcia, Benito Martinez, Ambrosio Guillen.
16 The Vietnam War Medal of Honor winners: Humberto Roque Versace, Daniel Fernandes, Alfred Rascon, Euripides Rubio, Maximo Yabes, Carlos James Lozada, Alfredo Cantu Gonzalez, Jay R. Vargas, Roy Benavidez, Hector Santiago-Colon, Jose Francisco Jimenez, Ralph E. Dias, John P. Baca, Emilio De La Garza Jr., Miguel Hernandez Keith, Louis R. Rocco and Elmelindo Rodrigues-Smith.

mander Everett Alvarez, the grandson of Mexican immigrants to the United States, was shot down over the Gulf of Tonkin in 1964; he was the first American prisoner of war in Vietnam and, held for eight years, was one of the longest-held prisoners of war in U.S. history.

AFTER WE UNDERSTAND THE ROLE of Hispanics and other immigrants in our military throughout U.S. history, it is shocking to realize that they and their families have not received adequate recognition and at times have even endured slights at the hand of the society they served.

In particular, I realized that some undocumented immigrants who served in our armed forces were not getting expedited treatment once they served or were discharged honorably from service. I promoted a bill in Congress that would grant permanent resident status to parents, spouses, or children of military men and women who have served in active duty. Such troops deserve special status, and priority. In some cases, close family members have been legally and patiently waiting in line to be reunited with their families here in the United States. I saw that immediate action would be a basic show of thanks and support for our troops.

I was impressed by profiles highlighted recently by the Veterans History Project of the Library of Congress. These are stories of common folk, deeply patriotic, committed citizens of our country. Eva Romero Jacques, for example, was attending the University of New Mexico during World War II. She decided to enlist in the Army Air Forces, worked in New Guinea, and rose to the rank of sergeant.

"When war was declared, we were very patriotic in New Mexico. Everybody was really involved," she told the History Project. "I went to mass one Sunday and the priest asked the mothers not to interfere if your daughters are willing to go, please don't keep them from going into the military because it's everybody's war. And that set me off. So I thought about it overnight and the next day I enlisted."

She actually thought the military might not accept her, because she was an inch shorter than the required minimum height of four feet eleven inches. "I didn't think they were going to take me. But because I had two years of college and was bilingual, they took me."

Sixty years later, she expressed satisfaction for her service; as with so many veterans, her military career was always a matter of pride. "My life wouldn't have been complete if I hadn't been in the military. I think I would have missed out on one of the biggest experiences of my life. Because I have a different impression of youth, I want them to be protected; I hate to see them go to war."[17]

17 http://lcweb2.loc.gov/diglib/vhp=stories/loc.natlib.afc2001001.18443/

CHAPTER 5

BASEBALL—
A TRUE NATIONAL PASTIME

Any time you have an opportunity to make a difference in this world and you don't, then you are wasting your time on earth.

ROBERTO CLEMENTE

As I've argued throughout, we tend to look to our heroes for inspiration, and sometimes we have not recognized the heroes who walk among us. There is one complicated realm in which we recognize people as heroes and role models but don't fully understand the value and import of what we're experiencing.

There is one segment of the Latin experience that enjoys a special role, and sometimes an exemption from the ill will and prejudice faced by too many of us. Even before Jackie Robinson broke the color barrier in baseball's major leagues, a handful of Latin players were playing professional baseball at a top level. Look at how the scene has changed. A good percentage of the starting teams of baseball teams everywhere in the United States are Latinos. They provide examples for all Americans, and cross over as role models for all young people. It is clear that the role of baseball in America and the Latino dimension go beyond the game itself.

Baseball occupies that unique place in American life—for African-Americans, for Latinos of the Caribbean basin, and for all of us. The game has a unique way of uniting our sense of history—the memories of games past, friends and family members cherished and departed.

Baseball, as with all the endeavors I'm talking about, is part of a process—every branch of American life carries deep Latino roots, flourishing more and more, growing in the light of understanding and truth.

Nowhere more successfully has the American experience tracked more closely and not always happily with the greatest and lowest points in American society. For a century, of course, baseball was an Anglo sport in the United States, almost without exception; African-Americans were particularly barred from the major leagues, depriving black heroes from participating in the highest level. The story of Jackie Robinson epitomizes the contradiction of America, and his courage and greatness transcend the game. Robinson's triumph also impacted Latino players, especially those who were both Latino and of African-American complexion.

Baseball helped break down the segregation barriers in this country. Robinson broke into the majors seven years before the Supreme Court decision in *Brown v. the Board of Education*. There are social tracks in baseball that go along with larger changes in society.

Even through the 1950s and onward, America has too often relegated minority standouts—whether it was Robinson or Louis Armstrong or Lena Horne or Jim Thorpe—to the entertainment pages, without offering broader recognition in all branches of society and not taking any of us particularly seriously. In this century, we now have different expectations and look forward to seeing our aspirations recognized and all glass ceilings obliterated.

Half a century ago, a few Latino players made it to the big leagues; now statistics tell us that a least one-quarter of professional baseball players have Latino roots. No question, Alex Rodriguez, Manny Ramirez, David Ortiz, Vladimir Guerrero, Alberto Pujols, Mariano Rivera, and Ivan Rodriguez are likely future members of the Baseball Hall of Fame, all of them role models for a generation of young ballplayers. For all young people, not just Latino kids. That's part of the concept of American roots, that as we grow together we create a shared experience and mutual understanding.

Nowhere has the Latino experience blended more happily and more influentially than in baseball, which is played from Canada to the shores of the Caribbean. At their best, these baseball players inspire us and provide role models for young people, guides for learning discipline and the determination to succeed. Of course we're going through a moment now when the scandal of performance-enhancing drugs has permeated our national sport. It is a tragedy and some of the players mentioned here are alleged to be involved. Latinos are no more or less culpable and no more or less likely to make mistakes and expose flaws in their lives. Let us hope that all these ballplayers can contribute to restoring the game to that role that it has held. The current generation of Latino players should inspire Americans on and off the field.

AND IF OUR HEROES ARE people of the rainbow of cultures in this country, as they are, our young people learn important lessons. The limited view of races and cultures breaks down—our heroes inspire not with their appearance but with their inner qualities. We see a portion of ourselves in a role model, just as I did in the people who inspired me when I was a child—study hard, set goals, right wrongs, and ultimately enter public service. Young people get it. The legendary Puerto Rican right fielder for the Pittsburgh Pirates, Roberto Clemente, was recognized as number twenty on the list of the hundred best major leaguers of all times, the highest-ranking Latino.[1]

Fans still remember Clemente, named twelve times a National League All-Star, gliding gracefully across right field, where he won twelve Gold Glove Awards; powering three thousand hits with a career .317 batting average; or dashing around the bases, then sliding into third base. His heroics on the field, of course, pale compared with his charity work, and the mission he undertook in 1972 to help bring relief aid to Nicaraguan earthquake victims. He died in a plane crash on December 31, 1972, en route to deliver supplies to the Central American country.

He gave the term "complete" a new meaning. He made the word "superstar" seem inadequate. He had about him the touch of royalty.

—BASEBALL COMMISSIONER BOWIE KUHN (1973 EULOGY)[2]

---

1 *Baseball Almanac*, "Baseball's 100 Greatest Players," http://www.baseball-almanac.com/legendary/lisn100.shtml.
2 Quoted in Patrick Ridgell, "A touch of royalty in right field," *Latino Leaders: The National Magazine of the Successful American Latino*, February–March 2002.

There is no better example of baseball crossing barriers and social lines. Clemente recognized his role as a well-known athlete, once saying, "It is my great satisfaction to be able to help erase hackneyed opinions about Latin Americans and African-Americans."[3]

He told the story succinctly, and better than most people could: "There is nothing so wrong in our homes and our country that could not be cured by a little compassion, concern, and love. We are all brothers and sisters and should help one another whenever it becomes necessary."[4]

Clemente was not alone among outstanding ballplayers of old: Rod Carew, Juan Marichal, and Lefty Gomez also made the top-hundred list, and players now will continue to make their mark in history, not only on the field, but also in terms of service and humanitarian pursuits. Many of our multimillionaire ballplayers work with youth groups or donate money and time to worthy causes, whether working with the infirm or sending money for hurricane relief in this country and back home.

Baseball is not just some latter-day acquisition among Latinos. The game arrived in Cuba well before the start of the twentieth century, probably with the inspiration of Cuban students returning to the island from the United States. Some Cuban historians trace the first baseball game in Cuba back to a game in Matanzas between a local team and a visiting club from Havana on December 27, 1874.

In the next decade the game spread and grew in popularity. Of course, what is known the national pastime in the United States is equally so in Cuba, and all the years of hostility since Fidel Castro's takeover in 1959 have done nothing to dull the interest in the game. By the way, there are grave doubts about the old tale that somehow history would have been

---

3 *"Mi gran satisfacción proviene de ayudar a borrar opiniones gastadas acerca de los latinoamericanos y los afroamericanos."* Wikiquote, s.v. "Roberto Clemente," http://es.wikiquote.org/wiki/Roberto_Clemente. Author's translation.

4 *"No existe nada malo en nuestros hogares y país que un poco más de compasión, cuidado y amor no puedan curar. Somos todos hermanos y hermanas y debemos ayudarnos mutuamente cuando es necesario."* Author's translation. *The Puerto Rico Herald*, Puerto Rico Perfil: Roberto Clemente, 1999, http://espanol.geocities.com/elpelotero_online/reportajes/roberto_clemente_herald.htm

changed forever if Castro had been signed to a minor-league contract in the United States in the 1940s. There is no evidence that Castro was really a serious contender for professional baseball in Cuba, much less in the United States. Roberto González Echevarría of Yale University writes in his 1999 book *The Pride of Havana*: "Cubans know that Fidel Castro was no ballplayer, though he dressed himself in the uniform of a spurious, tongue-in-cheek team called Barbudos (Bearded Ones) after he came to power in 1959 and played a few exhibition games. There was no doubt then about his making any team in Cuba. Given a whole country to toy with, Fidel Castro realized the dream of most middle-aged Cuban men by pulling on a uniform and 'playing' a few innings."[5]

González Echevarría's scholarship is an example, in and of itself, of the Latino contribution to our cultural heritage. González Echevarría earned his Ph.D. at Yale in 1970, and is Sterling Professor of Hispanic and Comparative Literature at the university. His award-winning books include *Alejo Carpentier: The Pilgrim at Home*, and *Myth and Archive: A Theory of Latin American Narrative*.

González Echevarría is quick to remind us that Hispanics in America come in many varieties and from many backgrounds, and that they may disagree in ways large and small. That is certainly true of baseball players. Oswaldo José Guillén Barrios, better known in the United States as Ozzie, the quick-handed shortstop of the 1980s and 1990s, has as different a background as possible from Alexander Emmanuel Rodriguez, better known as Alex or just A-Rod.

Guillén was born in Ocumare del Tuy, Miranda State, a forested, farming area of northern Venezuela. But he spent most of his major-league career with the Chicago White Sox, and became the team's manager in 2004. Guillén became a U.S. citizen in 2006.

Rodriguez, the star infielder and home-run hitter for the Seattle Mariners, Texas Rangers, and New York Yankees, was born to Dominican

---

5 Roberto González Echevarría, *The Pride of Havana: A History of Cuban Baseball* (New York: Oxford University Press, 1999), 6–7. This comprehensive book is an enjoyable review of Cuban baseball, its relationship to the major leagues, and the Cuban players who crossed the Straits of Florida to play in the big leagues.

parents in the Washington Heights section of New York City, and spent most of his childhood in Miami, where he attended Westminster Christian School before going directly from high school to professional baseball.

Ozzie and A-Rod are Latinos, or Hispanics, as you prefer; they are also, respectively, Venezuelan-American, Dominican-American. There is sometimes a debate with sensitivities close to the surface about such matters—let's start out by saying they are Americans.

Trying to deflate the matter, González Echevarría turns to the story of the interviewer who asked Kermit: "Are you an amphibian-American?"

"No," replied Kermit, "I am a frog."

Baseball tends to lead the wave of social and ethnic integration in this country. I observed during the spring of 2009 the joyous celebration of international baseball known as the World Baseball Classic—sixteen teams from six continents. Some of the players are from the major leagues—others are wannabes—but I was most interested in the national pride displayed by the Latin players who joined up with teams of their countries of origin, at the same time establishing home bases in the United States. As often throughout our history, we find our roots transplanted firmly, but our lives are grafted products of the lives of those who came before us.

Hispanic or Latino, we come from many different cultural backgrounds, and we have certain things in common, first and foremost, a connection to one degree or another with the Spanish language. A majority of us are Catholic; some were immigrants of another generation and may be Protestant, Jewish, Muslim, or other religions. We bring along a love of family and traditions that are shared by many. But don't expect us all to agree.

Just ask the ballplayers: Pedro Martínez, born in the Dominican Republic, one of the great power pitchers of his era for the Red Sox and the Mets, and Jorge Posada, the Puerto Rican–born mainstay catcher of the New York Yankees. Five years after the fact, the headstrong rivals were still fuming over a bench-clearing incident in 2003 when Posada claimed Martínez gestured to him that he was going to throw at his head.

Martínez denied this. "He's a human being, he has a family, and I'm a professional. [The pointing to the head] was because he cursed my mom. I was telling him, 'I'll remember that.'"

Martínez continued: "He knows—he's Latin, as much as he pretends to be American, he's Latin—that cursing your mom in Latin America will get you into a fight. That's something I would never do to his mom, because she doesn't play. She's not on the field. She's someone you admire and respect, and I didn't like that."[6]

Besides wishing I could mediate and get Pedro and Jorge to make up, I point to the incident as a perfect example of the beauty of sports—particularly baseball—in the United States.

THE NATIONAL PASTIME HAS SERVED us well as a mirror on our society. Jackie Robinson broke the barrier of racism in baseball in 1947, signaling a change forever toward civil rights.

Latino players did not suffer in the same way as did black players, but their entrance and increasing dominance in the game have accompanied the growing role and power and positive influence of Hispanics in the country.

Baseball has never been far from politics in this country.

The fascination with Cuban baseball has brought much pride to Cubans on the island and Cuban-Americans. Baseball has always been involved with the heritage and cultural climate in both countries. U.S. teams sometimes took spring training in Cuba, such as in the memorable 1946–47 season when Jackie Robinson traveled to Havana with the Brooklyn Dodgers, preparing to break the color barrier in the major leagues that year.

In the first century of white-only professional baseball, there was a strange contrast in the treatment of Cuban and other Latino players on one side and African-American players on the other. According to the unspoken rules of segregation, Latinos could play in the majors if they

---

6 Bart Hubbuch, "Pedro Livid over Posada Diss," *New York Post*, September 16, 2008, http://www.nypost.com/seven/09162008/sports/mets/pedro_livid_over_posada_diss_129274.htm.

passed as white; African-American players were banned from the major leagues for most of the sport's history until Robinson came to the Dodgers. But they sometimes were able to play if they were lighter-skinned and claimed to be Latino or even American Indian.

Surprisingly enough, the first Latino player in the majors was not a Cuban but Luis Castro, a Colombian, who played briefly in 1902. He was followed by a number of others, many of them from Cuba, including Rafael Almeida and Armando Marsans in 1911. But the earliest great Latin baseball stars in the majors were Adolfo Luque, a pitcher, and Miguel Ángel González, a catcher, whose fame was such that Ernest Hemingway mentioned them in *The Old Man and the Sea*. Both men were of humble origin, and both were born in 1890. Luque was from Havana and won the nickname "the Pride of Havana," and González was born in Regla, just outside the capital. Both men played in the Cuban leagues, and also had careers in the majors. Luque finished his career with the New York Giants in 1935, with a record of 194 wins and 179 losses. González, who played more than a thousand games mostly in the National League in his career from 1912 to 1932, finished with a batting average of .253.

There were a number of Latino players in the majors throughout the early part of the twentieth century, but not until the influx of Hispanics into the majors after World War II did a Cuban player come along to equal Luque's fame. In 1949, a twenty-six-year-old Cuban, Saturnino Orestes Miñoso Armas, from Matanzas province, debuted with little fanfare with the Cleveland Indians for a few games. But traded to the Chicago White Sox, he burst through in the 1951 season, batting .324 in 138 games. As soon as he settled in and the league took notice, his name was just too complicated for the majors, especially for sportscasters who Anglicized the ñ—pronounced "en-yea"—in his family name, Miñoso, and forgot about his given names. He became known in 1950s America as Minnie Minoso (the Spanish letter "ñ" dropped). Miñoso closed his career with a batting average of .298, and holds a remarkable distinction. After retiring from the majors in 1964, he returned as a pinch hitter in 1976, when he got his last hit, at the age of fifty-four the oldest person to ever get a hit in the major leagues. He appeared in two more games in 1980.

Think of some of the other players who inspire us—Liván Hernández, the Cuban power pitcher who fled Cuba in 1995 and started his major-league career with the Florida Marlins. Steve Fainaru wrote about Hernández with Ray Sánchez in their book *The Duke of Havana: Baseball, Cuba, and the Search for the American Dream.*[7] Fainaru spoke to Liván about the freedom to be in the United States and his reasons for defecting. "The first was to seek freedom, the second was to try to help out my family and the third was to play baseball in the major leagues."

When Fainaru pressed Liván about what he meant by freedom, he said he thought it was obvious. "Freedom is a word that every Latino and every American knows. It means the same in Spanish as it does in English. It's the freedom to do whatever you want, everything that you would ever want to do. This is the point and nothing more and nothing less."

When asked by reporters about how he pitched so well, he replied, "If you think I play well, wait till you see my brother." He was right; his brother is Orlando Hernández, better known as El Duque. El Duque left Cuba in 1997. Once a star with the Industriales of Havana, he had been suspended from Cuban baseball, and cast into obscurity. He wanted to play baseball, and referred to the sport as the son he never had. His debut in the major leagues came on June 3, 1998, with the New York Yankees.

Baseball has always reflected our values and a deeper sense of being Americans: playing the game well and challenging ourselves to do our best. It was in that spirit that President Franklin Roosevelt decided to go ahead with the 1942 baseball season, months after Pearl Harbor brought the start of World War II. The president knew that the game would provide a diversion and a sense of normalcy at home. On April 15, 1942, a young man named Hiram Bithorn took the pitcher's mound for the Chicago Cubs at Sportsman's Park against the St. Louis Cardinals. He was the first Puerto Rican to play in the major leagues. Bithorn pitched for

---

7 Steve Fainaru and Ray Sánchez, *The Duke of Havana: Baseball, Cuba, and the Search for the American Dream*, New York: Villard Books, 2001. 171.

two years with the Cubs, entered the U.S. military in 1944, and played several more years after the war ended.

Eventually, thanks to Jackie Robinson, Puerto Ricans and Latin players with darker skin tones than Bithorn were also able to play in the major leagues. Bithorn was honored in Puerto Rico in 1962 when the largest baseball stadium on the island was built and named after him.

Baseball will continue to reflect American values and pride, and act as a mirror for the progress of Latinos and all Americans. Of course, Latinos increasingly began standing out in other sports, whether it was Henry Cejudo, a Mexican-American who won a gold medal in Olympic freestyle wrestling; Anthony Muñoz, an NFL Hall of Fame offensive tackle with the Cincinnati Bengals in the 1980s; boxing champion Oscar De La Hoya; tennis legend Pancho Gonzales; or golfers Juan Rodriguez, better known as Chi-Chi, and Lee Trevino.

But baseball seems to track the lives of Americans and sublimely links all of us; it is bigger even than politics. In his book about the history of Cuban baseball, Roberto González Echevarría points out that not even a Communist revolution could slice this most American spot away from Cuba. Baseball shows our persistent joint experience. "American culture is one of the fundamental components of Cuban culture, even when historically there have been concerted and painful attempts to fight it off or deny it," Echevarría writes. "Even in periods, such as after the revolution, when Cuban culture tried to separate itself from American culture, it was being defined by it. Baseball is the clearest indication of this."[8]

The pride of sports, then, is significant and part of our heritage, the heritage of all Americans, just as Latinos are part of the mosaic of American life. And as Ted Williams, that most American of American baseball heroes, told us, "Baseball gives every American boy a chance to excel, not just to be as good as someone else, but to be better than someone else. This is the nature of man and the name of the game."[9]

Williams, whose mother was of Mexican descent with roots in the

---

8 Echevarría, *The Pride of Havana*, 12.
9 Ted Williams, acceptance speech at Cooperstown, NY, July 25, 1966, on his induction in the Baseball Hall of Fame. http://www.tedwilliams.com

Spanish Basque Country, is thought by some to have been the greatest pure baseball hitter in history. But he also served as a combat pilot in the U.S. Marine Corps during World War II and in the Korean War, where he served with former Senator John Glenn. This is how General Douglas MacArthur described Williams: "not only America's greatest baseball player, but a great American who served his country."

CHAPTER 6

GROWING AMERICA'S PROSPERITY

We must lay hold of the fact that economic laws are not made by nature.
They are made by human beings.

FRANKLIN D. ROOSEVELT

As in time of war, it is absolutely clear that no American, increasingly no citizen of the world, can be immune from an economic crisis of global proportions. The problems of Wall Street and of major financial institutions around the world certainly reverberate on Main Street in America and are felt by all of us. So before we talk about the Latino component in America's economic future—helping them to make progress in creating jobs and businesses and to develop a healthy environment for rational investments—we need to discuss our national responsibility to ensure a stable economic system for all.

The lesson we have learned from the recession of 2008 is that America must move away from the Reagan-era model of extreme, unregulated financial trading that brought us to the brink of disaster. Let's take a look at the global problem facing us; once we do that, we can focus on how Latinos can be and need to be at the forefront of the recovery.

It was evident to me at least as early as March 2007 that we faced a tsunami of unprecedented proportions that was leading us to economic collapse. I warned on the floor of the Senate at that time that unscrupulous mortgage practices presaged a major crisis, and had "a chilling ripple effect across our nation's economy, leading to sharp declines in the stock market." Without prompt action, I said, "we put not only more individuals at risk of deceitful predatory lending practices, but we put our financial markets and entire economy at risk."[1]

I recall this not in a tone of self-congratulation or successful soothsaying. It was all too evident that Wall Street was already in trouble, and our financial stability was already questioned. The Bush administration, in its neglect, had given lenders the chance to invent new ways to make bad loans, and pass off the risks on investors. The Federal Reserve had the power to fight predatory lending, but failed to act. With responsible controls, the lenders wouldn't have been allowed to peddle bad loans, which investment banks bought, and then went bust, and spurred this crisis.

If Congress or the White House had in fact intervened at that early moment, I wonder how things might have been different. Instead the Bush administration turned its back on regulation and oversight. Instead of being a cop on the beat, patrolling corporate accounting, the administration disastrously allowed Wall Street to police itself. Instead of overseeing mortgage lenders, the Federal Reserve also looked the other way—so much so that even though they had the power to stop rapacious lending for fourteen years, they didn't use that power until July 2008. In short, instead of keeping an eye on the regulatory system that had kept our financial system on sound footing for seventy years, the administration and its allies recklessly dismantled it. They passed it off as trusting capitalism—but really what they were doing was capitalizing on our trust. It was a level of incompetence that left us on the brink of an economic meltdown.

We wasted time in attacking the problem in the last year of the Bush administration. The Republican Party acknowledged the depths of the problem only after banks started collapsing and foreclosures became an epidemic. So by January 2009 we faced one of the most perilous economic times any of us have ever seen. Major financial institutions had collapsed, the stock market saw its biggest drop since the 1990s, home

---

1 Robert Menendez, "Floor Statement on Predatory Lending," http://menendez.senate.gov/newsroom/record.cfm?id=270765&&.

foreclosures rose at the fastest rate since the Great Depression, and hundreds of thousands of Americans lost their jobs.

The failure in leadership and the trickle-down effect hurt almost every American home. We were forced to rescue Wall Street from its profit-seeking failures in order to rescue homeowners, many of whom were in trouble through no fault of their own. A foreclosure in one neighborhood affects all the surrounding homes and can create that dreaded ripple effect we have seen, engulfing the greater economy. Foreclosures are at the core of a crisis that affects us all.

Recession and the credit collapse are especially tough for minority communities. Millions of Latinos, either just arrived or in the process of making the dream work for them, were among those in need of help. A report by the Center for American Progress sums it up well: "Although all U.S. households are hurt in the economic slowdown, Latino and African-American households are more vulnerable; they are likely to suffer first and to suffer more."[2]

Latinos and other immigrant groups are facing the toughest economic climate in years. During the Clinton administration, Latino family incomes rose consistently; in the Bush years, they fell steadily. Unemployment among Latinos rose twice as fast as among whites. In midcrisis, the rate of unemployment overall surpassed six percent by the end of 2008, but it was eight percent among Latinos. Government estimates said that a total of two million people will have lost their homes to foreclosure by the end of 2009; Latinos are expected to be hard-hit. I have promoted the concept of deferring foreclosures for up to nine months for qualifying homeowners. The goal is to provide help to responsible borrowers who are struggling with some subprime or adjustable-rate mortgages. It has been clear to me that relief and support for homeowners starts to get to the root of the economic crisis we have inherited.

Meanwhile, credit card debt is a hidden danger to the recovery; credit card debt grew an estimated twenty percent from 2007 and was ap-

---

2 "The State of Minorities, How Are Minorities Faring in the Economy?" by Amanda Logan, Tim Westrich. Center for American Progress, April 29, 2008. http://www.americanprogress.org/issues/2008/04/minorities_economy.html

proaching one trillion dollars at the start of 2009. Victims of excessive credit card debt are often the poorer segments of our society that are unable to meet minimum monthly payments when rates go up. If a consumer misses a payment or two, he or she is unable to get a home loan or any other form of credit. The credit crisis in this country involved a crunch of the big players on Wall Street and around the world. But the problem for individual credit card holders threatened to become another major consumer crisis. It was another in a series of financial dangers frightening all Americans—as they saw their life savings plummeting in value.

On January 20, 2009, President Obama took office and we crossed the threshold toward real leadership. The president's recovery package was the foundation for a new, stronger twenty-first-century economy. As more and more families faced foreclosure, and as housing values bottomed out, the administration moved quickly to cushion the fall.

The failure of Wall Street and the greedy practices of financial institutions were an awakening. The administration moved to reestablish accountability and regulation that protect American families while allowing our market-based economy to run smoothly.

Much more has to be done, with the goal of averting the next crisis. We need new regulations to catch developing storms before it is too late the next time; for example, we have started implementing credit card reform. I authored the Credit Card Reform Act, seeking to halt a vicious cycle of credit card debt that was drowning too many Americans. The goal was to end dangerous credit card practices that permitted excessive fees and retroactive rate increases, among other deceptive practices.

Despite the measures of the president's stimulus, government certainly can't do it all; any economic recovery also has to depend on the innovation and hard work that Americans do every day.

We have to target relief to those who need it most. The health of our economy requires help for homeowners, as the housing market is a pillar of our society. We can't sit back and watch families get thrown from their homes and their children pulled from their schools.

Again, the Latino community stood to suffer more than the general population. The fact is that our community is one of the most under-served, and has one of the lowest participation rates in the financial system. Latinos are more likely to be without a bank account than any other group,[3] and a greater percentage of Latinos goes without health insurance than any other group.[4]

ALL SAID, I'M OPTIMISTIC THAT we can learn and change after the failure of the past, once we recognize and repair the damage and negligence of the previous eight years. And while tough times are ahead for all Americans, we must work to make sure that rational recovery takes into account Latinos and others who are of limited means. We need to guard against foreclosures, provide solid credit opportunities both for Latino businesses and individuals. It is critical that we continue to advance policies that will empower our community and unlock the potential of America's fastest-growing segment. Latinos are an expanding populace that will continue to generate rising salaries that produce the purchasing power, disposable income, and entrepreneurship and job generation to spur American growth throughout the twenty-first century. All of this is possible with the required incentives.

My friend Cid Wilson understands these issues, and focuses particularly on the need for small-business relief. Cid is a Wall Street analyst in New York by day and has been one of the leading advocates for Latino economic empowerment. "The way to deal with the issue is that the government needs to remove some of the barriers to small business. Small business is a major driver of employment, especially in our community. The government needs to provide more opportunity, including a focus on protecting minority contracts. It needs to expand promotion in the private sector—offering tax incentives for large corporations that do business with minority contractors. That process fuels business and allows companies to employ more people."[5]

3 http://nubank.cust.digitalwest.net/hispanicbankmarketing/fed_reserve_article.php?articleid=bankingimmigrants
4 http://www.nclr.org/content/policy/detail/1785/
5 Cid Wilson, October 17, 2008.

He's right—stimulating business feeds into an economic cycle that is good for all American workers. Given the right jump-start and support for initiative, small business grows. Meanwhile, there is an essential point to be made. As corporations raked in record profits by marketing goods and services to our communities, they have neglected and sometimes mistreated the middle class and those working at the start of the economic ladder. Corporate America depends on the growing purchasing power of the Latino community, yet when we look at the number of Latinos in corporate leadership, or on corporate boards—we are rarely represented. Corporate America is hereby placed on notice—that must change. We can learn from significant economic models already in place in the community and I propose adapting such solutions on a broad basis nationwide. If we're looking for an inspiring blend of entrepreneurship, community development, mentoring, and philanthropy, we would need go no further than The East Los Angeles Community Union (TELACU) and its visionary founder, Dr. David C. Lizárraga. I'm proud to know David, who founded TELACU, a non-profit corporation, in 1968. TELACU serves as a model that combines business acumen and community development.

David, the grandson of Mexican immigrants to California, is also chairman of the United States Hispanic Chamber of Commerce, which represents about 2.5 million businesses with revenues approached a quarter of a trillion dollars. TELACU was created originally as a Community Development Corporation under funding legislation sponsored by New York senators Robert F. Kennedy and Jacob Javits. The goal has been to recognize that community development is successful when it is carried out in an economically viable model—one of its mottos is to create "profitability that is inseparable from social impact." The corporation has focused on real estate development, financial services, and general construction, with an important community service component.

He calls it "a progressive community development philosophy. We've put together a system here that is fully integrated that allows us to finance and build a multitude of things, industrial parks, first-time home buyers, senior citizens, and a construction management firm that builds schools."

When we examine the community impact in Los Angeles in the forty years since its inception, we get an idea of how much a model TELACU can be. It has created affordable homes for first-time homeowners and families, access to funding for small businesses and educational programs. The real estate segment of the TELACU project extends to multi-family housing and senior housing. The organization also provides funding for "green" improvements to real estate, including weatherizing existing homes, and analyzing energy efficiency to save resources and money.

The best of all-encompassing development programs such as TE-LACU recognize from the onset that buildings and physical resources cannot be separated from social programs, job opportunities and municipal services. The goal is to produce an integrated development system that answers all needs of a community.

What does that mean? TELACU negotiates new, rational rules of the game, building industrial facilities and apartment complexes; it has provided and negotiated loans for small businesses, and even saved a land-mark building in Los Angeles and turned it into a restaurant, named for the Mexican artist, Rufino Tamayo. The scope is enormous and in the end, infrastructure is given back to the community—empowerment becomes a dynamo, in turn building more infrastructure, then more development, and more empowerment.

David says the goal is to serve as an advocate "while providing a voice for this tremendous asset we call the Hispanic community.

"We're entrepreneurs. We'll make a business out of anything to help our families. Most people don't realize that first and second generation individuals are just starting to build on that natural base. They come here and work hard usually in a service industry. But somebody in the family is already creating a business, even if it starts out as a pushcart."

In 1983, TELACU created its education foundation, and since then has promoted schooling from childhood into graduate school. The foundation sponsors two thousand elementary and secondary school students every year, and offers 600 college scholarships to Latinos. Along with the scholarships, the foundation pairs up mentors with students according to their needs and interests. It's clear that the TELACU process has gotten it all right; investing in education, mentoring programs, measuring student progress—it provides a long-term payback for everyone. While we continue to work on high dropout rates among Latinos, TELACU has the system working. It has sponsored students at all levels to keep studying through high school, and graduate from college.

TELACU works with partnerships at all levels, in the community, among traditional business, the banking and financial sector and working with government. In the case of the education foundation, dozens of companies, including major U.S. corporations, help fund the scholarships and guidance programs. The system gathers profit and noprofit organizations, local, state and government entities, the widest possible reach of getting the job done.

The process focuses on human capital; engagement of energies, in turn, feeds the success of our nation. TELACU is a fine prototype for what I've been describing—this concept of global, shared solutions that feed and nourish our goal, Growing American Roots.

David describes it this way: "Our Return on Investment grows exponentially when we invest in human capital—developing and preparing our youth for the new challenges of this 21st century." He deeply understands the need, the responsibility of business leaders to create a long-lasting, self-perpetuating model. "We have the responsibility to empower our young men and women with the educational opportunity they need to succeed in the emerging marketplace. Ultimately, we are helping ensure continued prosperity for them, their families, and our entire nation."

Could TELACU serve as a model? David thinks so.

"There are a number of things that need to come together to create the TELACU model. TELACU is a unique model for economic development. It is based on the fact that a viable business interest coincides with sound initiatives and enhances the community. It positively impacts people's lives. And that's really important. We're stewards. We call it a double bottom line—getting involved in economic ventures that enhance the community and have an impact on the lives of people.

"Each and every business that TELACU operates has that double bottom line—profitability that is inseparable from social impact."

Organizations such as TELACU and the Hispanic Chamber of Commerce, along with The National Council of La Raza, focus on the important issues surround wealth development and preservation. Government and private industry need to work together to help Latino families develop savings, mortgages and assets for the future. We should be advocating programs that provide low-cost financing to people with worthy credit histories. Such organizations provide counseling and partnerships to encourage a greater percentage of Latinos toward having fixed assets. Despite the recession, future trends show that we will be able to generate credit support for mortgages, small business and commercial loans in our communities.

EVEN WITH THE DOWNTURN, AND despite the challenges of the credit crunch and connected issues, Latinos are advancing rapidly, well-grounded in this country as a driving economic force. I'm confident that Latino enterprise can lead the way toward new progress, contributing to the overall strength of our retooled American economy. There is ample evidence that many Hispanics in the country have graduated to the middle class and beyond. Before recent losses in employment across the economy, statistics showed us that the number of Latinos earning more than forty thousand dollars a year has been increasing at three times the national average. That trend will continue.

The number of Latinos in this country defined as earning more than one hundred thousand dollars a year has doubled since 1980. With a younger and booming population and with more disposable income, our appeal to corporate America is significant and growing. In 2007, for the first time, Latinos surpassed all other minority groups in terms of purchasing power—which rose to more than eight hundred billion dollars and was expected to exceed one trillion dollars sometime in 2009.[6] The

---

6 "Hispanic Purchasing Power Surges to $700 Billion," HispanicBusiness.com, May 2004, http://www.hispanicbusiness.com/news/2004/5/5/hispanic_purchasing_power_surges_to_700.htm.

increase of disposable income among Latinos was triple the overall national rate from 1994 to 2004.[7]

One estimate said that there were at least 2.2 million Hispanic-owned businesses generating close to $388.7 billion in revenues in 2008.[8] *Hispanic Business* magazine, a prominent monitor of Latino business activity in the United States, has profiled the top five hundred Latino-owned companies in the United States for twenty-five years. It reports that in that period, the total value of those companies has increased by seven hundred percent. Most startling is the difference in the median companies listed on that business barometer. In 1985, the magazine reported only 230 of the five hundred companies on its list had revenues of five million dollars or more. Eleven years later, five million dollars was the minimum revenue of companies qualifying for the list. This year the top five companies in their ranking exceed one billion dollars in revenues, and the top seventy have revenues of more than one hundred million dollars.

This is a dramatic sign of the power and growth of Latino economic enterprise in this country, and our contribution to dynamic growth. At the top of *Hispanic Business*'s top five hundred was Brightstar Corporation, based in Miami, founded in 1997, and employing more than three thousand people in forty-nine countries. Brightstar is a major reseller of wireless and cell phones for Latin America, and is increasing its operations worldwide. Its revenue was listed at more than $3.6 billion.

We find a recurrent theme when we discuss such success stories: Latino businessmen who have made it are reaching beyond their own enterprises to create new structures that will bring along a new generation of success stories just like their own. The founder and chairman of Brightstar is Marcelo Claure, an entrepreneur who has been honored internationally for his successful business innovating and marketing. A graduate of Bentley College in Massachusetts, he was cited by *USA Today* as Entrepreneur of the Year. He has been president of Small World Communications, an organization of independent wireless retailers, and has also

7 Ibid.
8 Ahorre.com, "2008 Hispanic-Owned Businesses," http://www.ahorre.com/dinero/business/marketing/2008_hispanic_owned_businesses/.

been active in developing business and economic opportunities in the United States and Latin America. He worked with Nicholas Negroponte of the MIT Media Laboratory and others to help create an organization called One Laptop per Child. The concept was to distribute and develop easily accessible portable computers for children around the world at a cost of one hundred dollars each, as a means of broadening educational opportunities, especially in the developing world.

Claure, the son of a Bolivian diplomat, told *Hispanic Business*, "You must have a vision and go at it with no fear, as if you have nothing to lose. In speeches, I tell young people that the only way to succeed is by taking risks."

His business trajectory was stellar. From his first cell phone store in Boston, Claure expanded to a chain of 134 stores, sold that business, and created Brightstar in 1997.

Moving up one ranking to number two on the top-five-hundred list was Molina Healthcare, of Long Beach, California. Created in 1980, the company employs 2,500 people and has revenues of about $2.5 billion. C. David Molina, an emergency room physician, was the founder. Molina opened his own clinic in 1980, dedicated to serving patients in Long Beach whether or not they were able to pay. The company now provides managed care, Medicaid, and Medicare plans to more than one million people in nine states.

There is no reason to focus on the top of the charts alone to see the vibrancy of Latino business in this country. Moving up on the ladder from number 495 to 480, for example, is Luis Auto Colors, an auto-painting and body-repair firm with six locations in Houston and Corpus Christi.

This is the kind of entrepreneurial spirit that inspires confidence now and supports the notion that, given a balanced, intelligent economic recovery, we'll be seeing geometric advances in Latino business expansion down the road. It is time to combine rational financial rules with opportunity at all levels of our society. Such empowerment will become as important as social justice is in our community. That means real access to capital and capital formation, expanded diversity on corporate boards, and real investment in our communities from the financial sector.

My friend Cid Wilson, in northern New Jersey, is rightly proud of the initiative and entrepreneurial prowess he sees among Latinos. He focuses on his own Dominican community, but the same is true of Puerto Ricans, Mexicans, Central Americans, the rainbow of Latinos who come to this country and slowly establish infrastructure and roots.

Paterson, New Jersey, for example, has a population of about 150,000, and half the residents are Latinos. An estimated eighty percent of the businesses are Dominican. Nor are Dominicans the majority Latino community in the Bronx, with a total population of 1.4 million. Latinos make up about half of the population, twenty-four percent of Bronx residents are Puerto Ricans, and about ten percent are Dominicans. And more than three-quarters of the businesses are Dominican.

"There is a common theme," Cid tells me. "Dominicans like to be independent. They own groceries, restaurants, beauty parlors, and are active in the taxi-limousine industry."

There is logic to this, and it follows the history of immigration in our country. First-generation arrivals are not likely to have advanced education, and look for opportunities with minimal schooling requirements. As immigrants move up the ladder, they start to develop strategies for financial independence. At the appropriate time, government can provide the impetus. If someone, for example, wants to start a small business, we can streamline regulations to provide access to capital, and to make it easier for legal immigrants to meeting licensing rules and other requirements.

With support and nurturing from government policy makers, Latino businesses can continue to be on the move. The success stories are beyond counting. Tens of thousands of Hispanic-owned businesses are created each year, all telling stories of the American dream. I was attracted by a recent report about a woman named Argentina Ortega, originally from El Salvador, whose determination took her from baking pastries at home to a company that has expanded into supplying food products to 150 Latino stores in Virginia and North Carolina.[9]

---

9 Juan Antonio Lizama, "Hispanic Bakery plans to grow and diversify," *Richmond Times-Dispatch*, September 26, 2008, http://www.timesdispatch.com/rtd/news/local/article/TOGO27_20080926-210740/91461/.

She started preparing pastries at home for four customers, and the popularity of her creations grew. She bought a small bakery three years ago, now has seven employees, and is talking about building an even bigger facility. Eventually she hopes to open a café with an assortment of pastries and cakes.

Then there is the success story of George Burciaga, president of smarTECHS.net, an information-technology consulting firm. Burciaga, a Chicago native, was named Minority Small Business Person of the Year in 2008, a designation awarded by the U.S. Small Business Administration. Burciaga's firm is one of the fastest-growing companies of its kind, and his expertise competes well beyond the realm of Hispanic businesses. *Inc.* magazine has also recognized Burciaga for its success.

He sounds like so many of the American business pioneers who continue to give our country the drive and power to grow. "You need a great idea as well as the focus and passion to turn that idea into reality. You have to be ready to risk everything to win it all."[10]

And he pays homage to his Latino roots for his work ethic.

"I grew up in a culture where working hard with a strong commitment to family and community was very important. It's where I get my work ethic."[11]

The story is repeated again and again. We can encourage our legal immigrants by providing the means to access capital, and by establishing training programs, and cutting red tape to smooth the way. Resetting the economic course will help us all.

We need to encourage people in our communities to build savings and build trust in financial institutions. On the flip side, we should encourage financial institutions to make themselves more trustworthy, so they can build bridges with our communities. The goal of our economic-recovery plan is to restore stability to our housing market, including tax credits for first-time home buyers, which I hope will help more Latinos achieve that piece of the American dream. And sometime in the near fu-

10 George Burciaga, interview, Hispanic Entrepreneur, May 27, 2008, http://hispanicen trepreneur.blogspot.com/2008/05/george-burciaga-wwwsmartechsnet.html.
11 Ibid.

ture, I hope to bring forward legislation to encourage low-income taxpayers to start saving more, earlier.

One of the greatest challenges in increasing access to credit is that people in our communities don't need just credit; they need *good* credit. This issue exists from Wall Street down. The financial sector should consider significant investment in our communities. I advocate measures to make credit applications and authorization more straightforward and equitable, while protecting lenders from unreasonable risk. I've introduced a bill to ensure regulators are doing their part to encourage the growth of minority banks, and a bill to provide low-cost capital to community organizations that fund projects in underserved communities. As a member of the Senate Banking and Budget Committees, one of my main focuses is a broad range of access to capital initiatives. We should be regulating and monitoring the work of payday lenders, check-cashing storefronts that can be found in every Latino community. People who deserve fair credit terms and need credit to grow should have that opportunity. The bodega owner in a disadvantaged area has the right to thrive by his own entrepreneurial skills and obtain the credit that will allow him to expand as the supermarket owner of the future.

Our challenges go beyond just dollars and cents. Following through on the projects we're discussing isn't just about strengthening America's economic standing, but renewing our moral standing.

Our immediate task is to get our economy back on track, but the real challenge for us is how we lift our community up, how we bridge the disparities that keep Latino-household wealth a fraction of that of Anglo households, how we bring those from immigrant communities into a banking system, and how we help Latinos think beyond today, to build for their future, their children's future, and their retirement.

Success will come only when we face these challenges united, whether we're Latino, white, Asian, or black; whether we're recent immigrants or our roots in this country extend back centuries. Many of us have already seen America's promise fulfilled, but there are still millions in America who have not.

With optimism and a drive for substantial changes in our financial system, we can do much more. Our responsibility to all of the most needy is to provide them with the wherewithal to succeed.

These must be our priorities as we create economic opportunity for families today and economic stability for families in the long term—a pledge for quality and affordable health care, education, and renewable energy. We're already on the road toward government measures that help provide for the economic well-being and safety of families.

THE HISPANIC COMMUNITY IS WITNESSING a swell in our economic, political, and social influence. Members of our community have become captains of industry and leaders in the political arena. That is to be celebrated. But we cannot let our celebration drown out the cries of our brothers and sisters who deserve the same opportunities provided to us. Our fight must be for them.

There are efforts to promote small business around the country, and Barack Obama has spoken of the need to spur on businesses just starting up. He has focused frequently on the issue. Even before taking office, he took steps to protect small business, and of course a majority of Latino businesses fall in that category. Part of the economic-recovery plan will expand loan guarantees offered by the Small Business Administration. The idea is to temporarily eliminate fees for borrowers and lenders, opening up easier sources of credit for small companies.

As always, there are important nongovernment organizations that work in tandem with federal programs. One organization that promotes Latino business, among many around the country, is the Latino Economic Development Corporation, a nonprofit operating in Washington, Maryland, and Virginia. It describes its mission as improving "the wealth-building capacity of low- and moderate-income Latinos and other underserved communities in the Washington area."

The organization, which started in 1991, seeks to strengthen small business, promote the ability of Latinos to purchase homes, and preserve the rights of tenants sometimes displaced by development. It advises small-business owners on loans and business plans, and provides microloans for startups and existing businesses. Affiliated with the National

Council of La Raza, the LEDC also promotes rental opportunities for families, and advocates long-term financing and government commitment to housing in underdeveloped neighborhoods; LEDC reports helping more than three thousand tenants stay in their apartments since developing its affordable-housing program in 2004. The nonprofit promotes apartment and home purchases where residents can afford it. It also conducts education programs intended to train future community leaders and advocates.

WHILE WE MAY BE IN the depths of a crisis unknown since the Depression, I am convinced that this year we are on the verge of a transformation in which we will see Hispanics take on a more important role in American public life than at any other time in history. This is not a matter of political muscle for the sake of exercising power. Our goal is to change the course of our lives, and those of our families, our children.

CHAPTER 7

OUR IMMIGRANTS AND THE MEANING OF LIBERTY

If a nation expects to be ignorant and free, . . .
it expects what never was and never will be.

THOMAS JEFFERSON

"With a few strokes of Thomas Jefferson's pen, we were told that life and liberty would be unalienable rights, that a chance to seek happiness would be something to which we were all entitled. Our rights grew over time—and over time we grew out of restrictions on who was entitled to those rights. African-Americans threw down the chains of slavery. Women marched to the polls. People came from all over the world to become full members of our society, because of the promise that our country held and the guarantees that our government made."[1]

With those words, I took the floor of the Senate on June 11, 2008, to appeal to my fellow citizens to consider the worth of all that we have built, to beg everyone to stand up for our highest values. I did so with passion and with hope that decency would win the day in our country.

The dream of comprehensive, sensible immigration reform is close to realization once we understand that it is in our national interest and that its enactment furthers the national security of our country. Our immigrants, much maligned throughout our history, are the lifeblood of America and have always been so. If we establish safe, orderly, and legal means of helping and integrating undocumented immigrants into the mainstream, we will engage the energies of highly motivated newcomers who want nothing more than to thrive and contribute to this country.

---

1 http://menendez.senate.gov/newsroom/record.cfm?id=299036

We do not support illegality, but in the case of undocumented immigrants who are already here, it is reasonable and pragmatic to offer them a path to residency and citizenship if they follow the rules for such an opportunity.

Consider the story of Juana Perez, documented by the Service Employees International Union.[2] It reminds me of the mother and father in Union City, New Jersey, who scrimped and struggled with great dignity half a century ago, and never could have dreamed that their son could be a U.S. senator. Juana knows that working is part of the American dream; listen to her words chronicled by SEIU,[3] which does so much to support immigrants striving to change their lives, or listen to the stories of Eleanora Parada, Veronica Taboada, or Ercilia Sandoval. Tell me if you don't understand or want to support them, and that you don't share their deepest efforts to succeed in life.

Juana Perez is a single mother, working two jobs and juggling commuting and low wages with keeping her home intact and taking care of her children, Lisa and Christian. She has a part-time job as a janitor in the evenings and works as a home-care aide during the day for the elderly. With all that, she takes Christian to school, runs home between jobs to clean the house, picks up her son, prepares dinner, and makes sure that Lisa does her homework, before she runs off again for her janitor job. Juana's story is the saga of a person who has learned how to survive, who is committed to hard work, expecting no more than to be paid and treated decently for her efforts.

How could anyone say that Juana is a burden on our society? Who can say that our Latino immigrants do not participate in our economic life? In 2005, immigrant households and businesses paid more than $300 billion in direct taxes to federal, state, and local governments.[4] And projecting into the future, the statistics look like this: Immigrants will have contributed half a trillion dollars to the Social Security system between

---

2 http://www.houstonjanitors.org/juana-perez/
3 http://www.youtube.com/watch?v=LOw_bxqi5J8
4 Immigration Policy Center, April 2008. http://www.immigrationpolicy.org/index.php?content=fc080412

now and twenty-five years from now and nearly two trillion dollars through 2072.[5]

Let us acknowledge the fact as well that some of those who contribute to our society are undocumented. Such is the case of Benita Veliz, whose story was reported in the *New York Times*.[6] Benita, twenty-three, has been in the United States since she was eight years old, and is in every way an American; she was in student government in high school, volunteers, studied hard to earn a college degree, has worked hard, and wanted only to attend law school. She was stopped on a minor traffic charge in January 2009, and faced deportation. In what way does that help America? Benita and others like her deserve to benefit from compassion translated into government policy, so she can remain and thrive in this home of hers in the United States of America. It's obviously unfair to expect that an eight-year-old child, as in Benita's case, should be held liable years later because of a choice made by her parents. Such is the situation for tens of thousands of undocumented immigrants who came to this country when they were children.

But there are voices in the land that would strike them down, and would encourage us to consider them as something other than participants in the American dream.

In this chapter, I want to examine the issue of immigration, pointing out that throughout history, the dominant immigrant groups of the moment have faced unfairness and prejudice. Second, I want to examine today's immigrants, with an emphasis, but not an exclusive focus, on Latinos—both documented and undocumented immigrants. I also want to stress that in the twenty-first century, we can no longer consider the United States as an island; the folly of political, social, and economic isolationism is simply not viable. We solve immigration issues the same way we solve problems at home—with global solutions, reaching out in this case to our neighbors, looking for synergistic ways of solving our problems. And finally, I want to convince my fellow citizens to explicitly reject

---

5 Source: National Immigration Forum, 2005
6 Lawrence Downes, "Don't Deport Benita Veliz," *New York Times*, March 28, 2009.

the language of hate and intolerance about immigration in this country. It is based on ignorance and misinformation.

I CAN SEE NO POSSIBLE way to restore our basic values and to recover our economic and moral equilibrium without a comprehensive immigration-reform program. Reform is long overdue. We need a sensible plan to reform our immigration system that is safe, legal and orderly, while reflecting both economic realities and American values.

We need to change the way that Americans talk and think about immigration: reject the hatred and intolerance, all based on ignorance. Without that, how can we expect that Latinos will be accepted for their full participation in the American experience? Rather than criminalizing immigrants and blaming them for our economic crisis, we need to make them part of the solution and help them along the path to full integration and responsible participation in society. It is time to break down the walls of intolerance, reminding ourselves of the oft-spoken saying that we must learn history to avoid repeating our mistakes. It is time to reject the idea that immigration is an attack on national sovereignty. That has never been true, and it is perilous to think so; it is time to recognize that immigrants are the soul of America.

All census reports tell us that as the nation grays and the proportion of the population that is Hispanic grows, Hispanics will be younger by a decade than the population overall. These hardworking immigrants will be a greater percentage of the workforce. It's not only humane to provide support—it is also practical and essential for the future. We will increasingly depend on this community. Understanding them, then helping them along, will hasten the social and economic pressures that they will make. Looking ahead to that bright future means integrating all Americans and working for common progress.

In terms of American history, that has not always been an easy task; as we seek to move forward in a more enlightened, more equitable way, we first need to understand that verbal condemnation and violent attacks on immigrants have often been at the center of American experience. When we talk about the immigration crisis these days, we're usually talking about the swell of immigrants to the United States, mostly for economic and political reasons, from Latin America over the last twenty-five years. Wars and U.S. policies, such as in Central America, have been a factor. But the longer view is that immigration has been debated since the earliest days of the republic.

During the colonial period, Benjamin Franklin fretted over the outsiders of his era, German immigrants, "generally the most stupid of their own nation," threatening the purity of the Anglo-Saxons of America.

"Why should Pennsylvania, founded by the English, become a Colony of Aliens, who will shortly be so numerous as to Germanize us instead of our Anglifying them, and will never adopt our Language or Customs, any more than they can acquire our Complexion."[7]

To us, it seems foolish to isolate and think of German immigrants in that way, and that precisely is the point. I suspect that bigots who target Latinos and African-Americans and Muslims in America will be considered one day in the same way.

Franklin, of course, was a Renaissance man, a Founding Father of our democracy, and one of our greatest thinkers, but he also was a product of his times.

Xenophobia has waxed and waned. In each case the most recent arrivals were certain to be the convenient targets of the moment. In the 1850s, the aptly named Know-Nothing Party won nine governorships in the North on the platform that America should remain pure and protected from Irish fleeing the potato famines. One of the governors, Henry J. Gardner, of Massachusetts, saw the Irish as a "horde of foreign barbarians." He pushed a bill through the state legislature that banned funding Catholic schools through tax dollars.

In 1881, the Congress voted to bar Chinese immigrants from entering this country, in what was known as the Chinese Exclusion Act. Congressmen discussed similar legislation to keep out Japanese nationals. The law was not repealed until 1943, in the middle of World War II, when the United States and China were allies against Japan.

---

7 "Observations Concerning the Increase of Mankind, Peopling of Countries, etc." by Benjamin Franklin. 1751. http://bc.barnard.columbia.edu/~lgordis/earlyAC/documents/observations.html

In the early nineteen hundreds, H. G. Wells, the British author of *The Time Machine* and *The War of the Worlds*—which can be read as a parable on the fear of immigrants—said that the arrival of Eastern Europeans, Jews, and Italians would cause a "huge dilution of the American people with profoundly ignorant foreign peasants."

Congressman Albert Johnson, a Washington Republican, warned in the 1920s against welcoming immigrants to these shores, saying, "Our capacity to maintain our cherished institutions stands diluted by a stream of alien blood."

Specifically mentioning an early round of Latino immigration, a 1925 report of the Los Angeles Chamber of Commerce stated that Mexicans are suitable for agricultural work "due to their crouching and bending habits . . . , while the white is physically unable to adapt himself to them."

IN THE HISTORICAL CONTEXT, THEN, and with an economic downturn, we find a new generation of dimmer bulbs than some of our forebears, but using the twenty-first-century immediacy of the airwaves and the Internet to stir up fears that are equally misguided and wrong. Divisive commentators distort the record, especially on talk radio and cable television; would-be populists and demagogues, such as Lou Dobbs and Rush Limbaugh, promote their ideas with the full protection of the First Amendment. When economic times are good, the din is quieter, but we need to get beyond the nonsense with some common sense.

But when I think of those men, I think of a quote from Carlos Castaneda:

> Self-importance is our greatest enemy. Think about it—what weakens us is feeling offended by the deeds and misdeeds of our fellow men. Our self-importance requires that we spend most of our lives offended by someone.[8]

---

8 *The Fire from Within* by Carlos Castaneda (New York: Simon and Schuster, 1984) page 12.

*   *   *

ONE OF THE GURUS OF the new immigration scare was Samuel Huntington of Harvard University, who warned wrongly that America is threatened with disintegration by the large-scale influx of Latin immigrants. "The continuation of high levels of Mexican and Hispanic immigration plus the low rates of assimilation of these immigrants into American society and culture could eventually change America into a country of two languages, two cultures, and two peoples. This will not only transform America. It will also have deep consequences for Hispanics, who will be in America but not of it."[9]

Those who worry about Spanish speakers and Latino holidays not only are prejudiced but don't realize their argument operates in reverse. In fact, Latino immigrants are successful enough at assimilating that some people worry about the future of their cultural memory. Despite the fearmongering of those worried about creating a separate Spanish-speaking state within a state, many Latinos are concerned about making sure that their children and grandchildren remember their language and heritage at all.

Dawn Oropeza, in Iowa, for example, wishes she spoke Spanish with less of an American accent. Dawn, an artist and a community organizer in Iowa, is of Mexican origin. "And my dad and uncle don't hardly speak. We have to work on it." I can relate to that. I had to work as an adult to perfect my Spanish-language skills.

Another example comes from David Madrid, a Mexican-American writer and youth organizer in California, who wrote several years ago that he was embarrassed as a young man when he got a job at a Target store and couldn't speak Spanish.[10]

"On my first day, a couple of coworkers attempted to have conversations with me in Spanish as we went about our work. To their surprise, they found I did not speak the language. That would be the first and last

---

9 *Who Are We: The Challenges to America's National Identity* by Samuel P. Huntington (New York: Simon and Schuster, 2004) p. 256
10 David Madrid, "English-Only Latinos Face 'the Shame' of Not Speaking Spanish," New America Media.

time I would have any contact with them. Now, they won't even look my way as I pass them in the aisles. . . . I know many Chicanos who feel ashamed of not being able to speak the language and are making efforts to learn—not to mention studying and embracing the culture and history of our people."

AND YET, WE HAVE THE onslaught of distortions. Lou Dobbs, the venting, self-appointed sheriff on behalf of the middle class, has refashioned himself as an everyday Joe protecting the common man against José. "Tough, relentless, independent," he calls himself. Tough, I don't know, independent, I doubt, and relentless, to be sure. He never stops emitting the same gruel. When Lou Dobbs says on the airwaves that "about a million aliens" cross the Mexican border every year, he's not being accurate. The authoritative Pew Hispanic Center reports that the number of all undocumented immigrants present in the United States with origins from around the world—not only Mexicans or Latinos—grows by about half a million every year. There is an important distinction—those five hundred thousand people are not all entering the United States illegally. Some enter legally and later overstay their visas. And not all of them are Latinos crossing the Rio Grande. Dobbs also claims that most of the heroin in the United States enters from Mexico. This is also wrong.

Dobbs has fellow travelers on the radio, such as Mike Savage, Rush Limbaugh, and Roger Hedgecock. All seem to revel in lies and vitriol—and ratings. It's a cheap and dishonorable way to make a living.

It is not just that I don't like the demagogues for what they represent; their words can incite hateful acts. Freedom of speech is sacrosanct, but when latter-day populist reactionaries tromp on the truth every day, let's not call them journalists just because they appear on the airwaves.

Talk-radio and right-wing ideologues feed listeners with baseless information, hoping it will stick—and it often does. Dobbs has a big platform and his employers allow him a solitary soapbox apparently because he helps them earn money. He goes too far. He went ballistic in 2008, for example, when I put a temporary hold on the expansion of E-Verify, a program run by the Department of Homeland Security and the Social

Security Administration. It is a voluntary plan for employers to prove their workers are legally authorized to work in the United States. I have serious concerns about the flawed E-Verify system, which is costly to businesses and American citizens. Among other things, E-Verify depends on Social Security records that have been shown to be prone to inaccuracy and could produce millions of discrepancies when attempting to prove identity and citizenship. Moreover, if the program were expanded, as was proposed by the Bush administration, the net cost of E-Verify would be $10 billion a year. Nevertheless, my action in the Senate in 2008 was procedural and did nothing to alter the reality of immigration policy; it was intended to promote debate about E-Verify in the new Congress on comprehensive immigration reform that would supersede that particular measure.

Dobbs raged against me in an on-the-air diatribe: "I just cannot imagine how Bob Menendez can manage to smile, even lightly, when he discusses the national interest, how he can even embrace the concept of being an American, when he is obviously putting his view of the illegal immigration ahead of the national interest."[11] Was he challenging my own right to citizenship, using my name as if I'm one of the people whose patriotism he wants his listeners to question?

THE ONLY THING THAT WE can do is persuasively present the facts.

You will hear that immigrants take away jobs, that they are a burden to our society, that they flood our schools and resources, and that they are taking advantage of our system, giving nothing in return. We have heard it all before, and you will hear it all again—all lies. You might hear that immigrants are on the dole in the United States, not paying their fair share, and hauling in welfare or stressing the health-care system. It is not true.

First of all, undocumented immigrants pay sales taxes and many pay property tax as well. They also pay their share of state and federal income

---

11 *Lou Dobbs Tonight*, CNN, Sept. 23, 2008, http://transcripts.cnn.com/TRANSCRIPTS/0809/23/ldt.01.html

taxes, and Medicare and Social Security payments, some through tax-payer ID cards, and many of them under false Social Security numbers from which they are unable ever to collect any benefits. The result is startling. The Social Security Administration has an account that is growing by billions of dollars every year, in which funds are deposited for irregular—often fake—Social Security numbers. Should we accept illegality in our country? Absolutely not. But the reality is what it is. People are paying into the system and receiving no benefits.

The picture in individual states is much the same. According to the Immigration Policy Center in Washington, D.C., undocumented immigrants in three sample states—Iowa, Oregon, and Texas—"pay more in taxes than they use in benefits."

Surveys by the center in those states found hundreds of millions of dollars in state taxes paid by people who will never receive the benefits. And the center cites information from the Texas state comptroller's office that undocumented people in Texas contribute $17.7 billion to the gross state product.[12]

After taking in those numbers, the angry talk-show host might reject that argument, complaining that immigrants, especially Latinos, are stealing jobs from other Americans. This is not substantiated by the facts as you can easily observe yourself.

Let's remember what jobs we're talking about. We have to face the economic realities in our society—undocumented workers are doing the work most Americans won't do. Latinos and other immigrants are doing the backbreaking work that makes our economy flow. The fruits you had for breakfast were picked by the hands of a bent-backed immigrant laborer. An immigrant worker likely cleaned the hotel room and the bathroom you used on your most recent vacation. The chicken you had for dinner yesterday was likely plucked by the cut-up hands of an immigrant laborer. If you have an infirm loved one in hospice or home care, the steady hands and warm heart of an immigrant aide probably tended to his or her daily necessities.

---

12 "The Economic Impact of Immigration." Immigration Policy Center, November 2007. http://immigration.server263.com/index.php?content=fc071115

Immigrants usually take the lowest rung of jobs available when they come to this country and—like my parents did, and the parents of most of us did—work their way up the ladder. Any American could do these jobs—but most choose not to.

Meanwhile, these entry-level workers on the first few rungs of the economic ladder are paying their dues and their taxes. At the same time, they are supporting higher-wage earners—the chef in a restaurant depends on busboys and people who clear the tables; a crane operator depends on pick-and-shovel helpers to clear debris on a construction site; a hotel manager depends on cleaners and maids to make his hotel more desirable. It is no exaggeration to say that low-level workers are crucial to those who hold higher-wage jobs; they are the underpinning of our interrelated economy.

WHAT IS THEIR REWARD? THE reward is a better life for their families and the hope that their children will have more and more of the benefits of American society.

These arguments deflated, the hard-liner will next say that immigrants come here to hop on the welfare train. That is simply not true. Undocumented immigrants cannot collect any of the services that two-thirds of them pay for with the jobs that they hold down. People who come to this country illegally cannot register for welfare, do not receive Medicaid, cannot obtain food stamps. The vast majority, more than ninety percent, of undocumented men are working for a living.[13] Moreover, statisticians tell us that by 2012 the largest component of growth in the workforce will be a result of immigrants entering the market.[14]

The intolerance preached by some has trickled into government policy on all levels. I am sorry to say that some members of Congress have been mean-spirited enough to propose laws that would convert any un-

13 "Common Myths about Undocumented Immigrants," National Council of La Raza, 2006. http://74.125.45.132/search?q=cache:Lkk70j6JdGAJ:www.wecanstopthehate.org/uploads/file_CommonMyths_Immigrants_FINAL.pdf+undocumented+men+working&cd=2&hl=en&ct=clnk&gl=us&client=firefox-a
14 "Labor force projections to 2012: the graying of the U.S. workforce," by Mitra Toossi, *Monthly Labor Review February 2004*, Bureau of Labor Statistics.

documented person in this country into a felon, and that would allow the government to prosecute almost any American who has regular contact with undocumented immigrants.

In such an atmosphere, starting with such misguided cues from the top, we hear hateful rhetoric that polarizes and divides us on this issue. This is far from the spirit that brought all of us together, and we must fight against policies driven by xenophobia, nativism, and racism. One of the more prominent cases was in Hazleton, Pennsylvania, where Mayor Louis J. Barletta tried to impose restrictions on illegal immigration in his east-central Pennsylvania city. He charged that Mexican and Central American immigrants had overcrowded local schools and social services. In 2006, he won passage of a law that punished employers who hired undocumented workers, and people who helped them find housing. He also declared that English was the official language of the city of thirty thousand. He vowed to fight after a federal judge overturned the law as unconstitutional. After that ruling, he said, "Hazleton isn't going to back down. . . . I will do everything that I can to make Hazleton the toughest city in America for illegal immigrants."[15]

It shouldn't go without mention that Barletta is the product of immigration himself. His family came to the United States from Italy in the last century, seeking equality and a better life for descendants. The irony doesn't seem to faze him. He apparently acted after two violent crimes— a murder and a shooting—that involved undocumented residents. He told *60 Minutes*: "When you start seeing serious crimes being committed, very violent crimes being committed and time and time again those involved are illegal aliens, it doesn't take a brain surgeon to figure out that you're experiencing a problem here that you've never had before, nor do you have the resources to deal with it."[16]

As a former mayor, I can sympathize with the need for state and federal resources to deal with a growing immigrant population. But Hazleton offi-

---

15 "Judge Strikes Down Town's Immigration Law," by Jon Hurdle, *The New York Times*, July 26, 2007
16 Daniel Schorn, "Welcome to Hazleton," *60 Minutes* Web site, November 19, 2006, http://www.cbsnews.com/stories/2006/11/17/60minutes/main2195789.shtml.

cials handled the case with out-of-bounds measures that drummed up prejudice and the potential that those feelings would spill over into civil rights abuses. Angry words produce intolerance and mindless acts of violence.

In the absence of congressional action, states and other municipalities like Hazleton may pass laws that violate equal protection laws, discriminate against U.S. citizens and permanent residents, and create conflict within otherwise peaceful communities.

Fearmongering promotes an increasing cycle of intolerance; this is not a theory or a matter of rhetoric. The result is a frightening trend: The more claptrap and half-truths are repeated, the more the public believes them to be true. If you are told time and again in alarmist language that there is a horde of outsiders stampeding the land (remember H. G. Wells and the invading Martians?), taking your jobs and your money, or seeking to reclaim the Southwestern United States, you're going to begin to hate the people that are being blamed. And you are going to start hating anyone who looks like them. It is not a small coincidence that as this type of rage has increased, so have hate crimes. A recent FBI report showed that the largest increase in bias crimes against any group was in those aimed at Latinos. The statistics show a forty percent increase in hate crimes targeting Latinos between 2003 and 2007, the same period in which Republican-fueled, cable-news- and radio-disseminated wrath targeted us for their special treatment.[17]

The Southern Poverty Law Center put it this way: "As anti-immigrant propaganda has increased on both the margins and in the mainstream of society—where pundits and politicians have routinely vilified undocumented Latino immigrants with a series of defamatory falsehoods—hate violence has risen against perceived 'illegal aliens.'" The SPLC noted those increases "even as a swelling nativist movement has become larger and more vitriolic."[18]

How, by the way, does Lou Dobbs respond to the SPLC? He defamed

---

17 Mark Potok, "Anti-Latino Hate Crimes Rise for Fourth Year in a Row," Hatewatch, Southern Poverty Law Center, October 29, 2008, http://www.splcenter.org/blog/2008/10/29/anti-latino-hate-crimes-rise-for-fourth-year/.
18 Ibid.

the organization in a chat with his friend Roger Hedgecock on *Lou Dobbs Tonight* on CNN on September 10, 2008: "We have been called racists, xenophobes, all sorts of nastiness from groups that—like the Southern Poverty Law Center, which has become a hate group of its own, referring to FAIR [Federation of American Immigration Reform] as a hate group simply because they want illegal immigration stopped and border security, port security, put in place."

It is outrageous though not surprising that such a person would malign the Southern Poverty Law Center, which is dedicated in part to calling attention to the lies of right-wing hate talkers on radio and television. Based in Montgomery, Alabama, the center has its origins in the civil rights struggle of the 1960s. Its founders, Morris Dees and Joseph Levin, have fought for the rights of minorities for four decades, and preach nothing more than tolerance and diversity.

What are the consequences of hate speech? Consider the tragic case of a mindless beating on July 12, 2008, in Shenandoah, Pennsylvania, twenty miles from Hazleton, involving racial slurs and resulting in a senseless death. A twenty-five-year-old man, Luis Ramirez, was attacked by a group of young people, including members of the local football team. Ramirez died of his injuries two days later.

Ramirez had been working steadily in Shenandoah after coming to the country six years earlier and had two children. But his fiancée told reporters in the town that he had faced racial and ethnic slurs occasionally. "People in this town are very racist toward Hispanic people. They think right away if you're Mexican, you're illegal, and you're no good," Ramirez's fiancée told the Associated Press.[19] Local officials said the problem was that some people in town couldn't adapt as Latinos started moving to Shenandoah over the last decade. Witnesses said they saw young toughs taunt, then beat the young man, and kick him in the head.

"For many Latinos, this is a case of enough is enough," Gladys Limón, a staff lawyer for the Mexican American Legal Defense and Educational

---

19 "Illegal immigrant's beating death exposes tensions in Pennsylvania town" by The Associated Press. *Orange County Register*, Monday, July 21, 2008. http://www.ocregister.com/articles/ramirez-fight-town-2098432-shenandoah-police

Fund, told a *New York Times* reporter, discussing the death of Luis Ramirez. "And it can help us get attention to the wider issue that this is happening all over the country, not just to illegal immigrants, but legal, and anyone who is perceived to be Latino."[20]

This tragic story is in part a failure of our society and our leaders to preach tolerance. The American people are better than that, and the hatred must stop. Equality and ethnic understanding must prevail. I am confident that a majority of Americans will reject rhetoric based on hatred and polarization. Latino immigrants—as with Europeans of another age, and African-Americans, although their arrival on these shores has a different history—share the same goals. All want to succeed and share the wealth of progress. They pose no danger to this country. Let us not relive the mistakes of the past, the words that many of our ancestors heard, that are so reminiscent of what we're hearing all over again: you know, "No Irish need apply," "No Jews allowed," the disgusting Jim Crow laws, "Restrooms, white only." The list goes on.

There is an underlying reality that is not recognized by the mass of Americans. Many of us argue for immigrant rights because it is the humane, sensible course to take. Others take out their spleen and vitriol about society on a class that should not be singled out for legal consequences and worse. But many on both sides assume a link between impoverished immigrant neighborhoods and high crime. It turns out that one strength of Latino life—strong family values—tends to promote lower crime rates than anyone had expected.

Ramiro Martinez Jr., a Mexican-American from San Antonio, set out about ten years ago on a research project to analyze claims about inner-city crime and violence committed by Hispanics in this country. He is a member of the National Consortium on Violence Research and an associate professor at the School of Policy and Management at Florida International University in Miami.

After Martinez received his Ph.D. from Ohio State University, he de-

---

20 Sean D. Hamill, "Mexican's Death Bares a Town's Ethnic Tension," *New York Times*, August 5, 2008.

cided to take a look at Latino crime statistics. At the outset, it wasn't at all easy to find reliable information. The problem was that many police departments hadn't been flagging information based on whether the people involved in crime were Hispanic. So he decided to do it himself. He chose several major cities with significant Latino populations—San Antonio, San Diego, and Miami among them. With the help of friendly police departments, he was able to go right into the homicide files and calculate data for himself.

When he began, the data collection was time-consuming, and computer crunching wasn't as easy as it is now. Eventually, computing power caught up with the painstaking paperwork, and a trend began to emerge. "We were looking at data gathering in so-called bombed-out communities, dilapidated areas which had been abandoned in the 1980s and 1990s, then repopulated by Latinos who rebuilt their communities in these places."

It became clear that the rates of violent crime—homicides and drug-related violence—were much lower than expected, despite the fact that in the poorest neighborhoods, there are large numbers of immigrants, education is limited, and, specifically, young people frequently drop out from school. Those factors have traditionally been thought to promote high urban crime rates.

"It was quite frankly amazing to me. This is a group that is stereotyped as being a major source of violent crime. . . . But in each case, and across the board in national data gathering of violence across America, it just wasn't the case."

As he continued gathering information on overall Latino crime patterns, Martinez found that the data was pervasive across the country. All along the southwestern border of the United States, even in Chicago's poor and increasingly Latino inner-city communities, the same results were evident, even where old, traditional Hispanic communities faced an influx of immigrants. The rates of violence were relatively low and the immigration of the 1990s was not changing the picture much at all.

Neither Martinez nor I would whitewash the realities of misdemeanor crime, issues involving alcoholism, and crimes that are a product of poverty and unemployment. These are factors we need to fight, with education and programs to raise up the economic standards of all Americans.

But the statistics were clear, and Martinez produced the first major profile of Latinos and violent crime. It was a groundbreaking effort, knocking down prejudice and stereotypes about Latinos and all immigrants.

Martinez's analysis points to the reality of these newcomers to the United States, seeking, as we have said, a new start and a chance to create a better future. Yes, these new immigrants sometimes have trouble communicating in English; yes, life is hard, nor are all human beings perfect. But by and large, Martinez concluded, "these communities with a heavy concentration of immigrants are populated by people in search of work, not by people in search of crime or engaged in criminal activity. They are trying to work, overwhelmingly so in the service sector, and they are the working poor. They are disadvantaged and extremely poor but still working, maybe even two or three jobs, subsistence jobs sometimes, but working. That attachment to work, significantly among young immigrant males, is something that solidifies those communities—this was one of the more significant characteristics that I encountered."[21]

And what are the factors among Latinos that contribute to this reality?

Martinez said that it has everything to do with the tradition of Hispanic family life.

"High numbers of them have extended families. They may not in all cases live in situations with a traditional family—a mother and a father and their kids—but extended households. There's a mother, or one parent at least, and a grandparent, or at least one other relative in the household. That is clearly maintaining some sort of family control on Latino youth, especially young males in these communities."

I can't help being reminded of my own experience, remembering my mother always keeping a tab on me, looking out the window, or asking my sister to track my homework. It's nothing new, and not a surprise, but

---

21 Ramiro Martinez Jr., personal interview by phone, September 17, 2008.

we need to be aware of the lesson—family ties and responsibilities are at the heart of facing the future together, Latinos and all of us.

There is something else to learn from Martinez's academic approach. It suggests how policy can be made, how people can fix their ideas without any real information to back it up. When we talk about gang-related violence, we need to both combat the problem and not overgeneralize. Martinez says that while the growth of gangs nationwide is a problem, the reality versus the claims of national gang organization needs to be studied. "I hear people talking about the danger, and using anecdotes about crime, but how is that translated across the nation? If they have the data, let's see it. It's a mystery—how do they generate all of these estimates?"

Finally, the time has come to separate prejudice from reality. Do we want a society in which you run the risk of violence because of the way you look or the accent you have, or the ability to speak Spanish makes you a suspect? That is the danger today and I fear that there is a slippery slope toward extending the threat to people who wear a turban or a veil, who are assumed to look like Muslims, whatever that means, or, in the words of Benjamin Franklin, who "are generally of what we call a swarthy Complexion" (he was referring to non-Anglos: "in Europe, the Spaniards, Italians, French, Russians and Swedes").[22]

Looking at a group of people and classifying them on the basis of who they are, not what they have done, is a dangerous encroachment on the Constitution of this nation. People born in the United States—American citizens by definition—and legal permanent residents play by the rules but can still fall into a trap. U.S. Immigration and Customs Enforcement stages raids of supposed undocumented workers in which some American citizens and legal residents are detained because of their physical appearance. Sometimes legal residents and citizens are even deported when they are unable to provide immediate evidence of citizenship or residence and look like foreigners.

---

22 Benjamin Franklin, "Observations Concerning the Increase of Mankind, Peopling of Countries, &c." (History Carper), http://www.historycarper.com/resources/twobf2/increase.htm.

We've heard the rhetoric and the hate-laced speech used to polarize our country. But we must never make the mistake of buying into the rhetoric—we can never subscribe to the notion that there are "good Hispanics" and "bad Hispanics."

America is a proud nation of immigrants and we must do everything possible to reject immigrant baiting and intolerance; such hatred takes us on a road that is unimaginable in our society. Let us live by the inspired words of the late Pope John Paul II, who warned against targeting immigrants. He lived through the suffering of migrations in Europe during the twentieth century, and visited every continent, speaking out in favor of those who are the least powerful. And one focus was immigrant rights in the United States: "The Church in America must be a vigilant advocate, defending against any unjust restriction the natural right of individual persons to move freely within their own nation and from one nation to another. Attention must be called to the rights of migrants and their families and to respect for their human dignity."[23]

I am banking on the best instincts of Americans; I appeal to all citizens to recognize the mistakes of the past. We have relegated millions of immigrants, and not only the undocumented, to a subclass unbefitting their worth and value to our society. Let us consider the state of our immigrants in the first decade of the twenty-first century. We must repair and remedy their plight.

The time has come in this country, a nation so great, so influential, so soaring in its promise, to reject prejudice once and for all. Our emerging multiethnic society will soon again be the envy of the world.

---

23 The Church in America, Pope John Paul II (Washington: USCCB Publishing, 1999) page 109.

CHAPTER 8

HOW TO FIX THE SYSTEM

We ought to think that we are one of the leaves of a tree, and the tree is all humanity. We cannot live without the others, without the tree.

PABLO CASALS

I believe this amounts to one of the great challenges of our time: We face the dilemma of an immigration system that is broken. At the same time we call for all Americans to reach to their highest sense of morality, combining compassion, reality, and pragmatism to find a solution. This is a multicultural nation, and our task is to honor our heritage for now and for all time.

That was what Barack Obama meant when he spoke in stirring tones during his campaign for president:

> We may not look the same and we may not have come from the same place, but we all want to move in the same direction— towards a better future for our children and our grand-children. . . .
>
> I have brothers, sisters, nieces, nephews, uncles, and cousins, of every race and every hue, scattered across three continents, and for as long as I live, I will never forget that in no other country on earth is my story even possible.

We all want to find a solution that protects our borders and our economy and our American values, but we must have a productive civil debate about it. We have to come to the table with facts and with respect for one another, not hatred. Unfortunately, some of the people who have the loudest bullhorns in the media are using them to promote an atmosphere of suspicion. If the light of tolerance in this country continues to fade beneath the shadows of fear, we will see terrible consequences for all. Not just for the Latino community, but also for the ideals and values this nation was built on.

We have every reason to ensure that a revamped immigration system is tough, but at the same time our laws must not demonize immigrants— they must be fair and humane. Comprehensive immigration reform should reflect economic and social realities while preserving the rule of law. I am convinced that what this country does on immigration represents our core; we are a country of immigrants and how we treat these immigrants will show either the best or the worst of America.

Logical reforms would relieve pressure on law enforcement, which now spends a lot of policing and investigative time on the issues of day laborers, forged documents, and driver's licenses, not to mention exploitation and cross-border trafficking. We need to aggressively curtail unauthorized crossings at the border, protect both undocumented immigrants and American workers from corporations exploiting undocumented labor, and provide a pathway for immigrants to earn permanent residency in order to ensure that our immigration system is safe, legal, orderly, and fair to all.

I have supported legislation that has increased the Border Patrol over recent years to an estimated strength of around twenty thousand people. I've also supported various efforts to protect the border; as early as 2006, I worked with John McCain and Ted Kennedy on a comprehensive bill to secure our borders; among other things, that measure envisioned a path to permanent residency for undocumented immigrants if they remained employed, cleared a criminal background check, paid their taxes, paid a fine and learned English. After eight years of shoddy management by the Bush administration, we didn't get very far.

SECURING OUR BORDERS IS THE first step to ensuring an orderly, fair immigration system, but by no means is it adequate in isolation. We must also crack down on companies that illegally hire undocumented workers—

something that is long overdue. Under the Clinton administration, employers were held accountable for hiring undocumented workers, as 417 businesses were cited for immigrant violations in 1999 alone. In contrast, only three employers were issued notices of intent to fine by the Bush administration in 2004 for similar violations, making it twenty-two times more likely for an American to be killed by a strike of lightning in an average year than prosecuted for such labor violations.

What happened in the span of those five years? Did companies suddenly decide to start abiding by the law by not hiring undocumented immigrants? The truth of the matter is, as with the issue of border enforcement, the Bush administration looked the other way, serving the interests of corporate America to the detriment of the average American citizen. Unscrupulous companies intentionally hire undocumented immigrants, knowing they can exploit these people without fear of retribution. They know this because undocumented immigrants are forced to hide and subsequently have no avenues to report labor abuses. This not only hurts the immigrant being exploited but also impacts American citizens, who must compete in the market with exploited labor. We must immediately end these abuses and in doing so create an equal playing field to ensure that the wages, benefits, and health and labor standards of the American worker are not undercut.

Improved enforcement on our borders and strengthened regulations in the workplace will enable us to control the influx of new immigrants; but those actions alone do nothing to solve the dilemma of the estimated twelve million undocumented immigrants who currently reside in the United States. Immigration policy must go beyond enforcement to provide a safe, orderly, timely, and legal process that deals with the economic realities of our time.

There are those who advocate the idea that the U.S. government should expel all twelve million undocumented immigrants; that would amount to the most massive roundup and deportation of people in the history of the world. The idea is impractical, costly, and inhumane.

Such a mass deportation, even if we assume twenty percent would leave voluntarily if such a policy was enacted, would cost at least $206 billion over a five-year period, according to the Center for American Progress. That amount is a large percentage of the recent financial rescue package intended to salvage the disastrous legacy of bank deregulation and accompanying Wall Street greed that brought on our financial melt-down. It is an impossible cost. Even if we could pay for it, the loss of workers and the cruelty of dividing the families involved would be much worse. And it wouldn't work, not even with completion of the multibillion-dollar fence across the U.S.-Mexican border.

In no way would I suggest that our laws should promote illegality, but if the system is broken, we all are at risk. The answer involves a universal approach to immigration. We all agree that we must catch criminals or terrorists who try to slip across the border. Rational changes in our law can strengthen the screening process of people seeking to enter the country. We should promote better technology along our borders, and make sure that our agencies have both the necessary staff and the resources to do their jobs.

Border protection is impossible unless efforts include a temporary guest-worker program and a path to compelling undocumented immigrants to come forth, register, and earn their residency. Without a chance at the American dream, immigrant workers already in this country would be driven underground and could be exploited, creating yet another underclass of undocumented workers. A solution will push immigrants out of the shadows and force them to legalize their status. The vast majority of those who cross our borders come looking for work, just as many of our ancestors did. These immigrants contribute to our economy, provide for their families, and want a better life for their children. The idea is not at all to promote illegality or to issue a blanket amnesty. The pathway to earned legalization means applicants will wait years at the end of the line behind legal immigrants.

THE MILLIONS OF UNDOCUMENTED WORKERS in this country are already contributing to our nation. They perform backbreaking work and pay taxes. They deserve the chance to fully participate in our society, and I think a majority of them will be willing to follow the stringent rules that will be laid down. They should not live under the constant threat of deportation, and the accompanying fear of losing their children, or being humiliated, injured, or killed in the process.

Latinos need to understand that when the pundits on the airwaves or members of Congress talk about "those people," they are talking about all of us as Latinos, whether we are citizens or undocumented. The opponents of immigration reform can't distract us when they issue their false warnings.

There is a bright side to the picture. A growing number of people in this country favor comprehensive immigration reform. Public-opinion polls show Americans want to see Congress enact measures that would strengthen border security, and they agree that employees should pay a heavy price if they hire illegal workers. Americans want to see legislation that really works—a system that also includes employment verification, a revamped visa program, along with family reunification so that children and parents are no longer separated. Legislation has described conditional legal status for undocumented people already in the country, and giving them six years as they prepare for permanent residency and citizenship. One new requirement would be part of the package I favor—for the first time, people obtaining permanent residency would have to be able to speak English. That has never been required before full citizenship, but such a measure recognizes that people must be able to speak English if they are able to participate fully in this democracy. At the same time, we must vastly increase opportunities for immigrants to learn English. The Latinos of this country who do not speak English do want to speak English. So far, the desire and need has outstripped the government and private programs that can teach language proficiency. We must change that.

Americans realize the value of meaningful immigration reform for a variety of reasons. A poll commissioned by the National Council of La Raza in 2008 showed that three-quarters of Americans think that offering undocumented workers a legal path to residency and citizenship would help the national security. It's logical and people get it: For the first time, we would have a reliable means of knowing who is here. About three-quarters of those polled also think that legalization will help collect taxes from immigrants in the country. We'll take that positive sign, even though as we've said, undocumented workers pay billions of dollars into the national treasury in Social Security taxes and income taxes they're not eligible to benefit from, and they pay state and local sales taxes and real estate taxes around the country.

The reality is that newly arrived Latinos quickly become part of the American experience and begin to share in our national life.

This has always been the recipe for American progress. Immigrants are out to set up roots in America and Latinos have been no different from other immigrants throughout U.S. history. A fascinating study by Joel Perlmann, a professor at Bard College, takes the case of Mexican immigration to the United States—the largest component by far of Latinos in America—and compares it with the situation of Europeans who came to America at the turn of the twentieth century. In his book *Italians Then, Mexicans Now,* he concludes that the difference is not great. Successive generations of Eastern European Jews, Irish, Italians, and others struggled with menial jobs, stumbled their way through learning English, and made a better life for themselves and their descendants.

While Perlmann said Mexican immigrants are "progressing more slowly than" European immigrants of an earlier era, "a modest exertion of social will would accomplish the most good by trying to boost high school graduation rates," especially among the children of newly arrived Mexican immigrants.[1]

The reason for the slower assimilation rate is that challenges for new immigrants are not exactly the same as they once were. Opportunities are different now than they were at other times in the twentieth century. Jobs were sometimes more available, and different types of jobs were available. Meanwhile, it is plain wrong to say that Latinos would rather keep to themselves and don't want to speak English. The problem is that the demand outstrips the opportunity. Look at the ads for English-language lessons on Spanish-language television or check out the church programs

---

1 *Italians Then, Mexicans Now* by Joel Perlman. (New York: Russell Sage Foundation Publications, 2005), 117.

and adult-education classes around this country where Latino immigrants are working hard on language skills, even when they hold down more than one job. We want all Americans to speak English; Latino immigrants agree—they desperately want to speak English. It's logical. I come from a family where I was pressed by my Spanish-speaking parents to speak English. They knew that speaking English is the single best way to enter this society, and to enjoy the benefits they sought when they came here.

As a matter of fact, we now sometimes worry about remembering Spanish. I know there are millions of other children of Hispanic immigrants who wondered as adults if they could even remember all their Spanish verbs. Statistics show that by the third generation—that is, the grandchildren of Latino immigrants—everyone speaks English. Visit Miami, or Los Angeles, or talk to marketers seeking the English-language Latino segment. Our people speak English. Compare the story with that of a Polish immigrant in 1908—he or she learned to speak English, perhaps with an accent, and perhaps fled before finishing high school. That immigrant might not have been able to write well in any language. His or her children might have grown up in an industrial city in the North, and World War II—a war fought by the children of immigrants—would have interrupted opportunities. But their children in turn, the first baby boomers, attended schools in the new postwar suburbs and in increasing numbers went to universities. Their ethnic background is no more than a color and proud facet of their American lives.

There is no difference now. A family that once crossed the Rio Grande and set up house in San Antonio may have a number of children who speak Spanish, but quickly and increasingly begin translating English for the parents. That has been America and it still is the way we live.

OUR GOAL SHOULD BE NEITHER open borders nor closed borders, but smart borders. The specter of terrorism in a post–September 11 world creates an even greater imperative for us to succeed in this endeavor. And succeed we must, but we are failing to uphold our end of the social contract. We have all heard about and seen the lawlessness along our borders.

Crime in our border communities is increasing—sometimes a result of drug violence bleeding over the border from Mexico—overwhelming local law enforcement's ability to address the challenges. So-called coyotes, or human smugglers, charge thousands of dollars to bring people into this country, creating a multimillion-dollar industry for organized criminal operations to exploit and to fuel their other illegal activities. However, history proves that it is not enough to rely on enforcement only. Over the past two decades, the federal government has tripled the number of Border Patrol agents and increased the enforcement budget tenfold. Despite these efforts millions of people have overstayed their visas or are undocumented.

Now that we agree on the essential requirement of secure frontiers, let us get down to the ground level. Our borders must be protected by all reasonable means, but we are inundated by misinformation in this area as well—baseless posturing has already cost us money and prestige. The negative campaigning and deceptively dire warnings about Latino immigrants have forced unreasonable policies.

It is an understatement to say that borders are insecure, but the focus on the southern boundary with Mexico has left our northern border even more open to attack than ever. There is no plan I know of to build a twenty-foot-tall fence along the Canadian border, and of course I don't advocate such a foolish, wasteful enterprise.

But the decision to build a fence on our long southern border with Mexico is under way. The idea of trying to shut out poor people with a wall is wasteful and wrong. The Bush administration and its hard-right allies in Congress never realized what seems so clear—in the words of Homeland Security Secretary Janet Napolitano when she was the governor of Arizona, "Show me a fifty-foot fence, and I'll show you a fifty-one-foot ladder." Building a wall harms U.S. interests, and is a terrible symbol for us and for Mexico and the rest of Latin America. A containment wall hurts everyone—farmers on the U.S. side of the Rio Grande, families who have lived on both sides of the border for generations—and alienates a new generation. A wall symbolizes exclusion and it makes it less feasible for us to collaborate with Mexico in other areas, such as legal, balanced migration control and counterterrorism. We need to refocus on building friendships, not fences.

Good fences don't make good neighbors with this wall. The existence of the southern-border fence is bad enough, and its estimated four-billion-dollar price tag is mind-boggling. Meanwhile, Americans appear to fret little about those lightly patrolled 3,987 miles on the Canadian border from Atlantic to Pacific. Our border with Canada is twice as long as the border with Mexico. It doesn't take a rocket scientist to realize that if a determined terrorist wants to put all possible resources into entering the United States, he or she will seek the course of least resistance. If the wall is on the southern border, a terrorist will try again to cross over from Vancouver or Windsor or Quebec.

The Government Accountability Office tells us that Canada is just as likely a weakness point as the border with Mexico.[2] With or without the immigration fence in the south, the GAO found lax security and some checkpoints that were not even monitored.

Here's what the GAO said in a report from May 2008:

> In testing ports of entry, undercover investigators carried counterfeit drivers' licenses, birth certificates, employee identification cards, and other documents, presented themselves at ports of entry and sought admittance to the United States dozens of times. They arrived in rental cars, on foot, by boat, and by airplane. They attempted to enter in four states on the northern border (Washington, New York, Michigan, and Idaho), three states on the southern border (California, Arizona, and Texas), and two other states requiring international air travel (Florida and Virginia). In nearly every case, government inspectors accepted oral assertions and counterfeit identification provided by GAO investigators as proof of U.S. citizenship and allowed them to enter the country. In total,

2 U.S. Government Accountability Office, http://www.gao.gov/new.items/d08757.pdf

undercover investigators made 42 crossings with a 93 percent success rate. On several occasions, while entering by foot from Mexico and by boat from Canada, investigators were not even asked to show identification. For example, at one border crossing in Texas in 2006, an undercover investigator attempted to show a Customs and Border Protection (CBP) officer his counterfeit driver's license, but the officer said, "That's fine, you can go" without looking at it. As a result of these tests, GAO concluded that terrorists could use counterfeit identification to pass through most of the tested ports of entry with little chance of being detected.

Even more troubling, the GAO said in 2008 that its investigators were able to easily cross the U.S.-Canada border with simulated radioactive material.

In four states along the U.S.-Canada border, GAO found state roads that were very close to the border that CBP did not appear to monitor. In three states, the proximity of the road to the border allowed investigators to cross undetected, successfully simulating the cross-border movement of radioactive materials or other contraband into the United States from Canada.

It is terribly alarming, especially since Ahmed Ressam, the so-called Millennium Bomber, attempted the northern route. His goal was to plant a bomb at Los Angeles International Airport on New Year's Eve 1999. Royal Canadian Mounted Police had tracked Ressam for years, and tipped off U.S. officials that he might pose a threat. Fortunately for all of us, Ressam was caught when U.S. customs officials on the northern border encountered him and noticed he appeared nervous.

How many more sleeper terrorists are out there, and will one of them manage to slip past surveillance? Their potential interest in using the northern border has been demonstrated. Solidifying the porous northern border should be a priority for the Department of Homeland Security. And yet, as of 2007, far fewer than ten percent of the fourteen thousand U.S. agents were patrolling the Canadian border. How is it possible that we haven't been focusing on the danger of terrorists crossing the U.S.-Canadian frontier? Instead we have been listening to hot air from Lou Dobbs and his allies, complaining about people who would cross that border in search of jobs as gardeners, busboys, hotel workers, and maids.

OUR COUNTRY BENEFITS FROM NEW workers and their families. As we look to the future under comprehensive reform, legal immigration will continue to welcome people to this country who are willing to work hard and participate in the democratic process. In the twenty-first century, we are also becoming more interdependent with our neighbors in Latin America. We need to work toward an immigration policy that isn't just tough, but smart. We should be working more with Mexico to control drug violence, youth gangs, and the smuggling of human beings. Rational immigration policies will help make that happen.

And so, after talking about border security, and the actual demarcation line, let us have a look at exactly what is going on and what our relations should be with our southern neighbors. The creation of the U.S.-Mexico fence has caused ill will, derision, and anger. We should have been working closely with the Mexican government to fight the causes of mass migration, while aiding the country in the fight against drug trafficking. However, the U.S. government did precious little in the first years of the twenty-first century.

Finally, in 2009, President Obama, Secretary of State Clinton, and other officials acknowledged that U.S. policy had to change. The agenda is long: Job creation is the key and we have to work on both sides of the border. A group of thugs in Ciudad Juárez, across from El Paso, is more heavily armed than the police. Drug dealers have spread their violence with impunity, forcing some Mexican officials to flee north of the border for their lives. Ironically, the drug criminals are freely armed with weapons shipped over from the U.S. side of the border; they kill hundreds of people every month in a reign of terror. They operate with impunity and seem to be able to corrupt as many people as they don't kill. In the interim, unfortunately, American demand for their drugs keeps them in business.

In 2007, the Bush administration proposed dealing with such issues with a new, mostly military aid program for Mexico and Central America. It would focus on cross-border cooperation in a variety of critical areas: intelligence sharing, counternarcotics, arms smuggling, and public security.

In theory, such planning and coordination was long overdue, and some aspects of the plan, mainly the long-term institution-building components, were a good start. But it focused too heavily on military forces rather than policing. While the heavy weaponry and sheer brutality of the criminals we're facing seem at first to justify the use of a nation's military, it's a deeply imperfect solution. Using a military command structure and ethos in domestic law enforcement represents a serious challenge to human rights.

There was hope at the start of the Obama administration that we would see a greater commitment and a more measured approach in relations with Mexico. Secretary of State Clinton told her counterpart during a March 2009 visit to Mexico City that "the United States and Mexico need a strong and sustained partnership, one based on comprehensive engagement, greater balance, shared responsibility, and joint efforts to address hemispheric and global issues.

"We need such a comprehensive agenda in order to make progress on the economy, on energy and climate change, on security, immigration, education, health, and other areas that are of great importance to our two countries and our two peoples."[3]

Perhaps her most memorable declaration in that trip was the admission clearly for the first time that the United States shares responsibility for the cross-border drug trade. "We know very well that the drug traf-

---

3 Secretary of State Hillary Rodham Clinton, Mexico City, Mexico, March 25, 2009, http://www.state.gov/secretary/rm/2009a/03/120905.htm

fickers are motivated by the demand for illegal drugs in the United States, that they are armed by the transport of weapons from the United States to Mexico; and therefore, we see this as a responsibility to assist the Mexican government and the Mexican people in defeating an enemy that is committing violence and disruption that is very harmful and which is something that all people of conscience should attempt to defeat."[4]

IMMIGRATION REFORM AND FOSTERING ECONOMIC prosperity in Latin America are really one and the same issue. To solve the problem of undocumented immigrants flowing to our country, not only do we need a solution in the short term to integrate those already here into our economy and society, but we also need to promote long-term improvement in the economic situations of those very countries that are being left behind. In doing so, we will not only create new markets for American goods and services, but we will also create economic opportunity that will stem the tide of undocumented immigration.

So I want to expand the nature of the conversation when dealing with cross-border issues. Our policy toward Latin America must be more than just free trade and counternarcotics—it must also be development assistance and teamwork to bring our neighbors out of poverty and into prosperity. We must promote investment in education, health care, and disease prevention, and the reduction of poverty, and broad support from the Drug Enforcement Administration.

Clearly, then, immigration policy must be truly comprehensive; it must be about more than simply enforcement—it must also be about providing a safe, orderly, timely, and legal process that fulfills the American dream for all. And it must be broad-based and deal with the root causes of unbridled immigration.

HOWEVER, AS WE HAVE ARGUED for and promoted the passage of such universal reform, something terrible has descended upon us. Stereotypes,

---

4 Ibid.

ignorance, and overzealous enforcement have been threatening the basic tenets of our nation. In the guise of fighting immigration, scattershot enforcement has led to the mistreatment in this country of thousands of human beings. In the pretext of enforcing the law, our government has overreached, and we have engaged in practices that threaten the very image of American decency.

CHAPTER 9

HUMANE TREATMENT—
THE ONLY WORTHY SOLUTION

Justice consists in doing no injury to men;
decency in giving them no offense.

CICERO

Among all the outrages and beyond all bounds of decency, the story of the federal immigration raid in 2008 at Agriprocessors Inc., the nation's largest kosher meatpacking plant, should be the rallying cry for immigration reform. On May 12, 2008, about nine hundred agents descended on the plant in Postville, Iowa, a town of two thousand residents, and a growing population of Mexican, Guatemalan, and other Hispanic immigrants. The raid illustrates the many painful aspects of a system that has failed, including harsh tactics and cruel conditions facing undocumented workers.

I want to focus on this particular case in depth because of the size and breadth of the questions it raises. This outrageous travesty of justice exemplifies everything that needs to be changed about the current system: the exploitation of immigrant labor by employers, the harshness and unlawfulness of the raids, and the degradation and inhumanity of the detention.

At the end of this exercise, I will pose a basic question: Without correcting injustices, without examining the unseemly underside of prejudice, how can we possibly aspire to a better future?

The story of Postville is a litany of the ills faced by detainees in this country every day. And as we examine the details, we can see not only how the process is unbecoming to our democracy but also that the implementation is counterproductive to our need for healthy, thriving, energetic people who want to work.

The Postville raid was bad enough, but the appalling conditions for workers at the plant hark back to the chilling stories of Upton Sinclair at the turn of the twentieth century, or even Charles Dickens decades before that. Among almost four hundred workers arrested during the raid, more than twenty were underage and some were thirteen years old. They spoke about brutal treatment, long hours, dangerous conditions, and horrendous injuries. Some of the detained workers said they felt as though they were slaves. In an interview with the *New York Times*, a Guatemalan worker identified as Elmer L. said he started working at the plant when he was sixteen years old. He said he worked seventeen hours a day at a rate of $7.25 an hour, and often did not receive overtime. He said he was kicked, was injured as a result, and didn't receive adequate medical treatment.[1] It is hard to decide which is worse: the treatment of employees as virtual indentured servants at the plant or the degradation and fears they suffered in detention. Anyone who doubts that would have only to read a dramatic open letter written by Erik Camayd-Freixas, a Spanish professor at Florida International University, one of about two dozen federal interpreters brought into Postville for a month. In his twenty-three years as a court interpreter, he never before had broken the vow of confidentiality about the cases on which he has impartially worked. But the misery he saw and the repulsion he felt compelled him to speak out in the highest patriotic sense of simply seeking redress for a wrong.

Summoned under rules of secrecy, Camayd-Freixas reported as instructed to the sixty-acre National Cattle Congress the day after the raid. The cattle grounds had been converted into a detention center. He counted twenty-three trailers set up on the site, two of them serving as makeshift courts for sentencing revolving lines of detainees. There were buses from the Homeland Security Department, dozens of federal agents, and the detainees themselves—about three hundred men sleeping on cots in the gymnasium, while women were taken by bus to local jails.

Camayd-Freixas's assignment was to act as interpreter and intermedi-

---

1 "After Iowa Raid, Immigrants Fuel Labor Inquiries" Bottom of Form by Julia Preston. *The New York Times*, July 27, 2008. http://www.nytimes.com/2008/07/27/us/27immig. html?_r=1&scp=1&sq=Elmer%20L.%20and%20guatemala&st=cse

ary for these illiterate, impoverished souls who had come to work in the United States illegally, but certainly with no criminal intent. By treating them as criminals, the government was able to use leverage on them to exact quick trials, and make sure they would be deported.

The proceedings changed his view of our system, and since the detentions were not recorded in any other way, his words serve as a historic document that may propel reforms. We can write legislation and give speeches, but this kind of testimony clearly portrays the fundamental mistake in which we equate immigrants with criminals, the regulations that dehumanize them and allow them to be relegated to a subclass, viewed as "the other." We see the waste of money and resources, the human toll, not only on the victims, but also on the officials forced into this sad service; we see the devastating effects of splitting families apart.

I hope that even people who reject my position will realize that the great irony of Postville was that the larger community had integrated the immigrant community as part of the fabric of their lives. When one actually examines the way life was in Postville before the raid, we find the basis of a model for how immigrants really can and do make our country a better place as they grow their roots. The immigrants of Postville had revitalized the local economy and participated in civic life and were good neighbors and friends to one another and their children.

But when Camayd-Freixas arrived, he saw broken, frightened people who were being forced into the depths of dehumanization. After a tour of the facility, he and his fellow interpreters began working with teams of prosecutors and more than a dozen detainees at a turn.

"Then began the saddest procession I have ever witnessed, which the public would never see, because cameras were not allowed past the perimeter of the compound (only a few journalists came to court the following days, notepad in hand). Driven single-file in groups of 10, shackled at the wrists, waist and ankles, chains dragging as they shuffled through, the slaughterhouse workers were brought in for arraignment, sat and listened through headsets to the interpreted initial appearance, before marching out again to be bused to different county jails, only to make room for the next row of 10. They appeared to be uniformly no more than 5 ft. tall, mostly illiterate Guatemalan peasants with Mayan last names . . . some in tears; others with faces of worry, fear, and embarrassment. They all spoke Spanish, a few rather laboriously. It dawned on me that, aside from their nationality, which was imposed on their people in the 19th century, they too were Native Americans, in shackles. They stood out in stark racial contrast with the rest of us as they started their slow penguin march across the makeshift court. 'Sad spectacle' I heard a colleague say, reading my mind."[2]

Sad spectacle and an outrage—in the guise of due process to the letter of the law, these uniformed frightened people were compelled to waive their rights to grand jury hearings. The U.S. attorney issued charging documents, which most of the detainees signed, hoping they could be deported quickly so they could continue working somehow, somewhere, to support their families. However, the government issued charges of identity theft and Social Security fraud, on the basis that undocumented workers obtained forged documents to work. Specifically, the government cited the Identity Theft Penalty Enhancement Act of 2004 to prosecute undocumented immigrants. This measure was intended to deal with credit card scams and the billion-dollar losses caused by identity theft in our modern technological age. The Supreme Court has since then rejected the use of the Identity Theft Act in cases such as the Postville raid.[3]

Camayd-Freixas became increasingly troubled as he learned more about the details of what the government had done. It issued 697 arrest warrants, but the raid had hauled in only workers on the day shift, among them 290 Guatemalans and 93 Mexicans. Fifty-six mothers with children were released; a few others were let go because they had medical problems. Only five of those arrested had a prior criminal record. These were humble, impoverished people, and the remaining 307 warrants caused terror and drove people into hiding.

---

2 A Personal Account by Erik Camayd-Freixas, Ph.D., Florida International University June 13, 2008. *judiciary.house.gov/hearings/pdf/Camayd-Freixas080724.pdf*

3 "Justices Limit Use of Identity Theft Law in Immigration Cases" by Adam Liptak and Julia Preston, *The New York Times*, May 4, 2009, http://www.nytimes.com/2009/05/05/us/05immig.html?scp=5&sq=identity%20theft%20penalty&st=cse

"Beside those arrested, many had fled the town in fear. Several families had taken refuge at St. Bridget's Catholic Church, terrified, sleeping on pews and refusing to leave for days. Volunteers from the community served food and organized activities for the children. At the local high school, only three of the 15 Latino students came back on Tuesday, while at the elementary and middle school, 120 of the 363 children were absent. In the following days the principal went around town on the school bus and gathered 70 students after convincing the parents to let them come back to school; 50 remained unaccounted for. Some American parents complained that their children were traumatized by the sudden disappearance of so many of their school friends. The principal reported the same reaction in the classrooms, saying that for the children it was as if ten of their classmates had suddenly died. Counselors were brought in. American children were having nightmares that their parents too were being taken away. The superintendent said the school district's future was unclear: 'This literally blew our town away.'"[4]

In his open letter, Camayd-Freixas quoted a nun: "Hundreds of families were torn apart by this raid. . . . The humanitarian impact of this raid is obvious to anyone in Postville. The economic impact will soon be evident."

Erik Camayd-Freixas became a compelling narrator of an agonizing disaster, in which a group of indigent men and women—undocumented to be sure—were victims nevertheless.

"THERE WAS LITTLE TO REMIND us that they were actually 306 individuals, except that occasionally, as though to break the monotony, one would dare to speak for the others and beg to be deported quickly so that they could feed their families back home. One who turned out to be a minor was bound over for deportation. The rest would be prosecuted. Later in the day three groups of women were brought, shackled in the same manner. One of them, whose husband was also arrested, was re-

4 "Town of 2,273 Wonders: What Happens to Us Now?" by Grant Schulte, Jennifer Jacobs and Jared Strong. *The Des Moines Register*, May 14, 2008, http://www.desmoinesreg ister.com/apps/pbcs.dll/article?AID=/20080514/NEWS/805140371/-1/SPORTS09

leased to care for her children, ages two and five, uncertain of their where-abouts. Several men and women were weeping, but two women were particularly grief stricken. One of them was sobbing and would repeat-edly struggle to bring a sleeve to her nose, but her wrists shackled around her waist simply would not reach; so she just dripped until she was taken away with the rest."

Camayd-Freixas's details portray the entirety of the injustice meted out against these people. One man he spoke to said he had started work-ing at the packing plant only that morning, and had been there for twenty minutes when the agents descended. He quoted the man: "I just wanted to work a year or two, save, and then go back to my family, but it was not to be. . . . The Good Lord knows I was just working and not doing any-one any harm."

The stories and the painful process wore down the interpreters, law-yers, and even some of the judges, who felt handcuffed by the law.

"Another client, a young Mexican, had an altogether different case. He had worked at the plant for ten years and had two American-born daughters, a 2-year-old and a newborn. He had a good case with Immi-gration for an adjustment of status that would allow him to stay. But if he took the Plea Agreement, he would lose that chance and face deportation as a felon convicted of a crime of 'moral turpitude.' On the other hand, if he pled 'not guilty' he had to wait several months in jail for trial, and risk getting a 2-year sentence. After an agonizing decision, he concluded that he had to take the 5-month deal and deportation, because as he put it, 'I cannot be away from my children for so long.'"

Most people in the process appeared to recognize the wrong that had been done in Postville.

"One of my colleagues began the day by saying 'I feel a tremendous solidarity with these people.' Had we lost our impartiality? Not at all: that was our impartial and probably unanimous judgment. We had seen attorneys hold back tears and weep alongside their clients. We would see judges, prosecutors, clerks, and marshals do their duty, sometimes with a heavy heart, sometimes at least with mixed feelings, but always with a particular solemnity not accorded to the common criminals we all are used to encountering in the judicial system."

My COLLEAGUE ON THE CONGRESSIONAL Hispanic Caucus, Representative Luis V. Gutierrez, of Illinois, studied the case extensively in his role as chairman of the caucus immigration task force. I agree that the federal government overstepped shockingly by issuing criminal penalties against plant workers whose only crime was possessing fake Social Security cards because they wanted to work. Most of the people arrested served prison terms and were deported. Luis said his investigation confirmed Camayd-Freixas's report; aggravated criminal identity theft was the prime charge. Certainly, the workers were breaking the law, but these were not hardened criminals, none of them.

There was concern and anger in Postville. It was a microcosm of the problem. Granted, many or most of the workers were undocumented, but did that warrant the treatment they received? These people are no danger, already contributing to this country, and many with children who are American citizens. That was evident. A day after the raid on the meatpacking plant, most Latinos of Postville's six hundred public school students were absent, probably because their parents were among those arrested or hoping not to be arrested. David Strudthoff, the school superintendent, compared the raids to a natural disaster. "People were in shock. Children were without parents."[5] He spent the day after the raid making sure that students were safe and cared for, in case their parents had been detained. He also recalled in interviews that the Iowa Division of Labor Services had subpoenaed school officials to provide information about students and employees a month before the raid.

Church leaders in Postville responded to what they considered a disaster. The Northeastern Iowa Synod of the Evangelical Lutheran Church in America, in fact, listed Postville on a main Web page about

---

5 Mary Ann Zehr, "Iowa School District Left Coping with Immigration Raid's Impact," *Education Week*, May 14, 2008, http://www.edweek.org/ew/articles/2008/05/21/38immig. h27.html?print=1.

their work in helping people affected by disasters, such as recent floods and tornadoes.

Bishop Steven Ullestad of the church focused on the trauma to children and families in Postville after the Immigration and Customs Enforcement raid. When I met with him, he told me that one of the most heart-wrenching parts of the story was the reaction of the non-Hispanic children in the community. They had been left behind, and had seen their little friends taken away. How could they distinguish between the niceties of the law and the political divisions that the government had so coldly enforced? They were frightened and wondering whether they would be next.

The church issued a statement saying that Postville had been a "model community," illustrating "the positive role that immigration can have in revitalizing a local economy and the capacity of very diverse groups to live together in community." The raid "exemplifies the humanitarian and economic cost of our broken immigration system."

Church members focused not only on the trauma to children and family members seized but also on the fear felt by everyone. "These children are having nightmares about their own parents being taken away and they are creating drawings of the intervention with the words 'Don't take my friends away.'

"Those who were arrested were active members of the community: shopping in Postville businesses, renting property or buying houses, attending the school functions for their children, and being good neighbors. People in Postville are asking if our government gave any consideration to the impact on this small town before they took this action. There simply must be a more humane way of addressing the concerns about undocumented workers."[6]

Indeed, there are more humane answers. What is the greater danger

---

6 Statement of Lutheran Immigration and Refugee Service and Bishop Steven Ullestad, Northeastern Iowa Synod of the Evangelical Lutheran Church in America Submitted to the House Education and Labor Subcommittee on Workforce Protection May 20, 2008 Hearing on 'ICE Workplace Raids: Their Impact on U.S. Children and Families," www. neiasynod.org/synod_news/pdf/LIRS.pdf.

to public safety here? What possible service can this be to a country that has no reasonable means of dealing with its immigration problems? It is much less than a thumb in the dam; it is a repressive show of force with no positive outcome.

But we can use this case as a rallying cry to take action and come to terms with the excesses and the criminalization of a class that is largely not criminal at all. Our treatment of the undocumented is shameful and a national disgrace. Such measures reached a peak of insensitivity in the latter years of the Bush administration, which was looking for an easy way to appease its political right flank. Doing so was playing to the basest instincts of our society. Once such measures are incorporated into the system, it takes concerted effort to wipe them out. But by the end of 2008, we had a long way to go.

A study by Syracuse University reported a seven hundred percent increase in immigration prosecutions during the Bush era from 2001 to 2007—11,454 prosecutions alone in September 2008.[7] In the fall election season of 2008, in California, in Texas, in Chicago, in Greenville, South Carolina, the raids continued unabated. The context was seen by many as a Republican play for votes among the most conservative, xenophobic elements of their party, who, as we have seen, wrongly label immigrants as somehow being to blame for our economic woes. Obviously, they might have looked elsewhere, starting with the deregulated financial system that led to the collapse of AIG, Lehman Brothers, unscrupulous mortgage brokers and major banks.

In a very early sign of a sea change in 2009, Janet Napolitano, the secretary of Homeland Security, initiated a review of the policy on immigration raids and enforcement. The measure gave a reprieve to immigrants who might have been caught up in planned immigration raids in the early part of the year; the hope is that the administration will not use undocumented immigrants as scapegoats. There is discussion about shifting the focus of enforcement, as we rightly should, to the actions of

---

7 Justin Akers Chacon, "Increase in Latino Federal Prison Population Reveals Flaws in Immigration Policy," *The Progressive*, February 25, 2009, http://www.progressive.org/mag/mpchacon022509.html.

employers and businesses that don't follow the law, while leaving workers in unconscionable situations such as those at Postville.

After examining the process of raids and the immediate impact on undocumented workers, we need to look at other travesties in the system. First of all, people are dying or suffering mistreatment in detention centers in this country as a result of inadequate medical care. Homeland Security statistics indicated that eighty-three people died in detention from 2003 to 2008, including fifteen people who committed suicide.[8] Many of them would be alive today if the system worked properly and had zero tolerance for inhumane, neglectful treatment.

Outrage upon outrage—I also want to describe a shocking side issue along with the raids: Some of the detainees are actually permanent residents and U.S. citizens, caught simply because of their appearance and because they're in the wrong place at the wrong time. In a climate of intolerance and misplaced fear, American citizens are being targeted for their appearance, detained, humiliated, deported, and injured.

FOR SOME TIME, I HAVE been following the treatment of people held at a detention center in my home state of New Jersey, just miles from where I grew up. But there are dozens of detention facilities around the country, mostly outsourced to private prison companies who only grudgingly and occasionally open their doors to oversight. As of 2008, these facilities were detaining thirty-three thousand people and a disproportionate number were Latino.

From the outside, the federal detention center in Elizabeth, New Jersey, is an unlikely place to be housing three hundred men and women, some of them for long periods of time. Not far from Newark airport, it is an old windowless warehouse that has been refurbished into what amounts to a prison. I visited in July 2008, accompanied by members of the clergy. The facility was established by U.S. Immigration and Customs Enforcement and is administrated by a private contractor, the Cor-

8 "System of Neglect" by Dana Priest and Amy Goldstein. *The Washington Post*. May 11, 2008. http://www.washingtonpost.com/wp-srv/nation/specials/immigration/cwc_d1p1.html

rections Corporation of America. It holds people who are waiting for determination of their immigration status, and they can anticipate a limited number of possible outcomes. One is that they will be held longer than they should be; two, that mistakes will be corrected and they will be released; three, that they will be confirmed as being in this country unlawfully, and they will be sent home. But there's another possibility: Some of them, whether or not they should have been held in the first place, might die of negligence.

As with the people rounded up in the ICE raids in Postville and elsewhere, these are not criminals, nor are they dangerous to our society. In fact, detention-center authorities screen and analyze the detainees to make sure they are peaceful and nonviolent. There are two classes: people seeking asylum for political reasons, and others who have entered the United States without documents or overstayed their visas. Some of them, as I have found, are held for long periods of time and eventually released for bureaucratic mistakes, or otherwise deported under court review. Could the greatest nation in the world find a more humane way to treat such people? There are obvious and easy fixes, of course, at a fraction of the cost. If you're dealing with nonviolent people with no criminal background, why not put them on administrative release with ankle bracelets or some other monitoring system to track their whereabouts?

The officials who greeted us during my July 2008 visit were courteous and willing to provide basic information. I spoke to dieticians, guards, and others, and it was evident that individuals employed there were trying to make the facility something other than the truly horrific setting it could have been. Nevertheless, there were shortcomings. Men and women were housed separately, but detainees were under constant watch and had a humiliating lack of privacy. Showers and toilet areas had low partitions, for example, making everyone visible to everyone else all the time. It is uncomfortable for anyone to be watched bathing and using the toilet, but people from some cultures are humiliated when forced to appear naked, or even partially clothed, before strangers. Remember, these are not people convicted of a crime.

*   *   *

THE DETAINEE POPULATION AT ANY given time is diverse. There are Africans, Eastern Europeans, Asians, and a large number of Latinos. In the course of my tour, I picked out the cases of three people that I had been told about, and they were not Latinos; this book is about Latinos, but these are issues in which humanity knows no borders.

One man, an African, said he had suffered for a long time before getting a doctor to examine an abscess in his mouth that was affecting his ability to eat and sleep. Finally he was taken to see an oral surgeon, who informed officials at the detention center that he needed a root canal. Detention-center officials did not authorize the treatment. The detainee said he was told that he would probably be leaving soon, and in any case, "We don't do dental work." Three months after the dental visit, the man was still there, the abscess was getting worse, and he was bleeding from his nose. If the infection entered his bloodstream and he died, what would officials at the detention center say?

The second person was also African. Despite assurances that detainees would be processed and have their cases adjudicated quickly, many, like this man, had been held for a year or more. He said he had been experiencing pain and muscle soreness for a long time, but that when he complained, guards told him he was only imagining he was sick. After he'd insisted for months, a doctor examined him at the clinic, which is run by the U.S. Public Health Service. The doctor said he was in fact ill and prescribed medication.

The third detainee I spoke with was a Tibetan monk who was caught in a sad cycle of misunderstanding and misery. Communication was extremely difficult; a translator interpreted his words via telephone and said he had difficulty understanding what the monk was saying. I imagined what it might have been like if the monk needed help after hours and had no way to communicate his needs with anyone. To the degree he was able to express himself, he said he had escaped a Chinese jail and paid someone to arrange his flight and passage to the United States. That person sounded like a "coyote," one of the human smugglers who charge migrants exorbitant amounts to sneak north across the Mexican border. Arriving in the United States, the monk presented a document that the smuggler said would allow him to enter the country. It was useless, and U.S. officials brought him to the detention center. He had been held for four months. Not only was he a danger to no one, but also the monk's case should have warranted his immediate consideration as a political refugee.

I'm shocked to say that there are those in the land, perhaps spurred on by hateful talk on the radio, who harshly criticize me for taking what I think is a most basic step in this democracy. And yet, after my July 2008 visit to the Elizabeth detention center, there were angry callers and messages posted online. These people seem not to care about the plight of the weakest, or to understand the democratic principles of our society. More than one critic complained that I was wasting my time in worrying about detained and illegal immigrants.

There are worse outcomes than those I encountered on this random visit. A man named Boubacar Bah, fifty-two, a Guinean tailor, for example, suffered a skull fracture at Elizabeth and was left in an isolation cell without treatment for thirteen hours. He died in May 2007, four months after emergency brain surgery.

There were other such cases, human beings who died and whose stories were buried in the statistics of detainee deaths around the country.

Hiu Lui Ng[9] was a Chinese-born computer engineer who had attended high school in Long Island City, and had lived in Queens, New York, since he arrived in the United States in 1992. He was detained in 2007 on immigration charges as he tried to get a green card. Ng, whose wife and children are American citizens, began complaining of severe back pain while in custody of Immigration and Customs Enforcement at a detention center in Rhode Island. His complaints went unheeded, cancer undetected, until five days before he died on August 6, 2008, at age thirty-four.

---

9 Nina Bernstein, "Ill and in Pain, Detainee Dies in U.S. Hands," *New York Times*, August 13, 2008.

The stories of Ng and others appeared in the *New York Times* and other newspapers. The *Times* documented cases such as the death of Francisco Castañeda, thirty-six, a Salvadoran whose cancer also went undiagnosed. The federal government admitted medical negligence in that case at a California detention center.[10] Castañeda discovered significant lesions on his reproductive organs. Officials denied Castañeda's request for help. After eleven months in custody, he finally obtained temporary release, paying for his own biopsy. Despite surgery and chemotherapy, Castañeda died of cancer in February 2008. U.S. district judge Dean Pregerson in Los Angeles said Castañeda's family had the right to seek damages, calling the case "one of the most, if not the most, egregious Eighth Amendment violations [involving cruel and unusual punishment] the Court has ever encountered."[11]

The United States of America essentially killed Francisco Castañeda by denying him the medical care he so desperately needed. Why? He had entered this country without the proper documentation at the age of ten. His mother brought him, fleeing civil war in El Salvador—a U.S.-funded war in the 1980s that brought thousands of refugees like him to our country. Whatever his offense was, in no way did it warrant his death. We cannot, in good conscience, allow these conditions to continue.

Washington Post reporters Dana Priest and Amy Goldstein[12] reported other stories about detainees in this country. One was Jose Lopez-Gregorio, thirty-two, who had a wife and five children in Guatemala. "Detained crossing the Mexican border and held in an Arizona immigration center, he felt guilty, he told guards, eating three meals a day. Lopez had been inside one month and eight days when he strangled himself with a bed sheet. Five days earlier, the staff had placed him on suicide watch, only to be overruled within hours by the center's psychologist."

10 "U.S. admits negligence in detainee's death," by Bob Egelko, *San Francisco Chronicle*, http://www.sfgate.com/cgi-bin/article.cgi?f=/c/a/2008/04/29/BANV10D87T.DTL
11 Emily Bazelon. "Prison Trauma: The epitome of cruel and unusual punishment," Slate, April 10, 2008. http://www.slate.com/id/2188745/
12 Dana Priest and Amy Goldstein, "Suicides Point to Gaps in Treatment," *Washington Post*, May 13, 2008.

The *Post* documented a shocking lack of medical care for detainees, and overwhelmed and undertrained staff, along with especially grim circumstances for people with mental illness. The *Post* revealed staggering deficiencies in our detention system that most of us couldn't dream up in our worst nightmares.

And the litany of wrongdoing goes on. Even when detainees are deported, the circumstances are beyond imagination. Employees of the government of the United States of America, the greatest democracy in the entire world, have been injecting people with heavy doses of drugs in order to deport them or just to move them around the system with more ease. Immigration officials drug some people so heavily that they have sometimes been observed collapsing on the tarmac after they disembark from airplanes.

PERHAPS YOU WILL SAY THAT such things happened in overcrowded facilities. Problems will exist. And certainly, you will add, the administrators and wardens of detention centers are God-fearing family men and women. Let us not malign their good intentions. But, unfortunately, good intentions are not enough. And you might think—though not be willing to say out loud—that illegal immigrants deserve to suffer the consequences. Or you may think that harsh treatment under custody will be a deterrent to others and even convince some immigrants to go back where they belong. We've been hearing these stories for too long. The excuses for institutionalized violence must be rejected and the abuses must stop. Our system fails when any portion of it allows atrocities to persist.

In 2008, I spoke about these atrocities on the floor of the Senate, and with my colleagues Senators Kennedy, Durbin, Akaka, and Lieberman introduced the Detainee Basic Medical Care Act. The bill would require the Department of Homeland Security to establish procedures for delivering basic health care to all immigration detainees in custody. It requires DHS to give people in custody access to any medications they urgently need, both during detention and during any transfers.

Currently, a bureaucrat can overrule a medical professional who is actually on-site and seeing a detainee. This bill ensures that the professionals who actually see the patients make the treatment decisions and requires that DHS report all detainee deaths to the Office of Inspector General and Congress.

As PART OF THE REMEDY to all these abuses, we also must face a blunt reality: Our legitimate desire to establish control over our borders has turned into a witch hunt against Hispanic-Americans and other people of color. Common sense repeatedly loses out to hysteria, and agents of intolerance frequently bypass and tarnish the legal protections to which every single American—and anyone in U.S. custody—is entitled. There is infuriating evidence to prove this is so—U.S. immigration raids are targeting people because of the way they look, the way they talk, and the spelling of their names.

In my speech about detention and immigration on the floor of the Senate in June 2008, I decided to focus on this particular violation—above and beyond complaints about undocumented immigrants, I was describing the treatment of citizens and legal permanent residents of the greatest country in the world. A shocking series of reports about federal enforcement efforts was boiling over. I said that if you were a Latino or another minority in this country in 2008, you might feel that you were liable for prosecution at any moment; you might very well feel that you were a second-class citizen. And that was my repeated, clear message. I was not there to talk about undocumented workers; I was pointing to the threat to our democracy when U.S. citizens and permanent residents are robbed of their basic constitutional rights. In a climate of intolerance and misplaced fear, legal residents and American citizens were being targeted for their appearance, detained, humiliated, deported and injured. I repeated it as many times as I could, hoping to broadcast a wake-up call— WE ARE TALKING ABOUT INHUMANE TREATMENT OF AMERICAN CITIZENS. Is anybody listening?

Untold numbers of American citizens are wrongly detained, sometimes even deported, because they appear to be foreigners in the eyes of those seizing them. Thousands of mothers and fathers have been separated from their children in the process, in overly harsh enforcement efforts.

On February 7, 2008, for example, more than one hundred American citizens were detained by ICE agents looking for suspected illegal workers at a computer company in Van Nuys, California. Those who looked like they were Hispanic, even the chief financial officer of the company—a U.S. citizen—were arrested, without explanation from agents.

An Urban Institute report in 2007 showed that five million children in the United States have at least one parent who is in the country illegally. Most of those children are U.S. citizens less than ten years old. And the report said that in the process of actual raids, parents in some cases have been institutionalized without even being able to contact or make provisions for their children.

The institute cited an ICE raid in 2006 in which an eight-month-old infant was taken to an emergency room in New Bedford, Massachusetts, for treatment after the child's mother was detained.

"The infant's pediatrician appealed to ICE officials to release the child's mother, citing medical reasons for which the child needed to continue breastfeeding. NCLR and our sister organizations in the Latino community wrote to the Department of Homeland Security after this incident to raise concerns; we received a response stating that the incident never occurred, despite extensive evidence, including video footage of the child and interviews with the emergency room physician who treated her."[13]

Some officials have claimed that these incidents are rare and that it is a reasonable price to pay in pursuit of undocumented aliens. I disagree; no matter how widespread this pattern of abuse turns out to be, it should never happen. Before we accuse someone of being undocumented, there's one other document we should inspect first: It's called the Constitution of the United States. It's time for Immigration and law enforcement on all levels to rededicate themselves to respecting the rights the Constitution guarantees.

That means respecting the need for probable cause and the right to be free from unreasonable search and seizure guaranteed by the Fourth

---

13 National Council of La Raza, "The Implications of Immigration Enforcement on America's Children," May 20, 2008, http://www.nclr.org/content/publications/detail/52035/.

Amendment, the right to due process guaranteed by the Fifth Amendment, the full benefits of citizenship and equal protection for anyone born or naturalized in this country guaranteed by the Fourteenth Amendment—and the entire range of rights and protections our Constitution grants. That's the only way that those who by birth or naturalization—Latinos or Africans, or Europeans or Indians—have a legitimate right to pursue the American dream.

How can we expect that Latinos and other people of color in this country will be comfortable and confident enough to go about the business of making ends meet, or improving their lives? Today, as a Latino, a person of color, or someone who speaks English with an accent, you might very well feel that your basic rights are worth nothing, subject to summary judgment by agents of the law. "Not me," you might say? "I am a citizen of this country." Well, prove it.

Let's suppose that at this very moment you are not home and have no access to your important legal documents. Can you prove this very moment that you are an American citizen? How do I know that you haven't sneaked into this country? Do you look like an American? What does an American look like? If you're Caucasian with a nonsuspicious name, you're probably okay. My name is Menendez and I carry a driver's license. I don't have a birth certificate or a passport in my pocket at the moment. Do you?

How would you feel if you were minding your own business one moment and, despite protestations, found yourself in a demeaning detention center the next, with no access to due process? It has happened in hundreds of cases we know of across this country. Such actions are simply un-American and violate the Constitution. All of us should be angry and concerned. The American people should stand collectively and say, "No more, we will not accept these affronts to our principles as a nation."

Could this be happening in America? Those loud knocks in the dead of the night hammered away their American dreams. Some might say once more, "This is what happens when people enter this country without going through the proper channels." I hear it all the time, because it is the mantra of people who defend these tactics.

Even worse, Latinos and people of color may not be surprised. Friends and relatives may have passed along the news. They may have heard stories about U.S. citizens or legal permanent residents who were seized in immigration raids, detained, and in some cases deported. They may have known that their accent, their names, the color of their skin, the place where they lived, would have put them at risk. They may have known that—regardless of what our politicians and historians say—fundamental constitutional rights still might not apply to them, in today's America.

I've focused in this discussion of inhumane treatment on the outright atrocities that are so shocking and strikingly wrong. But our broken immigration system creates other situations that may not be overtly violent but are still inhumane at the core. Four million people live outside this country in bureaucratic limbo, hoping to be reunited with family members already in the United States. They await entry visas and many of them are relatives of legal permanent residents or U.S. citizens. Close family members—parents, children, husbands and wives, and others—have the right under law to join their kin and participate in American society. Family life is central to our society, and Latino families thrive traditionally with such ties. They obey the law, follow the rules, but wait and wait and wait—sometimes for a decade or more for their family reunification.

I support laws that would guarantee that close relatives are quickly able to live together once more. There is a way of doing this without increasing the total of legal immigrants allowed to enter the country. It could be done by making use of thousands of slots for visas every year that have not been used. Such action would remedy the backlog of legal entry and would also resolve the emotional cost to American citizens and their family members. It would also discourage people in distress from crossing the line by overstaying a tourist visa or sneaking into the country.

Imagine the case of a woman who is waiting for the arrival of her mother and father. Perhaps there are enough resources to travel to visit with them from time to time; perhaps work schedules prevent it, or perhaps there isn't money to go back and forth. Imagine the practical cost—

such a situation also impacts productivity and the livelihood of people caught in such delays. Practically speaking, a breakdown of family structure often leads to a breakdown of social stability. It seems to me the essence of family should be given much more weight and points within the context of a whole new process of how we are going to move our immigration system forward.

IN SUMMARY, OUR LAWS ON immigration are counterproductive in every sense, morally, legally, and practically. I am passionate in my commitment to resolve the plight of detainees as a matter of basic human justice; I take this position on principle based on my love for this country. And as I said repeatedly on the floor of the Senate, many times those detained in raids and sweeps are actually legal residents and citizens of this country. But everyone who immigrates to this country, documented or not, deserves humane treatment. A detention should never amount to a death sentence. Action to prevent unnecessary deaths at detention facilities is long overdue.

Our job is to do all we can to secure our country while protecting the dignity of all human beings. If we fail to do so, we lose the moral high ground, the concept that our country must be a beacon of democracy and a leader in human rights around the world. It is astounding that human beings could be treated as badly as some are being treated on our soil. Critics should ask some simple questions: What if the detainee was a member of my family, arrested by mistake? What if that happened to us? Doesn't my U.S. citizenship, whether by birth or naturalization, protect me from this kind of abuse?

What methods could we employ in this century for dealing humanely with undocumented immigrants? Will we follow the prescriptions of the past, in which federal authorities—responding to fearmongering and base politics and bad leadership from the executive branch—rounded up human beings, imprisoned them, and gave them no chance to prove themselves innocent?

Or will we follow the law and follow the demands of humanity? That is what we must do and we can. Consider the billions of dollars wasted in the process of equating undocumented immigrants with hardened criminals. Beyond the inhumanity of their treatment, the process is economic and bureaucratic folly.

The Obama administration clearly understands the issue, and I've spoken to the president about the broader question of immigration reform. He understands that the system is dysfunctional and must be repaired. We agree that we must have both strong border controls and an immigration system that faces our economic realities. He also recognizes that part of the problem is working with Mexico and other Latin American countries to lessen the economic desperation that forces people to seek better circumstances on this side of the border.

He's also heard the calls from the rest of the Hispanic Caucus in Congress, and from our community, that there must be changes. He understands the political realties and emotions surrounding the issue. We now have a new chance, but will President Obama—assailed and deeply involved with the financial crisis he inherited—be able to address the problem and apply the necessary political capital? In the short term, the Latino community expects a resolution from Washington. The political reality is that a vote on such a contentious issue has to take place a distance away from Election Day.

President Obama knows that we need to act now, and there are many hopeful signs. We expect to be participating in a series of bipartisan working groups that would lead to new legislation in short order.

In the spring of 2009, two major labor organizations, the AFL-CIO and the Change to Win Federation, announced that they were willing to work on changing our immigration laws. There are competing proposals and questions, but those umbrella organizations acknowledged that a path toward legalization of undocumented workers makes sense.

Nevertheless, anti-immigration voices will still attempt to drown out good sense.

I sometimes worry that the purveyors of fear are having their successes. From many parts of the country people have answered my passionate call for humanity, callously saying in one way or another, "They

got what they deserved." Many people didn't even hear my constant re-
joinder: I am talking about U.S. citizens and permanent residents. Some
people cannot see beyond their hate, their irrational fear, of people who
don't speak their language or don't look like them. And yet if common
people could understand—erosion of due process in this country will affect everyone, families, mothers, fathers, and children. Where is the
outrage?

It is our moral business to defend the most fundamental principle on
which our nation was founded: that all of us are created equal. Stopping
illegal detentions of Americans based on their race is about more than
properly enforcing the law. Above all, it's about respecting people who
may be different from us, but who share the same birthright. As Martin
Luther King said, "We may have come on different ships, but we're all in
the same boat now." If we're worried about what to throw off the boat, it
should be our oldest enemy: fear. Once that's gone, we can resume our
course on the currents of freedom, and let our sails be filled with liberty
and justice for all.

CHAPTER 10

EDUCATION AT THE CORE— NURTURING THE YOUNGER GENERATION

A journey of a thousand miles must begin with a single step.

LAO-TZU

Everything in my experience brings me to one essential, overriding point: Education is the key that unlocks social and economic opportunity and upward mobility for all. How else could a child of immigrants, a young man locked in a small tenement apartment in Union City, New Jersey, ever have been able to make his way to the halls of the United States Senate?

It requires not only the unflagging support and prodding of teachers and parents but also the commitment of a society and a government to adequately support public education. Human beings have the right to recognize their full potential. Part of fixing and building our economy means investing in our youth, and at a moment of economic crisis, the role of education is more crucial than it has ever been.

I'm happy to say that President Obama recognizes the depths of the crisis in education, and plans urgent action. He made that clear in 2008 throughout the presidential campaign.

"This probably has more to do with our economic future than anything and that means it also has a national security implication, because there's never been a nation on earth that saw its economy decline and continued to maintain its primacy as a military power. So we've got to get our education system right. Now, typically, what's happened is that there's been a debate between more money or reform, and I think we need both.[1]

---

1 Barack Obama, third presidential debate, Oct. 15, 2008. http://www.debates.org/pages/trans2008d.html

"In some cases," the future president said, "we are going to have to invest. Early childhood education, which closes the achievement gap, so that every child is prepared for school, every dollar we invest in that, we end up getting huge benefits with improved reading scores, reduced dropout rates, reduced delinquency rates."

Swiftly on taking office, President Obama focused on education as a key portion of The American Recovery and Reinvestment Act. The president said this: "In a global economy where the most valuable skill you can sell is your knowledge, a good education is no longer just a pathway to opportunity—it is a prerequisite. The countries that out-teach us today will out-compete us tomorrow."[2]

Among other things, the Obama administration's $100 billion investment in education calls for new teachers with a focus on the sciences. He's spoken about the long-term goal of higher pay for our teachers, more training, and measures that will lead to standards that have fallen off in this country. He has also discussed yearly tuition credits for college students in an effort to decrease the indebtedness resulting from a four-year college career. One formula would include swapping such credits for participating in national service, including the military, but also programs like the Peace Corps and other such community activities.

It seems so self-evident, but to fully portray the Latino community, I'll state it clearly: All parents in this country would give everything for their children to be able to live happy, successful lives, to have a fair shake, regardless of their skin color or last name or the neighborhood they grew up in. Hispanic-American fathers and mothers have as much reason as anyone else in this country to believe that anything is possible for their children.

It should be no surprise, then, that a recent nationwide poll of Latinos by the Pew Hispanic Center showed that, after the economy, education ranks number two among vital concerns.[3] A publicly funded education

---

2 Barack Obama, Feb, 24, 2009. http://www.ed.gov/policy/gen/leg/recovery/presentation/arra.pdf

3 *The Latin Americanist*, "Poll: Economy Top Latino Concern," January 16, 2009, http://ourlatinamerica.blogspot.com/2009/01/poll-economy-top-latino-concern.html.

system shouldn't be in the business of choosing between the "haves" and the "have-nots"; learning should enhance individual drive and ability to succeed—that, after all, is the American dream.

I envision a future in which our country is flourishing as never before, because of the decisions we took now. Our goal is to provide all our children—every child of every creed—with a safe, nurturing environment, and the opportunity to have a quality education. If we are to make that happen, we must act now to provide the building blocks of a successful educational system. We need modern buildings, secure schoolyards, innovative programs, and well-paid, qualified, competent teachers to get the job done. We need that opportunity for all children regardless of the happenstance of who they are or what station in life they were born into. No other formula will assure us that the United States stands foremost as a nation of innovation and promise. A modern and effective education system will allow this country to maintain its leading role in the world economy and as a model of democracy.

There is some good news about progress among Hispanic children. When our children move into better schools and their parents advance toward the middle class, their educational opportunities expand. A recent report showed that Latino high school graduates who took the ACT college-admissions test in 2006 had higher average combined scores than Latino students who took it in 2002, and they also scored higher, on average, in each of the test's subject areas—mathematics, reading, science, and English.

But at the same time, far too many Latinos drop out of high school. According to the Pew Hispanic Center, forty-two percent of Latinos in this country do not graduate and almost a quarter drop out before they reach high school.[4]

In addition, consider the data on school testing in New Jersey, my home state. I'm sad to say this is no anomaly among major cities around the United States. These are the 2006 results of the High School Profi-

---

4 Pew Hispanic Center, "Statistical Portrait of Hispanics in the United States, 2007," March 5, 2009, http://pewhispanic.org/factsheets/factsheet.php?FactsheetID=46.

ciency Exam in Newark, our largest city, according to the New Jersey Department of Education: forty-two percent of Latino students failed the language arts portion, fifty-two percent of Latinos failed the math portion, and seventy percent of Latinos failed the science portion.

Too many Latino parents find it hard to be optimistic when only half of their children graduate high school, or barely pass, and most of those who make it to college don't finish. Latinos face a dire situation unless something radical is done. In a real sense, we are dealing with the competitive future of America. To change the trend line, we will be fighting to improve myriad factors—societal, economic, the happenstance of where one is born or lives. The outcome goes far beyond reducing a statistic, or instilling pride in the Latino community. It is a more general question. Are we going to have more scientists and engineers in the United States? Are we going to have individuals who are prepared to meet the challenges of America moving forward?

But the problem and the pressure to improve are even greater than the statistics measuring the present indicate. All estimates show that as our overall U.S. population grows in the twenty-first century, the percentage of young people will increase, and the component of young Hispanics will also increase. Statistics indicate that in about forty years, when the population of Latinos in this country grows from 45 million to 132 million, the median age of Latinos will be more than ten years younger than the overall population. Simply put, as the nation grays, the quality of life for all Americans will increasingly depend on this younger Latino population.

Studies around the United States show that dropping out of high school is more than just a lost opportunity for individuals who have not been reached by society. Social scientists say that such lowered horizons for a whole class of people create a drain on society—productivity is lost, there is a greater possibility that undereducated citizens will require public assistance, and they are statistically more likely to be institutionalized at public expense, including through the revolving door of the criminal-justice system.

One research organization, the Friedman Foundation for Educational Choice, dedicated to the ideas of the late free market economist Milton Friedman, described the cost to our society of not providing incentives for young people to stay in school.[5] For New Jersey alone, the organization extrapolates the cost of high school dropouts into the billions over a lifetime. More than 19,000 students drop out of school in New Jersey every year, a loss of $3,645 per dropout every year, based on lost tax revenue, Medicaid costs and the possibility of some of them entering the prison system, among other public costs. "Each year's class of new dropouts will cost New Jersey $69.5 million per year throughout their remaining lifetimes, or a total of $3.5 billion over fifty years."

Some groups in New Jersey and other cities have adopted the view that the high school dropout rate can be reduced with public school-choice options. This appears to be a viable concept—such choices develop competition among schools to survive by attracting the interest of both students and parents. Meanwhile, a lawsuit is pending in the state, seeking an end to assigning students to schools based on the districts in which they live. It would be a revolutionary concept, and would tacitly recognize a reality of American life. Local real estate taxes finance schools in our country—wealthy districts are likely to have larger budgets and better schools, and attract teachers with higher salaries and better work conditions. Impoverished neighborhoods have funding problems, their students are disadvantaged and undermotivated, and it is hard to attract and keep teachers in such districts.

The Hispanic Council for Reform and Educational Options, among other Latino organizations, supports the concept of school choice for failing school districts in this country. Rebeca Nieves Huffman, the former president of the organization, said, "School choice is the highest form of accountability that will offer low-income Latino parents the power to se-

5 Brian J. Gottlob, "The High Cost of High School Failure in New Jersey," Friedman Foundation for Educational Choice, February 1, 2008, http://www.friedmanfoundation. org/friedman/research/ShowResearchItem.do?id=10094.

lect a well-performing school that will help to stop harboring bad teach-ers and administrators."[6]

I UNDERSTAND THE PERSPECTIVES OF these organizations. However, I don't think that school vouchers are the right way to go. I am certainly focused on improving all schools in this country: raising teacher salaries, improving the quality of teacher training, seeking qualified, competent teachers in the subject matters they are teaching, and providing every possible resource toward establishing innovative, successful schools. Our goal of course is to promote all reasonable means to reduce the likelihood that students will drop out. One thing is clear: We have to deal with the issue of those children who are not being prepared for the future. About fifty thousand Latinos in the U.S. are turning eighteen every month, and less than one-third enter college. Any way you slice it, the economic and social health of this country depends on the viability of this ethnic group.

I used to cite statistics that by 2025, twenty-five percent of all the na-tion's schoolchildren would be Latino. Revised analysis shows that bench-mark will now be reached in 2017 and the number could change once more after the 2010 census. Project beyond 2017 toward the year 2050, and the percentage is certain to increase exponentially. The conclusion is obvious: The nation's competitive future and the quality of life for more and more Americans are going to depend on the quality of the education these children receive.

Lest we think that this population growth is a result of unbridled im-migration, statistics tell a different story. The changing of the American landscape with the growth of the Latino population in this country has a lot to do with Latino children born in this country. Most of the increase in the Latino population to forty-five million nationwide can be attrib-uted to Latinos born in the United States—U.S. citizens. Kenneth John-son of the University of New Hampshire commented on the growth of

---

6 "School Choice Lawsuit in New Jersey Raises Much Needed Public Awareness about the Crisis in Education," Hispanic PR Wire, Aug. 1, 2006. http://hispanicprwire.com/news.php?l=in&cha=15&id=6720

the Latino population in a 2008 interview with *USA Today*.[7] "In all of the uproar over immigration, this is getting missed," Johnson said. "All the focus is on immigration, immigration. At some point, it's not. It's natural increase."

We need to make decisions now based on the evidence that coming generations will be ever more integrated. When we look at the future, as we've said, U.S. productivity will increasingly depend on the Latino community. If you agree with me that education is the great equalizer in our society, then we must improve our results and enhance our commitment to our children. The pressures will only get more acute on our public schools and universities. We must be proactive.

Our dilemma is this: Too many schools in inner-city neighborhoods are overcrowded, deteriorating, and dangerous. We can't even begin to address the needs of students when the conditions for providing a quality education are not there. We need safe schools, reasonably sized classrooms, and federal funding to make sure we get qualified, certified in subject matter teachers.

It is imperative that we advocate policies that will create more and more opportunities for our community to create a new generation of Latino leaders—who aren't left behind by ill-advised policies or shortsighted initiatives.

The basic declaration of the Latino Leadership Alliance of New Jersey and its president, Martín Pérez, is that "an education is the most powerful antidote to inequality, poverty, discrimination, lack of health care, poor housing and most other ills of society; simply put, education is the great equalizer."[8]

That organization supports the concept of scholarships for students in need. I have advocated an expansion of education benefits, in line with President Obama's insistence that education cannot be sidetracked, even with all our economic burdens.

---

7 Haya El Nasser, "Births Fueling Hispanic Growth," *USA Today*, June 30, 2008.
8 Testimony of Martín Pérez, The New Jersey Senate Budget and Appropriations Committee, June 16, 2008, http://www.llanj.org/documents/testimonials/6-18-08_LLANJ_TESTIMONY_ON_URBAN_ZONE_SCHOLARSHIP_ACT.pdf

Many students are locked in a closed circuit, forced to attend under-performing schools, where otherwise gifted students are either not identified or not allowed to excel. There are problems even when these students are identified or with their own initiative attempt to surpass the expectations and limitations of the system.

My friend Cid Wilson, a member of the Dominican community in New Jersey, who would describe himself as an Afro-Latino leader focusing on philanthropy, points out the Catch-22 situation in which we find ourselves. Astutely, he notes that helping Latino youth is not simply a question of government aid to repair and renovate schools, or to provide more, better-trained, higher-paid teachers. "Let's say you live in an inner-city neighborhood with high crime," Cid relates. "In a high-crime environment, you could throw money into that school, but if the student leaves the gates of that school and has to worry about being a victim of crime, that is a deterrent to excellence. His or her environment is not conducive to getting an education."

He identifies the conundrum: We need to work at the problem from all directions—invest in safer neighborhoods, economic opportunity, and housing to support families. "You can throw millions and billions of dollars into schools, but it won't address the issue if there are a lot of other factors in the decision-making process for a student who otherwise could be a shining example."

What is the mechanism we need to raise up the students who haven't been making it? A program for action must become more than a speech or set of speeches. In terms of policy and in terms of sensitizing Latinos and the broader society, it is frustrating that so many people and excellent organizations have been unable to come up with a formula to tackle and resolve our crisis in education. I'm increasingly certain that there isn't a single silver bullet that is going to meet this challenge. We have been advocates for divergent parts of the issue, often successfully. I think we already have the elements of what the formula should be, but so far haven't been able to blend the ingredients. I'm talking about a comprehensive approach to solving our problems.

One of our challenges is consciousness-raising in the community. My friend David Lizárraga at TELACU in Los Angeles says it well. He reminds us that members of the community have a responsibility to help others who have not succeeded yet. "You get a hand and you've got to give a hand. If we help you take that elevator to the top, don't forget to send it back down so someone else can come back up with you." This is not a question of contributing money or words of support—I think we need to spend the time to promote change actively. This involves understanding and commitment. It is evident that we sometimes focus on the failings and challenges of our work so far, rather than focusing on the successes. We're fixated on the challenges because we're looking for progress, but in the midst of doing that, we don't look at the human resources we have. We must call upon people and institutions to be part of the solution.

I therefore advocate holistic tactics, finding multiple ways of dealing with the myriad issues affecting those children who live in environments that are so disadvantaged that they are already falling behind in early childhood. In other words, education does not exist in a vacuum—economic opportunity, jobs, health security, safety, and security all must be attacked at the same time and in a coordinated way.

The answer in part is organization—we need to put together disparate parts of programs that already exist. The studies and analyses exist: government agencies and advocacy groups have studied the data that tell us why Latino children are failing. We recognize that early childhood is important, and we understand that the disparity of wealth is an issue, particularly as it relates to underperforming school districts. Majority-Latino communities often don't have the budgets to promote excellence.

Many other factors are involved. The decision of whether to stay in school is often a matter of economics—do the students' families need them to go to work? Some face learning disabilities, others have problems with learning English. Some live in urban or very rural areas that are economically disadvantaged compared with other school districts where wealthier children are attending classes. In some cases, we need teachers and role models to provide guidance—giving students the sense of the possible. We need to jump-start programs that have fallen off with disinterest at times during the Bush years. In the 1990s, the U.S. Department of Education developed the Hispanic Dropout Project. The project sought to focus on the problem from all directions—schools, parents and families, and students themselves. We must revisit the project and see what we have learned. And as the project said, we must eliminate the excuses used to allow the problem to fester.

Among other things, we need to find ways to expand parental involvement in our schools. I recently met with a group of educators and parents, including one teacher who discussed encouraging parents to study English with their children. "If you're teaching English to my child, why don't we learn English together?" It's an attractive concept, and there are other ideas. Some schools are broadening the traditional concept by setting up computer labs after hours for members of the community, along with adult education programs. If we start to view schools as community centers, parents will be drawn naturally toward engagement with the process of educating their children.

Consider the relationship between education, poverty, and joblessness.

Despite evidence that Latinos are making strides in building new businesses, and reaching the middle class and beyond, we have a disproportionate number struggling to make ends meet. The statistics have particularly shown a decline during the Bush administration in earlier economic successes for Latinos and other minorities. The Census Bureau reported that the median income declined for all Americans between 2000 and 2006, but the impact was less for Americans classified as white. It reported the median income of Anglo households in 2006 was $50,673, a decrease of $745 from the year 2000. African-American and Hispanic incomes decreased more than that. The median for Latinos in 2006 was $37,781, down $1,043, while the median for African-Americans was $31,969, a $2,766 decrease.

Not surprisingly, the Census Bureau said that one in five Latinos is living in poverty, slightly more than the number of African-Americans in that category.[9] It is clear that the poor in this country have suffered se-

---

9 "State of the Union 2008: By the Numbers," PRNewswire.com, January 28, 2008, http://www.prnewswire.com/cgi-bin/stories.pl?ACCT=104&STORY=/www/story/01-28-2008/0004744513&EDATE.

vere reversals in this century, and by all measures the problems facing Latinos face all Americans, but every problem in our community is disproportionate. About eleven percent of white Americans do not have health insurance. But the number for Latinos is more than thirty-four percent.[10] Joblessness statistics also show the deep problem. In April 2009, the unemployment rate for all adults was about 8.5 percent, but the rate for Latinos was 11.4 percent.[11] The rate trended upward in the continuing recession, with no indication of immediate relief.

ALL OF THESE ISSUES ARE interrelated. There is a correlation in comparing access to health care and the probability of offering a decent home environment in which children can thrive and go to school. Latinos, meanwhile, are far less likely to have health insurance than any other group. It is also apparent that we need universal health care in this country. We need to line up with the other industrialized countries of the world and recognize that health care is a right in this country. More and more Americans are recognizing the problem and most of us are feeling the consequences; the United States spends more per capita on medical care than any other industrialized nation, but the health-care crisis is evident. The cries for change are justified, and even more so in the Hispanic community. It is unacceptable that more than forty-six million Americans do not have reliable health-insurance coverage. And the insurance they do have has been skyrocketing in cost. According to statistics from the Kaiser Family Foundation, the annual premium for family health insurance grew by sixty percent from 2000 to 2006 to $11,480.[12] The costs continue to pile up; health-care professionals themselves drop out of primary care because of soaring insurance premiums and Byzantine paperwork demands. At a time when the need is greatest, the disparities in health-care coverage are growing. The only answer is affordable, quality comprehensive health care for all Americans.

---

10 Ibid.
11 http://www.bls.gov/news.release/empsit.nr0.htm
12 "State of the Union 2008," PRNewswire.com.

*　　*　　*

I OFTEN THINK ABOUT AND describe the limits of government action, that mentoring and progress toward the future must be a cooperative affair that involves legislation, corporate and civic involvement, and innovation. There are many projects that can be tested, and some work better than others.

Part of doing the work of building roots involves building powerful organizations that represent the interests of the community. One of the oldest and most influential of such groups is the National Council of La Raza, which was founded in 1968. La Raza rallies smaller groups across the country under a Latino agenda that includes fighting anti-immigrant prejudice and hate crimes against Latinos, establishing health centers, job training, and promoting English courses.

Janet Murguía, the president of La Raza, knows well that while Hispanics are not a monolithic group, there are ties that bind, "a sense of culture and values that do bind many in the Hispanic community. You see that a sense of faith and family comes through. With our values and our traditions, we are very much American."

While Janet is of Mexican ancestry and my family is Cuban, she and I share an understanding of the value of education—based on the struggles and challenges in our family histories.

Janet has been president of La Raza since 2004, and her unique, impressive story fits well in the tapestry of America. Like so many other second-generation Hispanics, she is the child of poor Mexican immigrants. "My dad came to this country with a sixth-grade education and worked in a steel plant. Many other Mexicans in Kansas City, where I grew up, worked on the railroads, and when they laid the tracks down, steel plants followed. Hispanics served an important role in helping build the industries that powered this country."

Two of Janet's six siblings are federal court judges; her brother Carlos is the first Hispanic federal district court judge for the District of Kansas, and her sister Mary Helen serves in the U.S. District Court, District of Arizona.

"We didn't know when we were growing up that we didn't have money." Murguía is certain that her parents' lack of education precisely brought them a clear focus on obtaining for their children everything they never had. After law school, this child of immigrants was working in the Clinton administration as an assistant on legislative matters, and acting as senior White House liaison to Congress. "We know the American dream and we are committed to making the American dream a reality for others," she says.

National Council of La Raza is as close as it comes to the prototypical national organization for Latinos, rallying community groups around the country toward a new paradigm in representing and fighting for a Latino agenda. La Raza's programs focus on the full spectrum of educational opportunities, from early-childhood education to access to universities. They also work on keeping children in school until they obtain their high school diplomas.

It is clear that there have been improvements in educational opportunities for Latinos, but much more needs to be done. Janet acknowledges that it isn't easy work. "Where the kids are beating the odds and making it, you still have the statistic that seems hard to shake: the dropout rate among Latinos is still near fifty percent. There are a lot of difficulties, but we're committed to changing it."

A PARTICULARLY REMARKABLE BLEND OF innovative corporate and government action can be found in an inner-city neighborhood of San Diego, where Sol Price, a local businessman, brought his philanthropic vision of the future to the city government and created a pilot project that changed a neighborhood. Price, by the way, is the founder of FedMart and Price Club, the warehouse stores that were the prototype for Wal-Mart and Costco. His idea was that people had to be invested in their own neighborhoods. City Heights,[13] a neighborhood in the eastern section of San Diego, was for years the kind of low-income, high-crime neighborhood

---

13 Price Charities, "City Heights Initiative," www.pricecharities.com/City-Heights-Initiative/.

we find too often nestled within America's cities. Its population was around sixty thousand, and almost half the residents were Hispanic, about a third African-American, with an increasing number of immigrants from Mexico and other parts of Latin America, as well as an increasing number of non-Latino immigrants.

What happens when a bottom-line businessman decides to find a solution in such a neighborhood? In the 1990s, Price and his philanthropic arm, Price Charities, negotiated with the city of San Diego to create a model community that would change the complexion of the area. Slowly, the area was converted into something that would have been hard to imagine. Price and his team chose the kind of holistic approach I have advocated. He knew that it was necessary to establish a safe environment for residents. He worked with the city to build a new central police station in the neighborhood, asking that the structure have large glass windows—symbolizing transparency and changing the attitude between police and residents. He tackled the low median income of about twenty-five thousand dollars a year, by which more than a third of residents were classified at the poverty level. He financed low-cost housing, but was determined to make new dwellings more than a handout. He created a lease-to-own system in which the residents of new, low-cost, low-interest multiuse housing would have a special relationship with the place they lived. He instilled a sense of belonging in the neighborhood, and also set out to deal with other chronic problems, not only the basic issues of education and health care, but also the right of people to have cultural and recreational outlets.

City Heights today has a central state-of-the-art library, where residents can meet, read, and access the Internet. Adjacent is a cultural center, swimming pool, and sports facilities. Also included are a Head Start office and a continuing-education center for adults.

City Heights schools also applied the concept of local participation. Working with educators and parents, the Price initiative created an "Educational Collaborative," building local schools.[14] Working with San

---

14 http://www.pricecharities.com/City-Heights-Initiative/Education/

Diego State University, the city school district, and the teachers' union, the project applied theories on improving conditions through stimulating excellence with a rounded program at three inner-city schools. The schools function as community centers and have become comprehensive centers for health and social services for students and families. Results showed academic improvement at the three test schools by as much as fifty percent, based on standardized testing under California's Academic Performance Index.

On a given day, one could stroll by the modern, friendly-looking police station, see children of many ethnic backgrounds playing in the park, observe African and Latino immigrants using library facilities, all in a neighborhood where indexes of crime had dropped, and where an atmosphere of inner-city blight was slowly transformed.

No plan is perfect, and the City Heights initiative faced many issues, one of which was being a victim of its own success—the improved quality of life threatened to push gentrification of the neighborhood, and there is a real challenge that low-income residents, the original intended recipients, might be forced out by high prices. Yet the initiative seems to me to be worthy of study and replication nationwide. Again, government cannot legislate and change society from on high. Our future successes depend on common sense and partnership; the overall Hispanic community should join with corporations and philanthropists like David Lizárraga and TELACU, Sol Price and his family to pitch in with such innovation.

What would happen if partnerships were established on a pilot basis in the two hundred largest urban areas of the United States? Goodwill, sound analysis, and pragmatic decision making could transform our cities, and would serve as seedbeds for further innovative solutions. Let's get started.

There are other business initiatives that may not have the same focus but add important pieces to the question of how to connect with and inspire young Latinos, as a critical part of America's competitive future.

I was encouraged to participate at a meeting in 2008 that was just such an effort to draw together business, government, and leaders in education and community groups. Sponsored by IBM, Exxon Mobil, Lockheed Martin, and Univision, it sought to tackle ways to expand Latino participation in high-tech careers. Inevitably, the matter returns to basics, and is part of a larger problem affecting American education in general—the Latino component is just more pronounced, and more in need of remedy. First of all, education at all levels must strive to regain the American edge in science and mathematics. We have fallen woefully behind. By one measure, teenagers in the United States ranked in the bottom third in proficiency in math and science among students in thirty industrialized countries.[15] Latino children, as all others, must have access. We must have the option to pursue technical careers, heavy in science and mathematics—and interest in science and math has to be cultivated early and pursued throughout public school.

IBM, for example, committed to promoting studies in computer science and high technology, set up programs for Hispanic students in schools and universities that include access to computers and mentoring via the Internet. I like the multilevel approach of this initiative. IBM recognized that parents as well as students need training in order to share the task of educating children. For instance, the company provides an interesting two-way English-Spanish translation system to schools, called *¡Tradúcelo Ahora!* (Translate Now). The idea is to give parents the ability to communicate easier with their children's teachers. The corporate program also recognizes that students need mentors to be attracted to technology jobs. A program at the University of Arizona, Tucson, for example, established online mentoring discussions among professional engineers and Hispanic university and high school students. This type of initiative can not only promote computing skills but also attract students to the notion that high-tech jobs are something to strive for.

MEANWHILE, AS WE FOCUS ON the most disadvantaged, we must at the same time consider maximizing opportunities and challenges for children

---

15 Thomas Toch, "Community Colleges' Commitment to Teaching," Education Sector, August 18, 2008, http://www.educationsector.org/analysis/analysis_show.htm?doc_id=706801.

who are staying in high school. A report by the Tomás Rivera Policy Institute, which promotes educational opportunities in the Latino community, agrees that we must entice young people in this country to enter computer science, engineering and related fields to keep pace with efforts by other countries to establish highly trained workforces. This is in one sense a form of reaching out to children who might otherwise drop out of high school. Once we have a larger population of high school students, we should encourage them to move on to higher education with specific opportunities.

The institute report makes some key points in that regard. Researchers found that there is a need for building self-confidence among Latino students. Minority students in high school are sometimes relegated to less-rigorous public school programs than Anglo students, who are encouraged to take enriched programs in elementary schools and Advanced Placement courses in high school. Even bright Latino students can suffer as a result, unless their parents intervene, or their guidance counselors are highly sensitive to the issue. In addition, if a skilled student from a disadvantaged school is not adequately prepared with advanced courses in high school, he or she may not have the prerequisite skills to study alongside other students who choose science or math majors in college.

Every step along the way, teachers and counselors are obviously a first line of support for needy students, especially Latinos and other minorities. The Policy Institute report, created by its Center for Latino Education Excellence, said, "Students who are assigned to several ineffective teachers sequentially have significantly lower levels of achievement and fewer gains in achievement than those who are assigned to several highly effective teachers in sequence." That seems logical, but then the report identifies an additional bias that must be rooted out of our educational system. It cites evidence that Hispanic and African American students often are assigned to teachers who are considered to be less effective than other teachers.[16]

---

16 Maria Teresa V. Taningco, Ann Bessie Mathew, and Harry P. Pachon, *STEM Professions: Opportunities and Challenges for Latinos in Science, Technology, Engineering, and Mathematics* (Los Angeles: Tomás Rivera Policy Institute, 2008), http://eric.ed.gov/ERICDocs/data/ericdocs2sql/content_storage_01/0000019b/80/3e/55/99.pdf.

Despite the gloom, I see positive initiatives and positive signs. As much as we plan for the future, we also need to adapt to the changing landscape. We are facing changes that we must understand and take advantage of in the present. I recommend stopping by your local elementary school to have a look around. I bet it will be a revelation, whether you live in a wealthy suburb of New York, in Atlanta, in Des Moines, or in Sacramento. You might see something very interesting and hopeful. Across the country, not only in Los Angeles, or Miami, or New York, of course, you'll find large numbers of minority students; in Miami-Dade County Public Schools, for example, the fourth-largest school system in the United States after New York, Los Angeles, and Chicago, more than sixty percent of 385,000 students are Latino, twenty-six percent are African-American, nine percent are non-Hispanic white, and one percent are Asian and Pacific Islanders. Dozens of languages are spoken in the Miami school system, but everyone learns English, and children sit together, play together. The percentages are much the same in Los Angeles. The children in these schools come from backgrounds where their parents might speak an indigenous language of the Guatemalan highlands, or one of hundreds of languages spoken in India, or Haitian Creole, or one of dozens of other possibilities. The children have many skin colors and facial characteristics; they are united by the culture of America, speak English, and even become instant translators for their parents and other elder family members.

A generation later, these English-speaking, American-acculturated children will be able to advance economically and will blend into the larger society. It's a wonderful thing as we watch this new generation of Americans celebrating a shared culture, and calling upon the varied and joined heritage of their parents and grandparents. We will continue to be the ultimate melting pot. As that happens, we become more diverse, command more languages, and provide more opportunity in our own communities.

We in government have a responsibility to make sure that as many of these qualified minority students as we can aid graduate from school, have access to colleges, universities, and vocational schools. Their own children, in turn, will have even more access and more chances to improve on their economic power. This has always been the progression of economic growth for immigrants in this country.

For those students who don't go to a university, we need to expand vocational-education grants. Vocational state grants are critical for the institutions in our states that seek to develop a workforce that is able to compete in today's global economy. We need to restore cuts to education-technology grants, which George W. Bush called for eliminating. These grants help ensure that our children have access to technology in the classroom. New Jersey alone would have lost five million dollars in 2009 under cuts imposed by the Bush administration. In the global race to have the most well-trained, highly skilled, best-prepared workforce, we are losing ground. The earlier we can introduce our young people to technology, to help them gain fluency in areas that involve technology, the better off they will be in an evolving and increasingly technological world.

We also need an infusion of new funding for special education. We must guarantee that children with disabilities have an equal opportunity to receive a good public education, just like anyone else. It follows then that children must begin their school years on an equal playing field. We must focus on Head Start programs, which will help improve the school readiness of our young children to ensure they can get the skills necessary to succeed. Head Start provides child development, education, health care, nutrition, and socialization skills, all essential services that benefit more than one million low-income children in this country.

We need to support and publicize programs that provide important skills to the disadvantaged, and Latinos can make use of such measures. YouthBuild USA, established in 1990 with majority funding from the U.S. Department of Labor, for example, is an important training resource for young people. The organization supports nationwide programs for young people between sixteen and twenty-four who can earn high school diplomas or prepare for GED equivalency tests as they learn job skills. The organization strives for developing leadership by giving low-income participants the opportunity to work on housing projects for the homeless or low-income families.

YouthBuild focuses on students who are at risk, poor, with families on welfare, or in foster care, some already in touch with the juvenile justice system. The goal is for such young people to learn building and housing skills and prepare for postsecondary training.

It's always good to assess the value of such programs by listening to the words of beneficiaries. Consider the major benefits achieved when we make relatively modest investments in programs such as YouthBuild.

Eimy Santiago of Springfield, Massachusetts, ran away from home when she was fourteen, started using drugs, got pregnant, and dropped out of school. She found YouthBuild and the organization found her.

"A lot of people gave up on me. For a while, I even gave up on myself.

"That's when a program called YouthBuild changed my life." She earned a GED, became an AmeriCorps VISTA volunteer, and entered a community college.

Enter my colleague John Kerry.

"He listened to me, he shook my hand and he said, 'You can make it.' And today I am making it."[17]

Her words were all the more poignant because she spoke at the July 2004 Democratic Convention, supporting John for president.

Eimy had a role model and was supported by a cause. I think there are various ways that we can instill values and inspire change. Families play a key role; so do schools and teachers.

---

17 Eimy Santiago, Democratic National Convention, July 28, 2004. http://www.prnews wire.com/cgi-bin/stories.pl?ACCT=104&STORY=/www/story/07-28-2004/0002220654 &EDATE=

CHAPTER II

SERVING OUR COMMUNITIES TO BUILD A BETTER AMERICA

*At the heart of all that civilization has meant and developed is
"community"—the mutually cooperative and voluntary venture of
man to assume a semblance of responsibility for his brother.*

MARTIN LUTHER KING JR.

On the eve of his inauguration as president of the United States, Barack Obama, a onetime community organizer in a poor neighborhood of Chicago, called upon all Americans to observe Martin Luther King Day as a day of national service.

What a moment of symbolism, a declaration that this was the start of an unprecedented journey for this country, inspired by Dr. King's message of hope that *"all* of God's children, black men and white men, Jews and Gentiles, Protestants and Catholics, will be able to join hands. . . ."

President Obama reminds us of the underlying goodness of the American people, their kindness when they pull together, a spirit that is far distant from George W. Bush's uninspired exhortation after September 11 that the American people, in the depths of empathy and human concern, should instead take care of their business and go shopping.

Americans pull together in a crisis, whether the heroes who returned to ground zero after 9/11, or the volunteers who went to New Orleans after Hurricane Katrina, filling the gap at the community level when government failed.

Even with more enlightened leadership now, we must recognize in any case that we need citizens who can volunteer and shoulder the tasks ahead of us. Government cannot do it all. Our charge has more to do with commitment and a vision of the future than simply at voting, paying taxes, and feeding the economy.

Personal experience tells me that we need teachers and volunteers and mentors, in essence, a new, revitalized commitment to service that will propel us more surely and accurately to that better future. I was lucky enough to have mentors at key points in my life. How do we replicate that good fortune and convert it into a guarantee millions of times across the United States?

In some cases, the government will provide more support in jobs and in training programs, and President Obama has called for new emphasis on programs like AmeriCorps and the Peace Corps. In general, we must always focus on a public-private partnership, support from all possible sources, government, community groups, and business.

But at a more profound level, we need individual volunteers willing to donate their time and their expertise, and all Americans should apply; but let this include representatives of communities in need, people who have succeeded and are willing to offer their examples to young Latinos as a new sense of the possible. A universe of successful Latinos must be convinced that they have an obligation to the generation that comes after them. These are the role models—people who have fought and prevailed. The mentors we recruit should realize that giving back involves not only donating money but also giving time to help our young people understand why they must stay in school and how they can thrive in a new world. We seek to convince them by example; therein, we find part of the formula to keep our children in school. But that's not all.

I advocate creating a national mentoring program for Latinos; part of it would target students who are at risk of dropping out of school. But we are talking about that holistic approach: We need to convince parents and students that their decisions will have lifelong consequences. And we need to realize that our resources—human capital and funding—will be going toward an investment in the future, toward making the country itself more successful. We need to step up and to devise a call to action from within, creating a sense that we have the power to change some of our problems on our own.

While we promote policies and programs, I believe we should create a National Latino Service Foundation. There can be no more pressing issue; we must nourish and advance the welfare of all our people here and now, knowing that such conditions will affect our future. And that is an example of what we mean when we talk about "Growing American Roots."

In the course of this chapter, I'd like to offer specific cases of individuals and organizations that perform stellar, inspiring service to the community. Many talented people in wonderful organizations are already focusing on such things. I want to see regional pilot programs and concepts develop into a national strategy. If you're a Latino doctor, dentist, or still a medical student, how can you get involved in encouraging Latino youth to consider a career in medicine? If you're a lawyer, how can you involve students in focusing on a legal career? Teachers, scientists, engineers, and psychologists—all can do more to spark interest among new generations, using themselves as examples of people who made it.

A number of organizations in this country are working on these types of programs. Consider the Society of Hispanic Professional Engineers, or the various nationally and locally based Hispanic police officers associations; or the Hispanic National Bar Association. Such organizations are perfect models for attracting students to their respective fields and mentoring youth to established defined goals of future service.

A friend of mine, Jorge Mursuli, has been focusing on such civic action for some time. Jorge is the president of Democracia U.S.A., a nonpartisan organization that encourages community action through voting, organization, and leadership training. He started his campaign for greater involvement in Miami, but has expanded operations throughout Florida and to Arizona, Colorado, Texas, Nevada, New Jersey, and Pennsylvania, and cooperates with La Raza. The group has focused on voter registration in states with large Hispanic populations, and has managed to register hundreds of thousands of people. Importantly, they report that much of the success has been among the youngest voters, people from eighteen to forty years old.

Jorge and I share the same basic principles about establishing those American roots. And he describes the concept well. "The truth of it is that the only real road to fully realizing our role as Americans is through voting. There are a lot of ways we participate, through pursuing success-ful careers in business, through working in social services, maybe through our children's education, maybe through philanthropy. But there is no other way really to fully realize and put down roots as Americans without figuring out a way of maximizing the freedoms afforded to us in this democracy."

But something else is going on here. As Democracia U.S.A. trains canvassers to convince people about the prime importance of voting, it is also creating a new level of awareness and participation in these newly trained people. And that's what I'm talking about. We seed the commu-nity with expanding possibilities, and each of these new participants in the system can produce new generations of growth in the future.

When Democracia U.S.A. is not on the street canvassing during the election cycle, it is providing leadership training. That is the beauty of the system; trainees work themselves up the ranks, by first going out into the community and searching for votes.

Jorge's future leaders have already demonstrated a commitment to hard work—they've been out working on voter registration. Democracia U.S.A. takes the top performers in the election effort and offers them a nine-week leadership-training program. The first step is to analyze and understand the work they've already done—commitment itself is a form of leadership.

Soon, these future leaders study basic government issues, demograph-ics, and how they might apply their knowledge to their future work. Part of the story is encouraging people to understand that, as Latinos, and as immigrants in general, they are bringing an important lesson to the greater American family.

"We teach them to use their own stories. Many Latinos have faced tremendous sacrifices to come to the United States—and they can tell other Americans that they value the promise of participation in the Amer-ican system. If they come from a country where health care was degraded, they can argue all the better that we Americans have a reason to improve health care in this country. They use their own experience to strengthen themselves as leaders."

And having such people in our midst empowers all of us. Who are these people? They could come from any walk of life.

"That's the beauty of offering such leadership skills. We don't know what they'll do with it; perhaps they'll chose any profession, apparently unrelated to our work, but they will be inspired to remain very committed voters for the rest of their lives. Or perhaps they will continue to focus on voter registration and other social causes. Once you instill these values, once people really know they can impact this democracy, the possibilities are endless. And yes, perhaps one of these young leaders will aspire to be president of the United States."

I was impressed with a program at UCLA that encourages international medical students and other medical students who speak Spanish to move toward family medical practices. Imagine if medical students could be encouraged to dedicate some of their time to treating underserved Latino communities. The UCLA program offers a prototype that helps students earn medical licensing in return for a pledge to work in an underserved community for three years. According to the American Medical Association, thirty percent of Hispanics nationwide say they do not have regular medical care. It wouldn't be too hard to start a coordinated effort to use such pilot programs as a prototype to promote in every state. There are other programs in law and medicine at universities around the country in which young people can commit their time in impoverished, underserved communities in return for tuition allowances.

That effort in turn is only one of a range of programs at UCLA, appropriate in a state that is so immersed in Latino culture and where initiatives can broaden from local solutions to nationwide efforts. The Center for the Study of Latino Health and Culture at UCLA is a wonderful example of moving beyond one area into the kind of programs that attract me, dealing with comprehensive solutions. The center conducts health research, gathers data, and provides information to other organizations wherever it can. Visit their Web site, http://www.cesla.med.ucla.edu/, and find out about the efforts of this organization, part of UCLA's David Geffen School of Medicine.

The Center's director, Professor David E. Hayes-Bautista, is also the author of a fascinating social sciences study, *La Nueva California: Latinos in the Golden State*, in which he considers a best-case scenario for Latinos in 2040. In that year, he describes a fictional governor of California, María Isabel Rodriguez de Smith, her name itself representative of blended cultural identities in America's future.

The governor has declared one fine day that California, if analyzed separately from the rest of the country, would be the world's second-largest economy, thanks to the efforts and incorporation of Latinos.

The accomplishment would be hard-won, Hayes-Bautista writes, "the product of nearly forty years of intensive policy work and public investment that had built on the demographic foundation formed in the year 2000; the public decision to invest in a future workplace and society that shortly would be half Latino, so as to ensure California's prosperity throughout the twenty-first century."[1]

But without that hard work, he knows, the results could be an economic disaster for our country, and his chilling worst-case scenario assumes a lack of adequate funding, and the dominance of the worst instincts in American society.

In joining forces, we can succeed and these individual stories tell the story.

If we are to answer the call to national service, we do well to listen to and support the efforts of community leaders who adapt to the reality of what they encounter. Any given day, the most skeptical and cynical among us can see hope and are left with a sense of optimism by visiting any of these community organizations.

A prominent facility in the metropolitan area of Washington, D.C., is Mary's Center for Maternal and Child Care, a medical clinic and social services organization that treats women and their children in the mostly Latino neighborhood of Adams Morgan. Maria S. Gomez and a group of her colleagues established the center in 1988. Now serving as president and chief executive officer, she is a public health nurse and has worked with the District of Columbia Health Department, and at the American

---

1 David E. Hayes-Bautista, *La Nueva California: Latinos in the Golden State*, 209–10.

Red Cross, where she directed community education programs. Maria was born in Cali, Colombia, and came to this country as a young teenager. She holds a degree in nursing from Georgetown University and a master's degree in public health from the University of California, Berkeley.

What was intended to provide health care to underserved women became a much broader effort. Service requires adapting to reality. Maria and her colleagues understood that the best solution for treating women's health was to provide broader training and support that ultimately affects women's issues.

As with so many community organizers, and in concert with my vision of the future, Maria is convinced that mentoring is a key element. "We don't see enough Latinos who have made it coming back to the community, and they have such an important role that they could be playing."

Mary's Center has grown into being one of the most innovative and inspiring health organizations of its kind. With 132 staff members from thirty-two countries in the Americas, Africa, Asia, and Europe, Mary's Center has progressively grown beyond providing health care toward a whole-life experience. The center offers parenting training to mothers and fathers, day care and day-care training, preschool, English-language lessons, teen groups, and extends to dealing with social and family issues.

It is evident to Maria that the ethnic community served by Mary's Center has problems that are not unique to other segments of society. "People tend to think the only ones to come to centers like ours are recent immigrants or those who are very poor. But that's not so. The problem is that the health-care system doesn't work for anybody. We see people who have lost their health insurance. And the health-care system doesn't work for people who can't afford their portion of the premiums provided by their employers. The problem of obtaining health care is just as acute for people whose last name is Martinez or Gomez as it is for an American named Smith."[2]

---

2 Maria Gomez, personal interview, September 24, 2008.

The center operates in a part of Washington where many Salvadoran immigrants have settled. They were drawn there first in the 1980s during the violence in their country that killed and displaced hundreds of thousands of people. Maria speaks passionately against unwarranted, unjust charges about immigration. "Many people have the prejudice that immigrants are just coming here to have babies. They fact is that ninety-five percent of the people we meet are here because of unrest in their own countries."

These are not people that planned to come to the United States, and the prejudice against them is uninformed. Adams Morgan has been a microcosm of such migrations. "To the millisecond, you can see changes in our client base—when there are problems in Ethiopia or other African countries, we see more Africans. With the violence in Croatia, we saw an influx of many people from there."

Certainly, Mary's Center focuses on women. In America, one of every ten women is between the ages of eighteen and twenty-four; for Latinas it's nearly one in five—and that number is growing.

Women and Hispanics—a powerful combination, becoming more powerful every day. Latinas and all women are being asked to take on multiple responsibilities like never before. We know, as people know all across America, that a lot needs to change. On average, a Hispanic woman makes fifty-four cents on the dollar compared to a white man.[3] More than a third of Latinas don't have health insurance, more than any other group.[4] And Latinas are statistically just as likely to drop out of high school as their male classmates.[5]

Mary's Center, a model for such organizations around the United States, fits right in with the rising concept that we have to treat social issues in a comprehensive way. Maria learned quickly that health care in-

---

3 Gender Wage Ratio, U.S. Census & IWPR 2003, cited by National Hispana Leadership Institute, http://www.nhli.org/resources/labor.html.
4 HHS, cited by National Hispana Leadership Institute, http://www.nhli.org/resources/health.html.
5 U.S. Census, 2000, cited by National Hispana Leadership Institute, http://www.nhli.org/resources/facts.html.

volves a host of collateral issues. More recently, she says, she's been seeing people who have been sliding back into poverty during the economic crisis. One-concept solutions are not sufficient.

"The people we're dealing with have problems dealing with day care, issues with their children, with making rent payments, but also with finding a place to sleep or enough to eat. Here, they now have a center where all the issues will be addressed. If a person doesn't have a place to live, who cares at the end of the day that we give them good prenatal care?

"There's no value for me to be providing prenatal care without holistic resolutions to their problems. So our role is to say, 'What's going on in your life? If you have a partner and both of you are working, what happened?' And at the end of the day, they know they will have something to eat and someplace to sleep."

On a given day, there are sounds of children playing in the school day-care center, reciting their lessons in Spanish and English, or cavorting around office toys as their parents await a variety of health screenings, prenatal services, and gynecological exams available to them. Maria points to troubling data that shows immigrants arriving in the United States are often healthier than Americans on average, but their health gradually drops below the national average the longer they stay. She cites inaccessibility to health insurance plans, the pressures of long work hours, linguistic problems, and the general stress of being in a new country.

In all cases, the center's programs include helping new arrivals in this country to learn the English language and American culture, with an accent on civics and society. Maria Gomez knocks down the idea that immigrants are looking for handouts, and the center is dedicated to helping its clients reach self-sufficiency. The English classes, for children and adults, by the way, have a strong component of lessons on American civics, the voting process, and how government works.

"We also have children that may quickly be in danger of losing the roots to the societies they've come from. We know that it is important to preserve one's heritage and we like to help children learn Spanish as well."

This speaks to one central point we need to emphasize among the benefits of growing our multicultural American roots. The language skills of our community open doors in the twenty-first century—to our relations, for example, with twenty-one countries; our children will be American diplomats dealing with Hispanic nations and the future business people reaching out with the cultural and social skills to expand American commerce.

Maria has one general concern: Will she be able to meet the need, and will the government be there to provide adequate support? She is encouraged by President Obama's initiatives so far and hopes that the economic crisis will not produce funding cuts. We in Congress must do our part in the funding, but once again, that other element comes from volunteerism. I ask that Americans consider working in programs such as Mary's Center—yes, donating money, but also giving a deeper commitment when they can.

I'M POSITIVE THAT THE TRAJECTORY of Mary's Center, expanding from health care to universal services, is replicated around the country; as a result, community-service organizations understand the need for coordinated action. I've had the opportunity in my career to work with many organizations that are working at ground-level solutions. I had the privilege in 1999 to attend a founding conference of what became known as Latino Leadership Alliance of New Jersey, uniting the efforts of four hundred politicians, businesspeople, teachers, social scientists, and even police officers.

Martín Pérez is now the president of the Alliance. Martín came to the United States from Puerto Rico after graduating from the University of Puerto Rico with a bachelor of arts degree in political science and labor studies.

He obtained a law degree at Rutgers University and became a trial attorney and public defender. His professional focus on civil and human rights for the underprivileged crystallized with the creation of an umbrella organization for many disparate Latino organizations.

Martín's vision of uniting Latino development efforts stems from his long work in preschool programs for children, bilingual education, and assistance for migrant workers. That work led to a recognition that Latino groups needed to speak to one another, simply to discuss the matter of cooperating for common goals. "Everyone was in their corner— Dominicans on one side, Puerto Ricans over here, Mexicans to their own. There were Peruvians and Colombians, lawyers and nurses and police officers and members of chambers of commerce. It was the makings of a base organization, but there was no articulate voice for Latinos. So we basically decided to create the Latino Leadership Alliance, an umbrella group." The idea was to unite union members, educators, peace officers, doctors, and more. There are about 250 organizations now participating in the New Jersey–based alliance, which is certainly a model for other states.

Martín has striven for the organization to remain nonpartisan, and says that politicians need to speak to issues before receiving its support.

"It is a fallacy to believe that Latinos are only Democrats, and I think that's a big mistake for the Democrats to take us for granted or for Republicans to make assumptions and not pay attention to us. I prefer to call it a corporate approach, just as Johnson & Johnson donates money to both Democrats and Republicans. If the Republicans win, they say, 'We won.' And if the Democrats win, they say, 'We won.' In other words our official position is that we have no enemies, only permanent interests."

Another example of ground-level service organizations is Casa de Maryland, which has been an advocate for Latino immigrants in the Washington, D.C., region since 1985. That was a moment of expanding immigration from Central America—people were fleeing civil war in El Salvador and Nicaragua, while Guatemalans were fleeing political violence and repression that especially targeted impoverished Indians. The new arrivals needed basic help, clothing, food, legal counsel on their status in the country, and English lessons.

As the need grew, Casa de Maryland expanded with help from government grants and private foundations. From a small staff and almost no funding, Casa de Maryland now has more than fifty employees and a five-million-dollar budget, and has expanded its menu of support for the

Latino community. The award-winning organization has pioneered the creation of so-called workers' centers around Maryland, which have become a model for such operations around the country. The centers, five of them in Maryland, address the contentious issue of Latino day laborers, who need support and access to the job market. Informal day-labor-collection areas, in front of home-improvement stores, on street corners, and in vacant lots, offer an escape valve and an ad hoc means to solve a problem that sometimes brings community anger. But there are usually more workers than work, and the informal system sometimes lends itself to low wages and exploitation.

The Casa de Maryland blueprint looks for solutions. The worker-employment centers offer job training, language and literacy classes, computer courses, and health and legal services. Above all, the centers become a clearinghouse for job placement, helping create norms for both workers and employers.

The executive director of Casa de Maryland is Gustavo Torres, nationally recognized for his role in immigrant rights. Torres was born in Colombia, where he was a union leader before coming to the United States to avoid political violence in that country. He stresses that Casa de Maryland's method is to strive for self-sufficiency among Hispanic immigrants. He says, "We speak for the families in our community. More importantly, we provide families with the tools to speak for themselves."

There are other inspiring stories about organizations serving immigrants and solving problems across the country. In my home state of New Jersey, for example, the Focus Hispanic Center for Community Development, in Newark, focuses on jobs, education, and conflict resolution.

Volunteers and staff members at the Hispanic Center in Pittsburgh help immigrants prepare job résumés, set up e-mail accounts, and register at participants' job bulletin boards. They offer language help, job referrals and postings, counseling, and help on employment interviews. The center's vibrant outreach effort reflects a growing Hispanic community in southwestern Pennsylvania, and the need to promote growth and economic success stories in the Hispanic community.

Hundreds of such organizations are operating around the country, usually underfunded, and invariably unable to meet demand. We should be looking for ways to enhance service organizations, which often expand beyond the Latino community when new rounds of immigrants arrive.

Such programs include Job Corps, which provides job skills to young people, and services to help veterans' transition to civilian life. Many of our soldiers are in their twenties or younger, and a good percentage of them are Latinos. All of them need employment, training, and a chance to return to school.

In this chapter, I've focused on many promising initiatives that are the constituent parts of a new alliance of Latinos, and all minorities, with the larger American family. I've discussed the options for partnerships among government, community organizations, and individuals to build a structure capable of our energy, expectations, and dreams. And this in turn is part of a larger system that encompasses our future as Americans and citizens of the world. Because as we build better communities, expanding our roots, we can then use our resourcefulness to build bridges with other countries in this hemisphere.

CHAPTER 12

ENGAGEMENT WITH THE AMERICAS

Let us once again transform the American Continent into a vast crucible of revolutionary ideas and efforts, a tribute to the power of the creative energies of free men and women, an example to all the world that liberty and progress walk hand in hand.

JOHN F. KENNEDY

Almost fifty years ago, President John F. Kennedy declared an Alliance for Progress in the hemisphere, recognizing that the United States must engage fully with its neighbors to solve problems of wealth and inequity that affect all of us. I firmly believe that we have the opportunity early in the twenty-first century to renew President Kennedy's vision of that alliance. And I see a clear reason for Latinos in this country to take a leading role in making that happen, precisely in the same way that President Kennedy described the problem.

In a major speech to Latin American diplomats and members of Congress, he said: "Our continents are bound together by a common history—the endless exploration of new frontiers. Our nations are the product of a common struggle—the revolt from colonial rule. And our people share a common heritage—the quest for the dignity and the freedom of man. . . .

"As a citizen of the United States let me be the first to admit that we North Americans have not always grasped the significance of this common mission, just as it is also true that many in your own countries have not fully understood the urgency of the need to lift people from poverty and ignorance and despair. But we must turn from these mistakes—from the failures and the misunderstandings of the past—to a future full of peril but bright with hope."[1]

We now find ourselves in much the same situation. It was clear that during the Bush years U.S. policy was focused elsewhere and our esteem in Latin America suffered. President Obama has already recognized this and has launched an initiative to repair suspicions and questions about the U.S. role in the Americas.

In my view, this is the missing link: The Latino community should be deeply involved in this plan, as the one group in the United States that is uniquely qualified to understand and participate in this crucial social contract for the future. The Latino community in this country can be a catalyst for driving that agenda forcefully and successfully. We Latinos will not only establish and declare our deepest roots to this country but also teach our countrymen that we can no longer live in an age of cultural and ethnic isolation.

In September 2008, I proposed a bill before Congress that would be called the Social Investment and Economic Development for the Americas Act. That is a rather wordy title that boils down to this: To achieve our goals and assure the future path of all Americans toward a more stable, economically secure future, we need to recognize that the United States must reengage with the other countries of the Americas. My proposal has everything to do with our role as Latinos in the United States, and is part of the recipe for success in this country.

The proposal calls for a trust to be administered with $2.5 billion over ten years, working with existing U.S. funding and cooperative agreements with international agencies. I see it as a six-part plan, in which we recognize that military aid and spending are not enough to combat rising crime and issues of destabilization across the region.

That is where we fit in: My fellow Latinos have not been sensitized enough yet to this aspect of national life that I think can give us a mature and prudent new role in politics. Let us for the first time in a major way

---

1 John F. Kennedy, "Preliminary Formulations of the Alliance for Progress" (address, White House reception for Latin American diplomats and members of Congress, March 13, 1961), Modern History Sourcebook, http://www.fordham.edu/halsall/mod/1961kennedy-afp1.htm.

consider America's role in the world from the prism of Latinos in America. Over the last eight years, our engagement with Latin America has been mostly an engagement that begins, ends, and swiftly flops with a tacit attitude by the U.S. government: "We know best for you and we want to talk to you largely about only two things—trade and narcotics interdiction." For the last eight years, America's reputation in the world has taken a beating, sullied by the legacy of a war in Iraq that should never have been fought, dishonored by official admission that America, the city on the hill, got down in the dirt and committed acts of torture. Eight years of arrogance drove our prestige to a historic low around the world, and even in Latin America.

The Social Contract for the Americas includes six major headings:

- Primary needs—education, health care, disease prevention, and housing
- Crime reduction, focusing on violent crime, murder, kidnapping, gang violence, and acts against women
- Rural development to reduce poverty in farming and other nonurban settings
- Instilling the rule of law and independent court and legal systems
- Poverty reduction among the weakest sectors of societies, including indigenous groups and populations of African origin
- Stimulation and expansion of the middle class, using a mixture of investment and the promotion of small enterprises

Why should we discuss these topics of foreign policy in a proposal for establishing and expanding American roots in this country? For me, the answer is basic. We envision a future society in which the nations of the hemisphere, if not the world, are increasingly interdependent. The United States is not an island; communication, transportation, and immigration trends will make this ever more true in coming generations.

Directing Latino energy toward these goals also stakes out territory in which our community is uniquely qualified to help America.

Developing a Latino-inspired policy of engagement with other nations of our hemisphere would change the dynamics of America's relationship with the world. Too often U.S. government pronouncements have been based on dicta from on high, statements that come across to the ears of Latin American societies as the height of arrogance. Latin American governments hear pronouncements without diplomacy or engagement: "You've got to eradicate drugs; you've got to eliminate corruption; you must eliminate protectionism."

Latin American countries are proud and nationalistic above all, and they have their own agendas. In general, they face a great disparity and distortion in wealth distribution. They want us to talk about how we will work together in a common cause: how can we improve the lives of everyone in this hemisphere.

The issues that concern us may be serious, but without approaching diplomacy from a position of respect, we are lost at the start. Have we first approached our neighbors on an even basis, with the message "You are important to us as our next-door neighbors, not as an afterthought"? "What do you want to put on the table? What common ground can we identify toward an agenda for the future?"

In my view, our approach to our Latin American allies is far more important that what President Hugo Chávez of Venezuela might do or say. Sad to say, with his socialist diatribes and his railing against the United States, Chávez fills a vacuum in Latin American affairs that in some sense we have created by our absence and in many respects by our negative tone. Damage has been done, but fence-mending is a long-term proposition. And in that regard, I think that our burgeoning power as Latinos in this country can lead us to a prominent role. Beyond the next eight years of two Obama administrations, this can be the community that sets that new tone.

Who, after all, are the natural ambassadors for the linkages to change U.S. relations with Latin America? If we respond to the challenge and the opportunity, in the future Hispanic-Americans will be the natural interface with Latin America, employing their combination of shared language, culture, and business customs.

The classic joke about U.S. business acumen in Latin America is the case of General Motors and its marketing of the Chevy Nova. A car suited to Latin America, to be sure, and the price was right, no question, except for the comical detail: "Chevy *no va*" in Spanish translates to "A Chevy doesn't run." Few Spanish speakers with a degree in marketing would make that mistake. It's a revealing story—and not completely a joke. Understanding the language and the mores means something in making the sale. Latinos will be part of a big, growing opportunity for this country, as long as we generate a policy that understands and is sensitive to engagement.

Why should we be doing all of this? Engagement with the hemisphere makes good economic sense. Stronger Latin American economies will create new markets for American goods and services. Hispanic lawyers, for example, naturally can deal with issues about the rule of law; Latino public health officers can deal with medical issues in the language of the hemisphere and with cultural competency. These are natural markets that we can create and nurture: We build bridges with our native abilities.

But it goes much further. Latinos in America can declare that they understand the real issues and interests of Latin America, that we identify with our sister nations to the south, and that we can recognize and develop the interests we have in common.

I am not describing these issues in terms of foreign aid, or philanthropy, but as a new perspective on the Good Neighbor Policy, a perspective for the future as Latinos in this country exercise their power and take their rightful place.

I view this as a very bottom-line avenue of self-interest, one that makes sense for the United States. It is a key interest, because if we can help raise up the forty-five percent of people in Latin America who live below the poverty line to a higher standard of living, everyone will benefit. To the degree to which all Americans from various perspectives are upset about immigration, this is one answer. The best way to stem the tide of immigration is largely to help strengthen those countries, economically, socially, and politically. If we succeed, many people from those countries will change their perspectives on their lives; fewer of them may want to emigrate to the United States in the first place. The reason many Latin Americans leave their countries of origin is dire economic necessity and civil unrest. Greater economic opportunity and stability mean less civil unrest and obviously less need to go to a foreign country and find new, more secure opportunities there. They might want to come to visit, but they won't feel they need to stay.

AND IN REVERSE, CREATING A better, more stable climate in those countries makes economic sense for us. As we restore our own economy and create more jobs in America, we will be encouraging purchasing power in the rest of the Americas; secure growing economies will want more and more of what we Americans produce, particularly in high technology. People will rise to a level where they will have disposable income. It's an ideal complementary economic pattern. U.S. business wants to sell more of its goods and services because that will create jobs here at home. Latin America can easily become our best growing market for our goods and services. Latin Americans have a pre-disposition for American-style products and services, along with American expertise; they will want to buy what we have, and a rising middle class will be able to afford it. Stronger economies alter society: People will insist that their governments be more responsive to them, which creates greater stability; ultimately that transcends into rule of law, transparency, and a system in which people will want to stay in their countries. This policy of cooperative engagement with the hemisphere is based not only on being the Good Neighbor, but also on self-interest, national interest, immigration, health care, and national security. We don't have to worry about the hemisphere if it is stable, prosperous, and democratic.

To be successful, we must embark on a new chapter in our relations, not just with Mexico, but also with all of Latin America. It is time that we develop a more systematic engagement with Mexico and other countries in the hemisphere. It is clear, as Hillary Clinton said, that efforts to control drugs, or violence, or illegal entry into the United States, depend on working together.

If we just continue to fight the supply of drugs, we will not succeed. We must also fight demand in this country. The demand for drugs in the United States and the supply of weapons from the United States have helped fuel violence in Mexico for a long time. We have to think of Mexico and our friends in Latin America as complementary societies, where we have a stake in solving problems and promoting their successful economic progress.

Today we have an opportunity to readjust our policies toward Latin America. As members of the Hispanic community, we are in a key position to provide critical insight on our brothers and sisters in Latin America. As members of the Latino community, we have to make sure that our hemispheric neighbors are no longer neglected, in pursuit of our own national interest and security.

As a result, we also develop stronger alliances, because our neighbors in the hemisphere come to realize that America is joining with them on the basis of respect and common ground, based on common interests. I don't feel that the governments or the peoples of Latin America trust us that way right now. They've got a hangover from the early years of this decade. But the future can be bright, and Latinos in America can be in the vanguard. American Latinos have a real case to be made to the broader population. This is about the broader interest of all Americans.

The argument goes even further. Former vice president and Nobel Peace Prize recipient Al Gore came to speak to the Senate Foreign Relations Committee recently, and we discussed issues of the environment and global warming in terms of politics and economics. It's clear that we can't isolate ourselves in this world. Improving economic opportunity around the world enhances the ability of countries to choose green options.

Again, the Bush administration came late, if at all, to the table as the former vice president pleaded for changes in carbon emissions and the rate of global warming. We now have an opportunity to change course, hopefully in time. President Obama's economic-recovery initiative has taken steps to drastically reduce greenhouse gases, and in the process endorses new technologies, and promotes new jobs based on green industries.

Latinos in this country can play a similar role as in my proposal on economic changes in Latin America, promoting goodwill efforts by the United States, rather than allowing American diplomats to come across as authoritative scolds. The tropical forests and wildernesses of Latin America are a major objective for maintaining so-called carbon sinks that absorb emissions and protect our environment.

Gore said, "We must face up to this urgent and unprecedented threat to the existence of our civilization at a time when our country must simultaneously solve two other worsening crises. Our economy is in its deepest recession since the 1930s. And our national security is endangered by a vicious terrorist network and the complex challenge of ending the war in Iraq honorably while winning the military and political struggle in Afghanistan. As we search for solutions to all three of these challenges, it is becoming clearer that they are linked by a common thread—our dangerous over-reliance on carbon-based fuels."[2]

But what struck home was his reminder that the United States has a preeminent positive role to play—albeit belatedly—in this crisis, "that our country is the only country in the world that can really lead the global community."

So in the realm of employing our own Latino community as the best and most trusted ambassador to Latin America—as people who do speak the same language, in more ways than one—we can help countries find ways to make greener use of their resources, limiting deforestation while allowing farmers to earn money, limiting logging although encouraging balanced use of timberland, and in the end keeping rain forests intact. The essential point, once more, is reasoned diplomacy, not dictating terms, and employing the human resource of Latino emissaries.

And beyond environmental issues, we can apply these principles across the board. If we want to see changes in health care, we need to help Latin America; diseases have no boundaries. We had eradicated tuberculosis and other ailments in this country. We now see illnesses resurfacing be-

---

2 Al Gore, Testimony Before the Senate Foreign Relations Committee. Jan. 28, 2009. http://foreign.senate.gov/testimony/2009/GoreTestimony090128p.pdf

cause many people in the hemisphere don't have the health care that is necessary. This is a specific area with specific remedies, but at the same time it is tied to the social, economic, and political dynamics of the hemisphere. On collective security, if we want to ensure the hemisphere is not a breeding ground for crime, we need to provide real support in those countries and help them attack the sources of crime. If we want to stop the flow of drugs from Latin America, we need to pledge efforts to limit demand at home, and at the same time discuss and promote sustainable alternatives for the poor farmers of Bolivia and Peru, giving them something better to grow than coca to sustain their families.

I've made the case that Latinos should be naturally at the forefront of promoting U.S.–Latin American relations, but who will carry the message? Government is not the only answer. Engagement in solving problems will take the participation of Latino chambers of commerce, and international organizations like the Pan American Health Organization, the Inter-American Development Bank, and the Organization of American States. Businesses, community groups, individuals that want to improve the lives of their relatives back in Latin America—all must participate. As with mentoring programs, there are individual efforts to take up the task, but we need concerted efforts as a community. We should be meeting to discuss our possible role and entry points into the discussion. Foreign affairs is the new frontier for Latinos in this country, and in our expanding role, we must move in the direction of applying the power of numbers and the influence of our combined experience. It is not at all a revolutionary concept. Greek-Americans, Irish-Americans, people of Armenian descent, Jewish Americans, all understand how to use their citizenship muscle to influence the agenda that will inform and improve bi-national relations in a way that serves America's interests.

So LATINOS MUST COME TOGETHER and engage with the countries of South America; the hemisphere is waiting, and America needs your service. With a proper degree of advocacy, we stand at the brink of a new era in inter-American relations.

CHAPTER 13

IMMEDIATE ACTION

Representatives and direct Taxes shall be apportioned among the several States which may be included within this Union, according to their respective Numbers.

ARTICLE 2, SECTION 4, THE U.S. CONSTITUTION

There are some immediate-action items and initiatives on the agenda as we refine the quest for consolidating our Latino inheritance in this country. Sometimes, future success will depend on overarching plans, or on targeted legislation and on a commitment to joint action among government officials, private enterprise, and community activists. At times, otherwise overlooked details can make a big difference. Throughout this book, I've focused on ideas to set a course for the future; here I'd like to mention several areas that are on the front burner and can help adjust the course immediately. One involves the U.S. Census; two others relate to our most basic human rights.

In the spring of 2010, an estimated 1.4 million temporary government employees will set out in every corner of the land to conduct the twenty-third census of the United States. It seems like a simple process; perhaps two-thirds of census questions will be answered by mail; others will involve door-to-door visits. Enumerators will count males, females, adults, children, log the locations of where people live, ask basic questions about education, and, importantly for various ethnic groups, ask how people identify themselves. For Latinos, the key question is whether respondents are "of Hispanic, Latino, or Spanish origin." And if they are, would they specify their country of origin, "Mexican, Mexican American or Chicano, Puerto Rican, Cuban, Argentinean, Colombian, Dominican, Nicaraguan, Salvadoran, Spaniard, and so on"? The census collects data that affects employment and minority recruitment, bilingual election rules, health services, and voting rights, among other things.

The census, of course, has evolved since the first count in 1790, when the government determined there were 3,929,214 people in the United States. It was a brilliant, basic concept that will last for all time as the baseline for our understanding of America. How can we move on toward a brighter future unless we understand where we are at this exact moment? More than two hundred years ago, the plan was well thought out, but the concept of who exactly was to be counted was, to put it mildly, shocking and deplorable. Here is the full text of the establishment of the census:

> Representatives and direct Taxes shall be apportioned among the several States which may be included within this Union, according to their respective Numbers, which shall be determined by adding to the whole Number of free Persons, including those bound to Service for a Term of Years, and excluding Indians not taxed, three fifths of all other Persons.

Native Americans were not counted in that number, and each black slave counted as three-fifths of a person. Hispanics, if they weren't taken for some other disenfranchised group, might have been counted. While the census became more specific and complex over time, the question about Hispanics was not included in the questionnaire until 1970, when about 9.5 million of us were listed in this country. In this latest census of 2010, the number is expected to approach 48 million. But here's the problem. The census counts everyone in the United States on April 1, 2010—not just citizens and permanent residents—everyone. That includes documented immigrants and at least twelve million undocumented immigrants, most of them from Mexico. Undocumented immigrants are the most likely group to be undercounted, a large number of whom are either unable to receive a mailed questionnaire or difficult to find, and likely anxious and unwilling to meet with an employee of the government. But that group is precisely one that needs to be incorporated.

While the average citizen will hardly think about the ramifications of this fifteen-billion-dollar exercise, it is abundantly clear that the new census will be a milestone for Latinos. Determine the present count and designate plans for the future—we have strength in numbers and the Latino vote must be as accurate as possible. The Constitution declares that, at its most basic level, a ten-year census will determine the shape of the 435 congressional districts in the United States; it is also used to establish the proportional allocation of legislative districts in each of the fifty states. But beyond that, this new census will be incredibly important in terms of the distribution of four hundred billion dollars in funding education, Medicaid, and other federal programs and in terms of allocating spending by state and local governments. Businesses also make their decisions on where to locate services, manufacturing, and retail stores based on census results. All aspects of the census ultimately have major importance for the Latino community around the country.

There are few more seemingly mundane exercises that could mean so much to the future of our country, and the direction of resources for our people. When the enumerators send mailed forms or conduct house-by-house checks from Barrow, Alaska, to Cape May, New Jersey, and everywhere in between, their ability to conduct an accurate count will have a lot to do with how well Latinos are accessible.

The allocation of public funds has everything to do with Latino power. The Bush administration did almost nothing to prepare for an efficient census and underfunded the Census Bureau, which is an agency of the Department of Commerce. Senator Judd Gregg, a Republican colleague from New Hampshire, withdrew his acceptance after President Obama designated him the new commerce secretary; one component of his decision probably was that the Census Bureau would not be controlled by a Republican agenda. It's not too partisan to say that the Democrats and Republicans have a major ideological rift over the bureau and the usefulness of the official nose count. It's a simple matter: Democrats want every last body counted as accurately as possible. But what's the problem for the Republicans? If the count is accurate, millions of additional Latinos and other minorities will appear in the final census, and many of them live in neighborhoods that are traditionally Democratic strongholds. Pure politics.

It took several weeks for the president to regroup before choosing Gary Locke, the former governor of Washington, as the new Commerce Secretary. As a result of the delay, we had no Census Bureau director until the spring of 2009. The last time we were against the wall on organizing the census was in 1989 for the 1990 census. The disorganization led to an undercount for those most likely to be missed: Five percent of Latinos and Hispanics—millions of people—were not included in the statistics. We have to do better than that.

I am very hopeful that Robert M. Groves, the new director of the Census Bureau, will be able to move swiftly to organize the system. Groves is a respected academic and researcher and has previously served in the Census Bureau. He also understands that establishing the best possible count is crucial to our future. And despite the misgivings of Republicans who would tamper with the system on ideological grounds, Groves has promised that the bureau will have "the independent leadership it deserves and the professional oversight that Americans demand."[1]

The system is rife with shenanigans of all kinds—often favoring Republicans in rural areas. Generally, for example, the nation's two million prisoners are counted according to the locations where they are incarcerated. So, for example, the estimated 2,700 inmates at the Clinton Correctional Facility, a maximum-security prison in Dannemora, New York, are counted as being residents of Clinton County, New York, whereas most of them likely come from urban areas, and a significant percentage of them are Latinos. The inmate population is more than half the population of the farming community of Dannemora itself. Across the country, politicians use those types of inflated figures to build proportional constituencies based on prison populations that mostly can't vote.

I have fought alongside my fellow Democrats for the best possible outcome—an infusion of money and quick fixes to make sure the 2010 cen-

---

1 Ed O'Keefe, "With 2010 Census Looming, Obama Chooses Survey Expert to Run Bureau," *Washington Post*, April 3, 2009.

sus works well. Doing so, I know that I'm working for the future—the numbers will convert into revenues dedicated to education for a new generation of Latinos, small business loans, greater health care, and economic opportunity, all designated for areas that have been identified properly as being more densely populated with Latinos than ever before. In turn, real, solid census results are an investment for generations to come as Latinos pursue their quest to grow American roots. The product of an accurate census will improve the lot of the immigrant community for a decade. The fallout from a bad census would set us back, something we can't let happen.

IT IS DISMAYING TO REALIZE that our beacon of democracy has fallen to the point where its human rights record can be challenged. But that is exactly where we found ourselves at the end of the Bush administration. I would like to mention two other measures that have been on the legislative agenda; I'm shocked that we even had to wait until 2009 to consider these measures.

One is the Hate Crimes Prevention Act. Our nation must take rigorous action to protect everyone in this country, regardless of orientation or background. We've seen too many shocking incidents involving hate crimes based on race, ethnicity, religion, sexual orientation, disability, or gender identity. I took the floor of the Senate in 2007 to call for passage of what should be a very basic principle, but which had failed to pass in previous sessions. I said, "Hate crimes violate every principle upon which this country was founded. When our Declaration of Independence proclaimed that 'all men are created equal,' it did not go on to say 'except Muslim or Sikh Americans.' The freedoms we often take for granted—freedom of speech, freedom of association, freedom of religion—become empty promises if we do not protect all those who seek to exercise these freedoms under the Constitution."[2]

As Martin Luther King said, "It may be true that the law cannot make

---

2 Senate speech, Sept. 28, 2007. http://menendez.senate.gov/newsroom/record.cfm?id=284492

a man love me, but it can keep him from lynching me, and I think that's pretty important."[3] A single law cannot wipe out bigotry, but it can set our society on the proper course—hate crimes cannot be tolerated.

HUMAN RIGHTS WATCH, MEANWHILE, IN early 2009 released a report, *Detained and Dismissed*,[4] focusing on the failure to provide adequate medical care to women detained by U.S. immigration authorities.

The report, based on the kind of on-site inspections I have made, made a shocking but accurate assessment. "Most immigration detainees in the United States are held as a result of administrative, rather than criminal, infractions, but the medical treatment they receive can be worse than that of convicted criminals in the U.S. prison system."

The only thing I can say about this report is that it need not stop with women's medical care—as I've written in previous chapters, all detainees are subject to capricious, dangerous treatment, and they can die as a result. And as I've mentioned, some of these people at risk are wrongly detained to begin with—they may even be legal residents or citizens who were swooped up because of where they were and what they look like. We can and must change this tragic state of affairs immediately. We cannot act for our future common good with such a present blight.

As a result, I have proposed in Congress the Detainee Basic Medical Care Act, in response to what are evidently systematic problems in medical care for those detained in U.S. immigration centers, as well as those that may be segregated in local and county jails. Under this law, the Department of Homeland Security would be required to provide timely and effective delivery of basic health care to all detainees. Importantly, Congress would have a role in receiving timely reports and monitoring the improvement.

How can we talk about fairness and progress when detention in this country leads to suffering and unnecessary deaths? I am committed to

---

3 http://www.thespeeches.com/martin_luther_king2.html
4 Human Rights Watch, *Detained and Dismissed: Women's Struggles to Obtain Health Care in United States Immigration Detention* (New York: Human Rights Watch, 2009), http://www.hrw.org/en/reports/2009/03/16/detained-and-dismissed.

doing everything in my power to protect the dignity of all people in this country, especially the poorest, weakest, and most at-risk segments of our society.

The principal provisions of the act would require the following:

- Procedures for the timely and effective delivery of health care
- Decisions for detainee health to be based on the judgment of health-care professionals
- Monitoring and maintenance of care for detainees when they are moved or transferred from one detention center to another
- Timely reports by Homeland Security on detainee deaths, with Congress empowered to receive these reports

There is much more to be done than solving health issues for those who are detained; we also must deal with ensuring health care for the community at large. We have pressing problems in dealing with the young, the infirm, and the elderly and we must attend to all.

We should not labor under the illusion that poor health-care outcomes are limited to the impoverished. In our economic crisis, the middle class faces the fear of not being able to pay for health insurance, or for adequate medical treatment. As always, whether we're talking about the disadvantaged or the more successful middle class, Latinos and other minorities feel a proportionately higher percentage of the pain.

We need increased grants for community health centers and a focus on the nationwide value of the National Center on Minority Health and Health Disparities to address the health-care needs of our nation's minority and underserved communities. The center, which promotes health care for Latinos and other communities, is designed to coordinate and support government efforts to provide health care to all. It was singled out in President Obama's recovery package as an agency designed to provide support for proposals that invest in technological advances in health and science.

To the credit of the office of the surgeon general, the federal government recognizes as well that Latinos, especially recent immigrants, may not realize that they need to be able to evaluate their own health risks by obtaining family-health histories. Reports the surgeon general: "Health-care professionals have known for a long time that many diseases, such as cancer, diabetes and heart disease, can run in families. A detailed family history can predict the disorders for which a person may be at increased risk, and help to develop more personalized approaches to prevent illness or detect it early, when it is most treatable. However, with doctors and nurses spending less time with their patients, sufficient family information is seldom gathered to make useful predictions."[5]

The surgeon general has issued a guide in English and Spanish for organizing such information.[6] For some time, I've argued that the government must focus on evaluating its programs and work to improve the delivery of health care to all Americans. When we talk about public health, we are talking about not only potential injury and illness in our own families but also about the collective health of our communities, environment, and economy. Too often, when a federal program is implemented or when an agency acts, the focus is too narrow and the impact on public health is ignored. We always need to examine how federal programs impact or potentially harm public health.

A report from the National Hispanic Council on Aging describes an epidemic, for example, in diabetes among Latinos in the United States.[7] Latinos and people of Caribbean descent are "twice as likely to suffer the onset, complications and consequences of this costly and debilitating disease."

The organization describes the issues that make diabetes particularly threatening for Latinos. Sometimes cultural issues are at play: fatalism, a lack of understanding that obesity is a major factor in diabetes, a fear of insulin, and the idea that eating sugar is good for health and strength.

5 "Surgeon General Says Use Thanksgiving to Share Family Health History," SeniorJournal. com, Nov. 23, 2005. http://seniorjournal.com/NEWS/Features/5-11-23-FamilyHealth History.htm
6 https://familyhistory.hhs.gov/fhh-web/home.action?request_locale=es
7 "The Diabetes Epidemic in Hispanic America: Policy Recommendations," undated. National Hispanic Council on the Aging. http://www.nhcoa.org/pdf/The_Diabetes_ Epidemic_in_Hispanic_America1.pdf

But other issues also affect the overall picture of health care for Latinos and others—and not only those who are impoverished. There are millions of people in this country who either have no health insurance or are unable to pay their portion of the payments of employer-based health insurance. In such cases, screening for diabetes and other treatable diseases is left to slide. In other cases, working people, through bad priorities or lack of easy access to reasonable health care close to home, decide they cannot afford to take the time to get checkups, screenings, or even evaluations of warning signs of a potentially serious health issue. And sometimes for Latinos in rural areas, it may be impossible to travel the distance to see a doctor. Many times, language barriers hinder Latinos or make them shy to reach out for medical help. In many parts of the country, it is not easy to find doctors and medical services where Spanish and other immigrant languages are spoken.

With population growth, we face increasing concerns about the plight of the Hispanic elderly. Our Latino population in the United States is overwhelmingly youthful. Statistics show that of forty-five million Latinos in this country, fewer than three million are sixty-five or older. Nevertheless our parents, grandparents, and great-grandparents share the same issues facing other elderly people in our society, and as baby boomers reach retirement age, problems of elder care, Social Security pensions, and related matters will be more and more of a focus. Already census data show that percentages of Latino elderly are growing more than any other segment of the U.S. population. With that, Hispanic elders will increasingly be seeking health care as they face the characteristic challenges of their age group. Aged Hispanics also have a much higher incidence of many chronic diseases than the general population, including diabetes.[8]

I HAVE OTHER MAJOR ITEMS on my legislative agenda, and they usually cross and intersect with community initiatives. As a principle and guiding light of my public service, I believe that government officials and

---

8 Centers for Disease Control bulletin, 11/28/2003, http://www.cdc.gov/mmwr/preview/ mmwrhtml/mm5247a4.htm.

agencies must work in concert with community-based organizations, and respond to realities beyond the Beltway.

PRESIDENT OBAMA'S ECONOMIC-RECOVERY PACKAGE HAS overarching importance for Latinos and all Americans. The economic crisis reaches every aspect of the good works we can do as we plan for the future of greater integration of all members of our community in the larger American family. I will continue to reassert the special case of Latinos in this crisis and beyond—that Latinos suffer from the worst trials of our society. Whether we're discussing unemployment, foreclosures, the crisis of health care and insurance, or educational opportunities, Latinos feel the same pain as all Americans—but more so.

As I've said and I'll keep repeating, children are the key to our future. We have the moral obligation to bring along Latino and all underserved young people who live in poverty and tough situations through no fault of their own, and are victims of the economic crisis. If their parents lose their jobs, if they lose their homes, they are left without a net. President Obama's recovery plan sought to protect our children and our families as a priority. So even in cases of foreclosure, potentially millions of students were allowed to remain in their schools, rather than being uprooted; they were also given the opportunity to receive emergency financial aid to do so. I sponsored an amendment with Senator Ted Kennedy that would provide special transportation funding for students who might otherwise be moved to other schools. Our goal is to minimize the shock of moving from one school to another; we've seen studies that make it painfully clear that students who are forced to move repeatedly from one school district to another are less proficient in reading and other skills, and prone to being left back, developing behavioral problems, and eventually dropping out of school. We look ahead, cushioning them from the crisis and seeking new opportunities and programs to attract young people. Through government action, through community activism, and through mentor programs, I hope to encourage them; we need to provide Latino students with alternatives, to support new programs, improved school environments, so they will be able to succeed and grow.

I've focused for some time on helping communities combat the spread of youth gangs. Something is wrong when a gang is able to recruit children as young as eight years old. State police in my home state of New Jersey issued troubling statistics showing a marked increase of youth involvement in gangs between the years 2000 and 2005. I've sponsored legislation that would not only extend law-enforcement monitoring of gangs but also take steps to keep children out of gangs in the first place. The goal is to work with communities to offer safe alternatives to gang activity, while taking vigorous steps to halt gangs and decimate their ranks.

I view my work on the Senate Banking Committee as crucial to reorganizing and reining in our financial sector. This cannot be discussed in terms of benefits to one group over another. We must fix the system or we will all sink together. In that regard, we need to make sure the Securities and Exchange Commission is fully funded and capable of regulating banks, other financial institutions, and financial markets. The recession has produced unprecedented turmoil, unemployment and the loss of credit and tumbling stock values. Imagine if the Bush administration's sweetheart deal for financial institutions had been approved—our Social Security savings would have been set free on the stock market, which, by the way, lost half its value from a high of 14,000 points to slightly over 7,000 in March 2009. The losses, the unemployment, the lack of credit, all impact a Latino community that has been making great advances and will again, as long as we have the ability to lead our way out of the fiscal mess we were left with. Ideology during the Bush administration contributed to the SEC's lax enforcement as investment banks like Bear Stearns and Lehman Brothers collapsed under the weight of failed loans. None of us should ever again be exposed to the sub par mortgage and Ponzi schemes that led to fraud and a resulting recession. The recovery will focus on those hit hardest, working families and the poor—many of them Latino families that need immediate support. We aim to spur a new era of job creation and entrepreneurship that brings benefits to Latinos and all Americans.

A MANIFESTO FOR THE FUTURE

Preservation of one's own culture does not require contempt or disrespect for other cultures.

CÉSAR CHÁVEZ

I've spoken about inspiring leaders, extraordinary men and women who have persevered, and about role models we can honor and emulate. However, our inspiration must be accompanied by a sense of joint purpose, acknowledging the commitment to work together as Americans united toward that brighter future and more perfect union.

In that spirit, I'd like to end with a personal note about my experience of a remarkable day, January 20, 2009, the historic inauguration of Barack Obama, an African-American, as President of the United States.

The warmth of history and promise overcame that frigid morning on the Mall. I had a privileged position on the podium seated four rows behind President Obama. The view of the multitudes from that vantage point and the power they generated were sublime. The atmosphere was infused with optimism, with tears of joy, with laughter and celebration; we looked down on a gathering of Americans representing a rainbow of backgrounds, their warmth extending from the Capitol to the Washington Monument, and far beyond. We heard the stories of people turning to one another with hugs and laughter, the shared experience of people from all walks of life. I was told about one Spanish family that called relatives in Argentina and left the phone line open to share the moment in a special way as they watched President Obama speak, as did untold millions of people in the United States and around the world.

"On this day," the new president declared, "we gather because we have chosen hope over fear, unity of purpose over conflict and discord."

On this day, we come to proclaim an end to the petty grievances and false promises, the recriminations and worn-out dogmas, that for far too long have strangled our politics.

We remain a young nation, but in the words of Scripture, the time has come to set aside childish things. The time has come to reaffirm our enduring spirit; to choose our better history; to carry forward that precious gift, that noble idea, passed on from generation to generation: the God-given promise that all are equal, all are free, and all deserve a chance to pursue their full measure of happiness.

The euphoria as we considered the wisdom of President Obama's words amounted to shared experience and emotion to build on—the feeling that America's promise can be fulfilled. I came away with a lesson learned—President Obama has shown us that while we measure our progress incrementally, change sometimes grows beneath the surface, unnoticed. And suddenly we are reminded that we are graduating to a new level of achievement—the process has been creating a foundation all the while.

IN OTHER WORDS, BARACK OBAMA'S theme that day spoke directly to my title and theme: Growing American Roots. He reminds us that the parts of the American whole are indivisible. Our roots feed one another and we grow stronger as a result. This is more than a goal; it is never ending—our democracy depends on the ongoing process of moving toward perfection just beyond our grasp.

I take it as an article of faith that all of us, whether from necessity or concern for humanity or for common American values, will turn to one another. We suffer through the same problems and we can resolve them together. We need one another.

In the darkest times of doubt, we have pulled together; we must offer hope and substance when we hear from our neighbors that they fear for the future, for their jobs, and for the economic future for their children, that they will not make it through the economic crisis. They *will* make it if we take up a commitment to mutual assistance, recognizing that government must be wise and responsive to the needs of its citizens. Americans, in return, must contribute, knowing that laws cannot do it alone. I am convinced that the voices of divisive anger will be drowned out by those of civility and good sense. Change is already here, heralded in the words of our young president, in the essence of his call for Americans to turn *to* one another.

We create the building blocks for a future as we envision it. The individual factors for success are largely known. We must blend the answers to our problems, creating a model in which we bring the full force of the society to the task. This should be beyond political parties, a national commitment, government working with business and funding community organizations, which then reach down to the individual level, mentoring, inspiring, and engaging with our challenges.

It is time for us to consider our history and to broaden the American conversation to make sure it includes Latinos and all ethnic groups in the United States. All of us are capable of the mission at hand. Farmers, businesspeople, workers, all of us need to pull through, for our own sake and for the sake of our children. We cannot work alone, without the labor of others.

We've spoken about the essential need for a good education; Latinos, part of the multicolored ethnicities of this country, must be encouraged to stay in school. They are more likely to stay in school, grow and learn if their parents have financial security and the chance to improve their lives.

Children of working age must complete their education and we must legislate to make that happen. As a top priority, we will hammer down the high levels of dropouts among Latinos in this country. It is a question of values, and economic imperative.

I've used the examples of mentors and community leaders and organizations; we must have a commitment to volunteering to give time as well as money back to our communities. I've emphasized history and role models, past and present, the contributions of our people in all fields of endeavor—in cultural and political realms, and certainly in protecting the security of this country. The raw material of our cultural backgrounds contributes to the greater product of America. We find inspiration in the stories of success and trials through adversity.

I've mentioned the immigrant experience in this country and encouraged readers to recognize their role in building this country; furthermore, by recounting the history of this republic, we see that Latino immigrants have come to this land with the same values and aspirations that inspired every previous generation of Americans to seek his and her fortune here. Therefore, we must support our immigrants; they bring with them the strength and commitment we need to build the future we seek.

And I've taken considerable time to decry and condemn the harassment, mistreatment, and shoddy protection of immigrants and detainees in the United States. I've asked you to consider that often shocking reality and to share my outrage in a system that sometimes allows the innocent to suffer and die. I have reminded you that the task involves nothing more and nothing less than recommitting ourselves to the highest aspirations of a society that values the rights of all men and women as preeminent.

We've looked at cultural icons, professionals and visionaries, sports figures, and military heroes who are an integral part of the American story. We could never, nor should we, sever the intertwined cultural roots that are deeply seated in this country.

I've also discussed the larger economic problems all Americans face now. The government is committed to restoring a strong economy by promoting investments in business and credit and human capital. Looking forward, Americans must be protected from unregulated investing and banking fiascoes that threaten to drag all of us down.

It is in the nature of Americans to join together and win. We are making a positive statement, recognizing that we are working to contribute to the future of this country, still a young nation compared with many, in the process of growing and redefining itself. Latinos are increasingly central and important to the process and we won't shirk our shared responsibility. This process is integrated and irreversible. We are confronting the same issues that all Americans face.

In that spirit, I recall a stirring speech accompanied by a warning from former vice president Al Gore in Oslo on December 10, 2007, upon receiving the Nobel Peace Prize. His passion and commitment to global warming brought more than a prize. He forced us to start thinking about what a healthy future could be for us and for the planet.

He was talking about a commitment to world survival, and also about our future, the roots we all share. We are all in this together, he told us, and no one can be marginalized or separated from the rest. In focusing on the special concerns of Latinos in this country, my purpose is to project a vision of what that future can be if we all take the high road.

He said, "The future is knocking at our door right now. Make no mistake, the next generation *will* ask us one of two questions. Either they will ask: 'What were you thinking; why didn't you act?'

"Or they will ask instead: 'How did you find the moral courage to rise and successfully resolve a crisis that so many said was impossible to solve?'"[1]

It is time to summon up that moral courage—now. We are living at a time of unimagined hope and great danger; we have new, inspiring leadership, but we are faced with daunting challenges that range from issues of the pocketbook to personal safety to national security. It is clear that this is our moment—it is time to act decisively. We look to the future and we carry remembrance of those who came before us.

This is our manifesto for the twenty-first century, my challenge to all Americans. Let us rededicate ourselves to that American dream and recognize that we must work and grow together. Our goal is mighty: We seek to confirm the highest aspirations of our unique, pluralistic society, based on the historic values of the American experiment in which all of us share in the very same dream.

---

1 Al Gore, "Nobel Lecture" (Oslo: Nobel Foundation, 2007), http://nobelprize.org/nobel_prizes/peace/laureates/2007/gore-lecture_en.html.

APPENDIX

DATABASE

46 million: Latinos in this country, 15 percent of the U.S. population.[1] Latinos are the largest single ethnic group in the country and the fastest-growing minority group.

$1 trillion: in 2009, Latino purchasing power, according to government calculations.

1 out of 2: the ratio of new Latinos to the total increase of the nation's population between July 1, 2006, and July 1, 2007. There were 1.4 million Hispanics added to the population during the period. *Source*: Population Estimates 1

3.3 percent: increase in the Hispanic population between July 1, 2006, and July 1, 2007, making Hispanics the fastest-growing minority group. *Source*: Population Estimates 1

132.8 million: projected Hispanic population of the United States on July 1, 2050. According to this projection, Hispanics will constitute 30

1 U.S. Census Bureau, "U.S. Hispanic Population Surpasses 45 Million," *U.S. Census Bureau News*, May 1, 2008, http://www.census.gov/Press-Release/www/releases/archives/population/011910.html.

percent of the nation's population by that date. *Source*: Population Projections

22.4 million: the nation's Hispanic population during the 1990 census— less than half the current total. *Source*: The Hispanic Population: 2000

2nd: ranking of the size of the U.S. Hispanic population worldwide, as of 2007. Only Mexico (108.7 million) had a larger Hispanic population than did the United States. (Spain had a population of 40.4 million.) *Sources*: International Data Base 1; International Data Base 2 and Population Estimates

64 percent: people of Hispanic origin in the United States who are of Mexican background. Another 9 percent are of Puerto Rican background, with 3.4 percent Cuban, 3.1 percent Salvadoran, and 2.8 percent Dominican. The remainder are of some other Central American, South American, or other Hispanic or Latino origin. *Source*: 2006 American Community Survey

107: number of Hispanic males in 2007 per every 100 Hispanic females. This was in sharp contrast to the overall population, which had 97 males per every 100 females. *Source*: Population Estimates

National and state estimates by race, Hispanic origin, sex, and age released today by the U.S. Census Bureau also show that the Hispanic population exceeded 500,000 in 16 states.

U.S. CENSUS DATA AS OF 2007

Thirty-four percent of Latinos are younger than 18.

Twenty-five percent of the general U.S. population is under 18 years old.

The Hispanic population in 2007 had a median age of 27.6.

The overall U.S. population had a median age of 36.6.

Sixteen states have Latino populations of more than 500,000.

Twenty states have African-American populations of more than 500,000.

African-Americans are the largest minority group in 24 states.

Hispanics are the largest minority group in 20 states.

STATES WITH LARGEST LATINO POPULATION

California—13.2 million

Texas—8.6 million

Florida—3.8 million

STATES WITH HIGHEST PERCENTAGE OF LATINOS

New Mexico—44 percent

California—36 percent

Texas—36 percent

MINORITY GROUPS IN THE UNITED STATES

Latinos—45 million

African-Americans—40.7 million

Asians—15.2 million

American Indians and Alaska Natives—4.5 million

Native Hawaiians and Other Pacific Islanders—1 million

POPULATION INCREASE 2006–7

Latinos—3.3 percent

Asians—2.9 percent

Caucasians—0.3 percent

MINORITY POPULATION OF THE UNITED STATES

Total minorities—102.5 million

By state

California—20.9 million

Texas—12.5 million

States in which minorities are more than 50 percent of the total population[2]

Hawaii—75 percent minority

District of Columbia—68 percent

New Mexico—58 percent

California—58 percent

Texas—53 percent

---

2 U.S. Census Data 2009. http://www/census.gov/Press-Release/www/releases/archives/population/013734.html.

ACKNOWLEDGMENTS

Thank you to Peter Eisner, my coauthor, who captured my voice and thoughts and without whom this book would have never materialized.

To all those who gave of their personal time to be interviewed and in doing so enriched our story, including Maria S. Gomez, Roberto González Echevarría, David C. Lizárraga, Ramiro Martinez Jr., Salomon Melgen, Janet Murguía, Jorge Mursuli, Dawn Oropeza, Jeffrey Passel, Martín Pérez, Ken Salazar, Steven Ullestad and Cid Wilson.

Special mention to Erik Camayd-Freixas, whose open letter on Postville I quote from extensively.

To my former Chief of Staff, Ivan Zapien, who constantly urged me to write about our community.

To Danny O'Brien, my current Chief of Staff, and to my incredibly dedicated and talented Senate staff, whose commitment and idealism make my service so fulfilling.

To Rob Kelly, my personal assistant who makes my life a little more gentle.

To Donald Scarinci, my lifetime friend, whose example as an author, and his role in promoting the idea, motivated me to finally write this book.

To Dan and Sandy Krivit, two dear friends, who have been after me for some time to tell this story.

Thanks to Philippa Brophy, my determined agent, the president of

Sterling Lord Literistic; and to Raymond Garcia and Mark Chait, my editors, who provided guidance and vision throughout.

To the innumerable Latinos and Latinas, who I have met in my travels, and who in their ordinary lives perform extraordinary services to our county, inspiring us all.

To those Latino pioneers, who blazed the way, often against the odds, and on whose shoulders we stand today.

To that special someone whom I shared the manuscript with and who gave me both inspiration and constructive critique.

My thanks to all. *Sí se puede!*

6/16 (5) 6/15